Achhe Din? Ha! Ha!!

Achhe Din? Ha! Ha!!

Mani Shankar Aiyar

PALIMPSEST

Published by Palimpsest Publishers
Palimpsest Publishing House Pvt. Ltd.
16 Community Centre, Panchsheel Park
New Delhi 110 017, India

First published in Palimpsest in 2015

ISBN 978 93 82622 06 2

Typeset in Adobe Garamond Pro by Devdas, Goa
Printed at Thomson Press India Ltd

CONTENTS

FOREWORD

The 2014 general election started for me when on 17 January at the All India Congress Committee (AICC) plenary, a TV channel asked me what I thought were the chances of Modi becoming Prime Minister. With fervour and conviction arising out of my belief that a secular country would not vote in a man with blood on his conscience, I replied that it would never happen. I then added, as a joke with reference to what he loved calling himself from public platforms – a chaiwallah – that if, however, he wanted to serve tea we could always provide him a tea stall. The remark set off a storm. The joke badly rebounded on me. Independent observers like the veteran journalist Rajdeep Sardesai have even suggested that Modi send me a 'Thank You' note for having helped him win his election. My vanity does not extend to regarding myself as so influential as to determine, with one jest that backfired, the outcome of an election with 700 million voters.

But a year after I was proved wrong that a man like Modi could never become PM, I continue to be extremely sceptical about his ability to be an effective Prime Minister. However much he tom-toms himself, arms flailing as a series of acronyms, alliterations and slogans flow out on that deep, sonorous voice, I believe his penchant for self-praise and self-publicity will redound on him. People will start asking whether this is a PM or an EM – an events manager. As action trails far behind rhetoric, his credibility has already started its downward spiral. The momentum will get accelerated as the gap widens between his flair for clever lines and his inability to match words with delivery.

This is not a last-minute thought as the first anniversary of his being

Prime Minister approaches. Week after week, through my columns for NDTV.com and my regular column every three weeks for *The Week*, and several other occasional writings, I have been tracking the man. Of course, I have to accept that I went hopelessly wrong in thinking he could not possibly win. He did get the mandate to run the country. But as I have watched him from the sidelines, I persist with the view that he has not risen to the occasion and that the country would be well-advised to turn him down at the next opportunity. The reasons are spelt out in this little collection brought out to more or less coincide with the close of the new government's first year in office.

I have been greatly assisted in my endeavours by my research consultant, Vandana Seth, who has delved deep into the Internet where my incompetence with computers would not permit me to go. I am also deeply grateful to a young student, Naushad Qayoom Khan, who has helped edit the book, putting together the articles in chronological order and correcting errors that have crept in. The end-product, however, is my own, warts and all.

My grateful thanks too to Bhaskar Roy of Palimpsest without whose enthusiasm these articles would have remained buried in the caverns of the Word Wide Web. I am also grateful to NDTV.com, *The Week* and others for permission to reproduce pieces that were initially for them alone.

April 2015　　　　　　　　　　　　　　**Mani Shankar Aiyar**
New Delhi

SHAME SHAME PUPPY SHAME

27 July 2013

The 'oracle of development' has at last spoken out fully and frankly about the pogrom of Muslims in Gujarat in 2002, likening his own role to a passenger in the backseat of a car and the Muslims slaughtered to a puppy that accidentally came under the wheels of his vehicle.

What the chief minister was doing in the rear seat when his state was going through the tumult of a communal massacre reveals his invidious attempt at distancing himself from the carnage by describing the murderous mobs as the true drivers and himself a hapless passenger, just so as to escape all responsibility for the "puppy's" brutal end. It also reveals his mindset regarding large-scale killing as 'stuff happens'.

He does not think it was his duty as the head of the government to jump out to check if there was any life left in the poor victim. Or to take the victim to hospital or to reprimand the chauffeur. He just rushed from the scene of the crime to stop anyone from discovering that he was there. Now he is feeling a little sorry – largely for himself – and that too 11 years later. More a *maut ka saudagar* than an oracle of development, the man stands condemned in his own words.

By one of those telling coincidences that fate serves up when no one is looking, just days after Modi's infamous interview, PTI put out a story datelined Melbourne of a real-life incident involving a dog that came under the wheels of a car. "Steve Hunter," said the news item, "was making a delivery when a fox terrier suddenly ran out of a driveway and was clipped by an oncoming car." The car sped away. Hunter, however, ran to the puppy, found it still had a little life left, picked it up, carried it to the pavement, and, to use his own words, "did the deed". He gave the dying puppy mouth-to-mouth resuscitation, "pulling the dog's jaws apart and, by the way, he didn't brush his teeth"! The puppy recovered at a veterinary centre.

That, Shri 108 Modi, is what you should have done. You should have leaped out of the car the minute you heard of Godhra and recognised that there would be "action-reaction". Immediately, you should have picked up the puppy and comforted it. Immediately, you should have given an entire frightened community mouth-to-mouth resuscitation. Immediately, you should have ensured that no other car ran over any other dog. Immediately, you should have sacked the man at the wheel—your home minister (the one witness who actually knew what you were up to and was mysteriously killed for his pains). Or perhaps it was a woman at the wheel – Maya Kodnani (now serving a life term in jail for inciting the murder of innocents). Instead, you rewarded her by making her a minister in your post-massacre government.

Modi exculpates himself by claiming to be a "Hindu nationalist". I can understand an Indian being both a Hindu and a nationalist. But a "Hindu nationalist" can surely be no more than 85 per cent Indian. Would Modi accept Syed Shahabuddin calling himself a Muslim nationalist? Or a Mizo calling himself a Christian nationalist? Twenty years ago, an election pamphlet written in the Mizo language called for "Christian socialism" in Mizoram, whose native denizens are all Christians. The BJP went wild with accusation at the time and, although the term was withdrawn two decades ago, reverts to it every time there is an election there. (And, of course, Hindutva never has and never will win a single seat there.)

But none of us would or could object to Shahabuddin calling himself an Indian Muslim or to anyone from Nagaland to Goa and Kerala and Kanyakumari calling himself an Indian Christian. But how can our religious minorities be "Hindu nationalists", the only category in the vulgar mind of the Hindutvist that qualifies as a true Indian?

The Week

11

WE'VE BEEN FAR TOO POLITE TO MODI

24 January 2014

Obama made world-renowned his election slogan, "Yes, we can." With a hundred days yet to go for our own elections, we must learn to say, "No, we won't" to the Modi challenge.

Let us begin by remembering that at exactly this time ten years ago, everyone assumed that the NDA would have a walkover. Indeed, that is the only reason the BJP Prime Minister brought forward by six months, from October to May, the Lok Sabha elections of that year.

I remember a solitary article by Yogendra Yadav (then an intellectual of repute, now a pall-bearer of the Aam Aadmi Party) speculating in a really thoughtful, closely-argued article in a leading national newspaper that the outcome of that election was not yet a closed chapter. That, indeed, turned out to be the case. Soberly assessing the Party's own electoral prospects, the Congress stitched up a series of alliances in the run-up to the 2004 polls and emerged triumphant. I felt so sorry for Atal Bihari Vajpayee that after taking my oath as a minister, I walked up to him in Parliament and humbly touched his feet. There were not a few on our benches who reproached me for that gesture but I have not regretted it for Vajpayee was a good man and I felt the least one could do was offer an expression of human sympathy for one whose hopes had so suddenly crashed to the ground.

Modi, however, is not a good man. He is going to receive not a drop of the milk of human kindness from me when his hopes are equally dashed come the merry, merry month of May.

The pre-poll survey results that are flooding TV channels are all serving to indicate to all concerned what they need to do to turn the apparent outcome on its head, even as it happened in 2004, indeed even as it happened in 2009 when UPA II bested its own record as UPA I.

That would be at two levels – the tactical and the strategic. At the tactical level, the DMK would be seeing the stark prediction that its strength in Parliament might be reduced to a mere five, while its principal opponent's soars to perhaps the highest among the "Third Force" parties if it does not shed its present reluctance to join hands with others who are at least as interested in dampening the Puratchi Thalaivi's ambitions as they themselves are.

Equally, a divided house in UP has opened several doors for the BJP. Those doors could start getting shut if like-minded parties were to start getting together. The same holds for Bihar. Closing ranks in those two states could dramatically alter current predictions. The lesson is different but similar for the NCP and the Congress in Maharashtra.

On the other side, the resistance to seeing Modi toppling their own hopes is also a lesson that those, such as the Left Front, who want to see a secular government emerge are bound to learn and absorb. Thus, tactically speaking, the assumption on which the current surveys are based – that the present line-up is the final line-up – could well be changed in state after state.

But more than the tactical is the strategic offensive that all those who do not want to see a Modi-led government must mount. "No, we can't" must change to "No, we mustn't" to point to the dangers that lie ahead if things do not change over the next hundred days.

Ours is a democracy based on consensus, not an authoritarianism bent to serve one man's whims. Good governance is not the same as overruling all law, all alternative considerations, riding roughshod over contrary opinions and bullying the bureaucracy into violating not only rules and procedures but also all ethical imperatives. Whether it was the post-Godhra pogrom, the so-called "encounters", the stalking of a young woman, there are a myriad other instances to show that what Modi calls strong governance is in reality one man's rule based on retribution for respecting the law instead of that one man's imperiousness.

The cry comes loud from the jails where the victims of those who listened to Modi's illegal orders are lodged. Instances of this in his 12 years in Gujarat are numerous and must be documented and propagated so that the people know what he has been up to before deciding that they do not want that in their lives.

The merciless exploitation of Gujarat's tribals must also be highlighted. The Twelfth Plan document officially proclaims that 76 per cent – the highest in the land – of those displaced by the Gujarat model are desperately poor tribals, mercilessly exploited to make way for Modi's friends, the Wolves of Dalal Street and Nariman Point.

The obscene subsidies extended to Big Business must reach to the knowledge of every home. The highly respected *Economic and Political Weekly* has calculated that every Nano built in Gujarat has a subsidy from the government and people of the state amounting to ₹60,000 per car; that land acquired by the Gujarat government in Kutch and sold to a single private party at one rupee per unit has substantially been resold at 1500 times that price; that small enterprises have been allotted land in a Special Industrialization Zone at up to 700 times the value of the land allotted in the same SIZ virtually free to a giant engineering enterprise.

It also needs to be bruited about that Gujarat's growth rate under Modi has been lower than even under Chimanbhai Patel, that agricultural growth is only the result of operationalisation of the Sardar Sarovar Dam built by the Centre after the World Bank withdrew its funding; that many states, beginning with neighbouring Maharashtra and extending all the way to distant Bihar and Tamil Nadu have returned far better results than Gujarat; and that Gujarat's human development ranking is a pathetic 15 in comparison with the other Indian states.

Violations of human rights, beginning with 2002 and extending down the years till today, need to be rubbed into the Indian psyche to forestall the tragic mistake the German electorate made in January 1933. The fundamental values of our modern nationhood – the widening and deepening of our democracy; secularism as the bonding adhesive of our peoples; the forging of unity out of the celebration of diversity; non-discrimination; the pursuit not of the domination of any individual but the upliftment of the weakest; priority to the poor over the privileging of the rich – all this is in danger.

We shall overcome because everything Modi stands for is in opposition to the civilizational idea of India. We have been far too polite to Modi. We must show him up now for what he is.

NDTV.com

BJP'S FIRST AND LASTING MISTAKE

24 January 2014

In the most mealy-mouthed statement ever to emerge from the politics of hypocrisy, the BJP president, Rajnath Singh, has said his party is ready to apologize to our minorities for their "mistakes, if any". Rajnathji does not seem to recognize that his party's very existence hinges on their first and lasting "mistake". For the BJP is the political 'mukhauta' of the Sangh Parivar. And the Sangh Parivar's origins lie in the RSS. And the author of the RSS's political philosophy was VD Savarkar, whose one word, 'Hindutva', has for the better part of a century given the Sangh Parivar its distinctive character and its obnoxious manifesto.

What does 'Hindutva' mean? It does not mean "Hinduism" as a religion – for Savarkar was, after all, an avowed atheist. Savarkar, whose English was impeccable, himself translated this strange word he had invented into meaning "Hindudom" in, he said, the same sense as rule by Christians has been known in the West as "Christendom".

He was explicit in deploring what he regarded as a thousand years of Muslim rule that preceded colonial rule and, therefore, sought liberation from both the Brits and the Muslims (at the time when the Muslims constituted less than a quarter of our pre-Partition population). What Savarkar, therefore, postulated was the replacement of British rule by Hindu rule. The mainstream Freedom Movement stood, in sharp contrast, for the replacement of colonial rule by Indian rule, for a secular state not "Hindudom".

Fascinated with this concept, evolved by Savarkar while he was under house imprisonment in Ratnagiri after he secured his release from the Andamans by pleading with the British to have compassion for his youth, Keshav Baliram Hedgewar, then toying with the idea of creating the RSS, rushed to meet him – and became, in effect, Savarkar's first chela for this new philosophy.

In *We, or Our Nationhood Defined* MS Golwalkar, the leading ideologue of the RSS, further refined the concept of Hindu India's nationhood to exclude all those who were either not born in this land or who looked beyond its borders for spiritual inspiration. The target was explicitly identified as the Muslims who, it was stated, might continue to live here but only as "guests" and who would cease to have any rights if they transgressed any element of the quintessentially Hindu ethos of the country.

Golwalkar also expressed his great admiration for Hitler. After Hitler was defeated and the RSS came under scrutiny for its possible role in Mahatma Gandhi's assassination, the RSS distanced themselves from this publication saying it was not authorized. However that may be, Savarkar, in a statement from Nagpur, ironically datelined 15 August 1943, four years to the day before India was due for her tryst with destiny, said he completely agreed with Jinnah that there were in fact two nations inhabiting this land, a Hindu nation and a Muslim nation, and it was the Hindu nation that he wished to see privileged.

Fanning out from this poisonous proposition, several fringe groups came into existence, one of which spawned the assassin of Mahatma Gandhi. The germane "mistake" that Rajnathji should first apologize for is the systematic stigmatization and exclusion of our religious minorities that lies at the heart of 'Hindutva'.

It is such stigmatization and exclusion that led to the demolition of the Babri Masjid in December 1992. In the run-up to that demolition, LK Advani was quoted as saying that all Muslims who live in India are "Hindu Muslims" and all Christians must acknowledge that they are "Hindu Christians". Advani never answered my question as to whether he was a Hindu or a "Hindu Hindu" – but he certainly shed copious crocodile tears as his Rath Yatra led inexorably to the "mistake" of the Babri Masjid being demolished brick by brick in front of his eyes. Vajpayee earned himself the title of 'mukhauta' for distancing himself from this unforgivable insult and injury to our 15 crore strong Muslim community. (So also, PV Narasimha Rao was never forgiven for having sat on his hands doing nothing while this outrage was taking place.)

Rajnath Singh was a key BJP leader of Uttar Pradesh while all this was underway. Today, having lost the Hindu vote since genuine Hindus have nothing against their Islamic brethren, he hints that his attitude in 1992 might have been a "mistake".

That is akin to Narendra Modi dismissing the victims of the post-Godhra riots as "puppies" that came under the wheels of a hit-and run car (while he himself rested comfortably in the backseat). So long as Muslims are contemptuously referred to as "Mian" and told they cannot have their own Personal Law, as guaranteed by the Constitution, or that the special measures taken in favour of their community amount to "tushtikaran", it is the very existence of the BJP that remains not just their biggest "mistake", but the biggest sin the Sangh Parivar has to exorcise before we can cease accusing them of dividing the country on communal lines.

NDTV.com

WHY BJP CAN'T WIN

8 March 2014

This time 10 years ago, all pre-poll surveys were predicting that the BJP was well ahead of the Congress. Only one psephologist, Yogendra Yadav (now the AAP's Dronacharya), cautioned that the results did not mean a closed contest but an election in which the outcome was yet to be determined. Apart from the first-past-the-post seat-taking, which put the Congress comfortably in front (you should have seen the shattered expression on Vajpayee's face), there were two other factors that contributed – as they might do now – to snatching victory from the jaws of the frontrunner. The first is that election-eve polls results incentivise alliances among the runners-up to come together to overtake the frontrunner, while disincentivising the frontrunner from sharing his lead with others. The second is that the more geographically concentrated the vote-lead, the less the number of seats it yields.

It would be prudent to apply both these lessons to the current voting trends. Both the BJP and the Congress do not have a significant number of committed electoral allies. The BJP has only the Shiromani Akali Dal and the Shiv Sena. All other parties are keeping their options open. This is most vividly illustrated in Tamil Nadu, where Jayalalithaa has conspicuously distanced herself from close friend Narendra Modi. In what was billed as the BJP's major debut in Tamil Nadu, not even one party turned up to share the platform with Modi at his major rally in Chennai. Meanwhile, Congress' talks with the DMK are quietly gathering steam. In the key states of UP and Bihar, local rivals might further their edge by tying up with one of the two "nationals", one of which only Ram Vilas Paswan wants to touch.

Frontrunners in the states have all agreed that they want nothing to do with the national frontrunners. Apart from Haryana's Indian National Lok Dal, no one seeks the company of the National Democratic Alliance. And while many spurn the Congress, the Nationalist Congress Party has reaffirmed that it will be going with the party. Of course, the tainted Yeddyurappa has returned to the BJP, but whatever good that might do the BJP in Karnataka will be wiped out by the corrupt and opportunistic image it gives the party throughout the country.

I turn now to the second factor – geographical concentration. In our system of elections, where victory and defeat are determined at the constituency level, every vote secured above the last vote gained by the loser is wasted in terms of seat-gain. The BJP vote, with substantial margins, is concentrated in Rajasthan, Gujarat, Madhya Pradesh and Chhattisgarh. Here, the BJP will win many seats but all of its surplus votes will not translate into more seats. The BJP is not the frontrunner in peninsular India. Nor in the Northeast. Nor in the far north, Haryana upwards (except, perhaps, in the seat-starved Himachal Pradesh and Uttarakhand). The determining band thus narrows to UP and Bihar. In both states, the BJP is the dark horse desperately attempting to come from behind but being stalled by formidable hurdles – Mayawati and Mulayam in UP; and Nitish and Lalu in Bihar.

The BJP would have to take half the current Congress seats to emerge the clear winner, but much of the haemorrhage from the Congress would be in the direction of the Third-Front parties, not the BJP. Even if the BJP picked up half the Congress losses, it begins from such a low level that it will be stranded well below its ambitions.

The Third-Front parties would much rather take a shy at the coconut themselves than leverage one they loathe to the top post. And they would be supported from within the BJP by at least four leaders who want the top slot for themselves. It's open season and all bets are off!

The Week

BJP'S DODGY MATHS FOR TAMIL NADU

24 March 2014

I was amazed to hear a well-known commentator describe the motley crowd the BJP has put forward for the Tamil Nadu Lok Sabha elections as a "formidable" combo. Formidable? Really?

Apart from the one seat that the BJP won in Kanyakumari back in 1999 (the winning candidate being the son of Kamaraj's right-hand man in the constituency) the BJP has not won once from this state. It has now brought on to its side Vijayakant's DMDK that won some 25 Assembly seats in alliance with Jayalalithaa's AIADMK in 2011 but has now lost about five of them to the AIADMK following the falling out between Jayalalithaa and Vijayakant that took place almost immediately after the state Assembly elections were over. So much for alliances between film actors.

The DMDK loathes Dr. Ramadoss' PMK, a sentiment warmly reciprocated, despite both being in uneasy political wedlock with the BJP. The origins of the quarrel lie in the PMK leader's intense dislike of the domination of Tamil screen heroes and heroines in the state's politics. This led to his ordinance to PMK workers that they must eschew all cinema-going and badly hit the otherwise deep pockets of Vijayakant's fan club-turned-political party. The bad blood endures to the extent that Dr. Ramadoss failed to turn up at Rajnath Singh's stage-managed inauguration of an alliance that is fraying before it has quite been formed. Apart from personal dislike, there is also intense rivalry for the same political base in several of the northern constituencies of the state, including Salem, Kallakurichi and Villupuram. Also Puducherry. This rivalry has apparently been papered over with an alleged agreement brokered by the BJP president but is showing signs of wear and tear within a mere 24 hours of the papering over.

Witness the street fight that has broken out between the PMK's initially declared candidate for Cuddalore and the newly anointed DMDK candidate. In Coimbatore, a battle royale has started between rival BJP aspirants, CP Radhakrishnan and GKS Selvakumar.

The fourth member of this odd quartet is Vaiko's MDMK. There was a time (oh! so long ago) when Vaiko thought his fiery, chauvinistic oratory would enable him to replace the ageing Karunanidhi. However, Karunanidhi has just celebrated his ninetieth birthday while Vaiko sinks further and further into oblivion, his utterly opportunistic politics now having landed this great champion of secularism in the lap of the RSS. His ineffectiveness and limited influence was clearly demonstrated when, in the last Lok Sabha election, ManickaTagore of the Youth Congress, then not much over 30, took on the lion in his den and pulled out the lion's teeth. If Vaiko cannot win his own seat, how can he win the ones for his lesser mortals?

We thus have a party of no sitting Tamil Nadu MPs, merging with three Tamil Nadu parties of no MPs, each engaged in sawing the branch on which they sit. And this is the combo that has driven the hype that describes the BJP-brokered alliance as "formidable", marking the BJP's debut on the Tamil Nadu stage. Elementary maths would show that zero plus zero plus zero plus zero still equals zero!

What has further outraged those who on TV watched the BJP president reading (with great difficulty) the names of the combo's candidates, or saw the photograph on the front pages of newspapers next day, was that Rajnath had flung one dhoti-clad leg over the other and kept twiddling the soles of his well-shod feet at the eyes of the audience. In Tamil Nadu, this is just not done. You don't fling one leg over the other, certainly never in public, in a manner reminiscent of feudal lords showing the poor their place. The BJP President, in all his innocence of Tamil etiquette and propriety, only proved to his Tamil audience that he was what they had always suspected, a NNQLU (a Northerner Not Quite Like Us).

This is not a political alliance, just a bit of a nuisance that will probably not open its score and, if it does, not score above a run or two.

NDTV.com

THE DYING LIGHT OF FREEDOM

17 May 2014

It is in Parliament we can best thwart every effort of the incoming government to move towards its nefarious ulterior agenda. (Source: PTI)

Darkness descends. The idea of India gutters. The light that lit our freedom struggle and so defined the nature of our nationhood is going out. We are at a moment of history that can only be compared to Lahore, March 23, 1940, when Jinnah persuaded one section of our society to accept that India comprised two nations because nationhood had to be founded in religious identity. Thus was conceived a Muslim Pakistan. But Gandhiji resisted India cloning that example with a Hindu India. For that, he had to pay with his life at the instance of the very forces that are today most avidly celebrating Narendra Modi's victory.

The campaign has shown the incoming Prime Minister insisting that for any Hindu, India is his rightful home, thus equating India with Hindudom and reducing to sufferance those who regard India as their home but not Hinduism as their religion. My closest Muslim friend, viewing the imminent catastrophe, asks, "Was it for this that our parents decided to remain in India?"

I have reassured her that even if over a third of Indians voted for the BJP, nearly two-thirds did not. This is a low moment for us, but if Indian secularism is not a Nehruvian whim but the consequence of that secularism, that plurality, that inclusivism being woven into the warp and woof of our millennial civilisation, then this is not a moment of defeat but a moment of challenge.

We have to be on our utmost guard to spot the new government awaiting its Godhra opportunity. Godhra was to Modi what Marinus van der Lubbe's attempt to set fire to the Reichstag was to Hitler. It gave them the occasion to ride a wave of public anguish to accomplish the deepest purpose of their political lives. We have been forewarned, therefore, we must be forearmed. This is not a moment for armchair secularism. The issue is not a philosophical or polemical one. It is a red alert to be vigilant and activist. We must convert Modi's Reichstag moment, when it comes, into our Belchi moment. In the Congress, the Sadbhavana Sena died with its first and only chairman, Sunil Dutt.

That needs to be revived and converted into a rapid action force that reaches the spot the minute news comes in of a communal flare-up. Moreover, the sena must concert with other secular forces, irrespective of differences. India's secular nationhood is too fundamentally important to be left hostage to other considerations.

There are two other fronts on which vigilance is called for. One is development. The so-called Gujarat model blazed the path to unashamed crony capitalism. That is why those thousands of crores of rupees of doubtful provenance poured into the coffers of Modi's campaign, just as Krupp and Thyssen funded every step of the march of the corporal from the Beer Hall Putsch to the German Chancery. Hitler repaid them with the biggest bonanza ever. Modi waits to confer similar bounty on his benefactors.

Even as the nation's secular majority must concert its efforts to preserve the quintessence of our nationhood, so must the forces of equity, social justice and human development concert their efforts to keep the country from being gifted to robber barons. The Congress may be in reduced numbers in Parliament but along with others not on the Treasury benches, the voices of fair play for the aam aadmi will not be lacking in number. The socialist Lilliputians might yet tie down big business Gullivers and their political cohorts.

That brings me to the next, and related, imperative. Parliamentary institutions have been severely mauled in the BJP's clambering to power. The last Lok Sabha was rendered by their antics the most non-functional ever. The Rajya Sabha followed suit – and often led the way. The incoming opposition, of which the Congress constitutes the largest single fraction, must unchain the Speaker and Chairman and insist that both Houses function in accordance with the rules and regulations of the House, its propriety and precedents, with dignity and decorum. Happily the saffron shouting brigade is on the Treasury benches.

Hence the Opposition can ensure that democracy is restored to its throne. The priority of the largest opposition party must be to restore Parliament as the nation's highest forum for debate, not demonstration. And it is in Parliament that we can best thwart every effort of the incoming government to move towards its nefarious ulterior agenda.

On the external front, the first duty of every parliamentarian in this centenary year of the start of World War I must be to read all he or she can on the vainglorious strutting of jingoistic leaders that led those the Cambridge historian of the war, Christopher Clark, has called "The Sleepwalkers" blundering into a slaughter they never intended nor wished, a slaughter that began in 1914 and, with but a short interregnum, ended only in 1945, after nearly 50 million people had lost their lives. Shrill and narrow nationalism, as Gurudev Rabindranath Tagore warned, are the worst enemies of peace and humanism.

Yet, those two qualities are precisely the stock-in-trade of the party now coming to power. There is no Atal Bihari Vajpayee — surely the last Nehruvian — to rein in the chauvinism of what passes for "patriotism" in that party. The ideological extremists have taken over and will seize every chance to convert external events into the grand opportunity for flag-waving and mindless brinkmanship. Catastrophe worse than the two World Wars awaits this subcontinent, if those fortunate enough to not be on the Treasury benches fail to be ever-vigilant and ready to risk immediate popularity for the larger cause. We have our work cut out for us. Let us put our shoulders to the wheel.

Indian Express

SWEARING-IN OR SWEARING-AT?

27 May 2014

Almost a year ago to the day, and in the wake of his convincing victory in the Pakistan general election, Nawaz Sharif stretched out an exceptional hand of friendship to India pointing to neither Kashmir nor India having been an election issue in Pakistan, seeking a resumption of intensive dialogue with India, and demonstrating his earnest by inviting the Indian prime minister to his swearing-in. The invitation was not taken up then or subsequently, largely because of pressure against engaging sincerely and in depth with a Pakistan that had not brought Hafiz Saeed to book, nor proceeded with the expeditious trial of those involved in 26/11, nor handed over Dawood Ibrahim and Tiger Memon, besides being responsible for the beheading of Indian soldiers, the bludgeoning to death of Sarabjit Singh and more than one incursion into Kashmir across the Line of Control. None of that has changed. And yet, the very elements that most opposed even the courtesy invitation to lunch at 7 Race Course Road to outgoing Pakistan president, Asif Zardari, before he proceeded to perform *ziarat* at Ajmer Sharif, are now preening themselves at having pulled off the coup of getting the Pakistan PM to hop across to the Rashtrapati Bhavan for what is being described as the "coronation" of the next Indian PM. They might have delusions about this being a repeat of the 1911 Durbar for the Laat Sahib with the feudatories all in attendance, but ours is a republic, not a monarchy, and the seven heads of government who have come are not salaam-ing maharajahs.

What then is the import of the visit? Has Pakistan changed its spots? Or has the Sangh Parivar undergone a lobotomy? I still remember with horror the twisted fury on the face of Arun Shourie, spokesman for the BJP in the Rajya Sabha on the morrow of 26/11, as he railed against the Pakistanis that we should not seek a tooth for a tooth but the entire jaw for a tooth in any Pakistani terrorist attack. Has that fury abated?

For Nawaz Sharif to accept the invitation is no more than

consistency with the stand he has always taken: that any contact with India is welcome and that dialogue with India is a must. But without preconditions – that is fundamental. The Sangh Parivar, on the other hand, has thus far insisted that without Pakistan making amends for past outrages and giving iron-clad guarantees of no repeats, how can India engage with this monster to our west? Is, therefore, the invitation to Nawaz Sharif no more than yet another empty gesture in keeping with the event-management style of the BJP's election campaign or does it mark the dropping of preconditions to dialogue that Pakistan can neither accept nor fulfil?

This is the year of the centenary of the outbreak of World War I. The casus belli was the Austro-Hungarian Empire's allegation of the Serbian government's involvement in the assassination of the heir to their throne in Sarajevo by Serbian terrorists. It is now clear that although the Serbian government shared with the terrorists the broad national goal of uniting all Serbs under the roof of a single Serb state, the assassins were acting on their own and not at the instance, or under the direction of, the Serbian authorities. That is exactly what the Pakistanis say.

Short of bombarding Islamabad, as the Austrians bombed Belgrade to bend the Serbs to their will, there is nothing New Delhi can do to compel the Pakistani government to admit it is complicit in crimes against India it says it has had nothing to do with. And parallel to Hafiz Saeed in 2014, loomed in 1914 in Serbia the dreaded figure of Apis, the don of all Serb terrorists, who covered his tracks so well that the Serbian government never figured out, or was aghast at the thought of finding out, just how compromised individual officials of the Serb government in aiding or abetting the assassin Gavrilo Principe and his five teenage companions were. (Even in age, the assassins who fired the bullets in Sarajevo that sparked the death of a hundred million through the first half of the 20th century resemble the gang that spread its net of terror through Mumbai that ghastly night of 26/11).

Remember, Pakistan may be the hub of Islamist terror but it is even more a victim of its own terrorism than the outside world. It is futile to pretend, as some Indians who ought to know better do, that the terror groups who train their sights on India are different to those who train their sights on Pakistan; in effect, all these groups are inter-linked and share the same objectives and sources of sustenance, even if their different targets are nuanced. Nawaz Sharif is engaged simultaneously in defanging all of them. But the chances of his success are remote. If, therefore, the Pakistan government has to prove itself more successful at reining in its terrorists than India has been at reining in its own home-grown terrorists, whether in the jungles of Dandakaranya or in the Northeast, or even among the Indian Mujahideen, imagine how much more horrendous the challenge before the Pakistani government is in proving its anti-terrorist credentials to the Sangh Parivar's satisfaction.

Pakistan just cannot do all that the Sangh Parivar demands before serious talks commence. Therefore, either the Parivar dilutes its demands or Nawaz Sharif pulls off the impossible. Neither is feasible. The only way out is an "uninterrupted and uninterruptible dialogue", as I have been urging for decades. Pakistan, under Hina Khar of the PPP, accepted and articulated the proposal. The successor government of Nawaz Sharif has endorsed the phrase. Neither the previous UPA government nor the incoming one were or are ready to touch such a proposal with a barge pole. Thus, we are left stranded where we were – whether Nawaz Sharif prefers last night's chicken chettinad to his own Lahori biryani or not. The swearing-in is but a prelude to the resumption of the swearing-at.

Indian Express

WILL THE REAL SHASHI THAROOR PLEASE STAND UP?

8 June 2014

Of the 44 Congress MPs elected to the Lok Sabha, the most highly educated is undoubtedly Shashi Tharoor. His IQ is way ahead of any other Congress MP. His good looks have left armadas of women swooning in his wake. When he brushes his mop of hair from his impressively high forehead, and lights up his charming smile, men roll back in wonder. He writes with matchless skill. He speaks even more impressively, in a voice as deep as Amitabh Bachhan's and with eloquence as fluent and witty as Winston Churchill's. Indeed, the first time I heard him, which was his 125th anniversary address to our common alma mater, I walked up to him to say, "That was a better speech than any even I have ever made – or could ever make!"

When, therefore, the Congress picked him to be one their candidates from his home state of Kerala for the 2009 elections, it was a political coup of sorts. We were to get in our ranks one who had made his name at the highest echelons of the UN, one who had had more international leaders eating out of his hands than Sushma Swaraj is likely to encounter as Foreign Minister.

Inevitably, and notwithstanding his being a rookie MP, he was named immediately after his convincing win to the glamorous, high-profile post of Minister of State for External Affairs and given the responsibility for more than half the world: West Asia, Africa, Latin America. He brought all his abundant energy to becoming perhaps the most peripatetic minister the MEA has ever seen, clocking up flying returns at a mind-swirling pace. Then came the denouement of the IPL cricketing scandal, and the Government felt obliged to put its blue-eyed boy on the back-burner to escape the singeing it might otherwise have got. But as soon as the heat died down, Shashi was back, perhaps not in his natural fortress of South Block but in charge of the UPA's flagship programme, the Right to Education Act.

Then, notwithstanding simmering public doubts over the tragic death of his warm, gregarious wife Sunanda, he was selected again for Thiruvananthapuram, where he won a handsome victory over the BJP veteran, O Rajagopal, the Left being left far behind, a straggler. With two successive resounding victories behind him, Tharoor returned to the Congress benches in Parliament invested with the highest hopes of his party that he would prove himself a doughty warrior at the nadir to which the party has sunk.

Instead, a mere 10 days after the new Government was sworn in, and long before it begins to be sworn at, Tharoor has poured encomiums on the new Prime Minister that even the most ardent of BJP supporters might have been too embarrassed to proclaim quite so fulsomely – an *abhishek* of the like that Raja Rajarajendra Chola arranged for the Nandi at the Brihadeeswara temple he built in Thanjavur!

Modi, it seems, has emerged in a mere 100 hours as an "avatar of modernity and inclusiveness". Why did this not occur to Tharoor earlier? This is exactly what Modi had been saying of himself right through the election campaign, that his programme was "development" and that this would include all 125 crore Indians. If Tharoor was going to be taken in by such unctuousness immediately after the campaign ended, why not while the campaign was on? Then, Tharoor could have replaced Rajagopal and emerged today as a top BJP minister. So, will the real Tharoor please stand up? The proto-Tharoor who lambasted Modi and the BJP till but a fortnight ago? Or the deutero-Tharoor that finds so much virtue in the other man within a week of his investiture as PM?

What did Tharoor expect? That Modi would unleash a pogrom on the morning after? That he would ban *ziarat* at Ajmer Sharif? That he would abolish the Ministry of Minority Affairs or call it the Ministry of Appeasement? (Although giving it to Najma Heptullah is, perhaps, the same thing). That he would abolish Parliament and declare himself Absolute? Of course, Modi will not reveal his ulterior motives on walking into 7 Race Course Road. He will await his Godhra moment, just as Hitler needed his Reichstag moment to befool his Parliament into giving him the Enabling Act which enabled Hitler to institute his one-man rule. How can such a dyed-in-the-wool Hindutivist (remember his comparing the victims of the 2002 riots to puppies that come under the wheels of a car?) so suddenly emerge as a Nehruvian secularist? Is Modi 2.0 a caterpillar turned into a butterfly? Has he left his ideological baggage, accumulated over a lifetime, in the attic of his Ahmedabad home?

For a man as bright as Tharoor to not ask himself whether Modi has undergone a lobotomy in the week of his inaugurations is bewildering. Does he seriously imagine that this mendicant pracharak, who abandoned his child-wife and lonely mother in adolescence, did it all as a lark and is no more serious about Hindutva than Tharoor is as a Congressman? Can a leopard change its spots like some quick-change artistes the Congress has allowed to sneak into its ranks? What is this "modernity" and "inclusiveness" that Tharoor sees? Is it not exactly what Modi preached as the "Gujarat development model"? That model is 12 years old. Its flaws are 12 years old. The same Tharoor who presumably pointed to the flaws of the model in his campaign speeches (I don't know for certain if he did for I speak no Malayalam and was as busy losing my election in neighbouring Tamil Nadu as he was busy winning his). But assuming he, like all Congressmen, examined the Gujarat model and found it wanting, what has got him believing that the worst excesses of crony capitalism that the Modi model comprises will not be replicated from Delhi? One estimate has it that each Nano car includes a generous support of ₹60,000 from the government, banks and people of Gujarat; that land acquired for a rupee a square yard was so abundantly made available to a big business house who sold the surplus at more than ₹700 a square yard; that at the Hazira Special Industrial Zone, the tiniest enterprises were allotted land at 700-800 times the rate charged from the largest industrial houses; that the callous displacement of tribals in the interest of the fat cats led to 76 per cent of those displaced being tribal people in a state where the tribals' share of the population is a mere 8 per cent?

The renowned Gujarati economist, YK Alagh, former head of the Institute of Rural Management, Anand has shown that agricultural growth has averaged nearer 6 per cent than the claimed 10 per cent, and even this is on account of the Sardar Sarovar Dam sanctioned by Rajiv Gandhi and financed by the Narasimha Rao government after the World Bank withdrew support on account of Medha Patkar's Narmada Bachao Andolan. And how the project, fortuitously for Modi, came on stream the year he became CM. How can agricultural productivity not increase when water for the first time ever flows into parched and arid wastes? Or even how the growth rate of SDP was faster under previous Gujarat regimes, as also several other states in contemporary times, even as human development indices under Modi stagnated at about 15th position of all Indian States?

Being taken in by Modi's promises for the future that belie his track-record of the past is not what is expected of an alert Opposition. Tharoor's statements and clarifications have reduced the strength of the Congress in the Lok Sabha from 44 to 43. We shall struggle on.

NDTV.com

GOVERNANCE, MODIJI, IS ABOUT MAKING CHOICES

12 June 2014

The Constitution obliges the President to read out whatever the government dishes up as the "President's Address". For a man as intelligent, sensitive and experienced as the present President, it must have been painfully embarrassing to be forever associated with the tissue of empty slogan-mongering and meaningless alliteration ("Democracy, Demography, Demand" – what does it mean?) served to him by the incoming Modi government. Tired clichés, pinched from electoral platforms, were recycled as "policy", and continuity of government, the cornerstone of the democratic process, was given the go-by as programmes that have been underway for decades were warmed up and put on the table as fresh new ideas. The dilemmas of governance were conveniently ignored in the rhetoric of what they choose to call "good governance".

It will boomerang on them as they get down to real business. "Cooperative federalism" has already met its first test and failed. Jayalalithaa met Modi and demanded the immediate establishment of the Cauvery Management Board mandated by the Supreme Court. The Karnataka BJP, led by Anantha Kumar, who had worsted Nandan Nilekani in the recent election, rubbished the idea. Modi is caught in a bind – a bind with which he is going to get increasingly familiar as he learns that his job as Prime Minister is, for the most part, the reconciling of the irresistible force of one state government with the immoveable object of the other.

Why would the Centre wish to interfere in a matter that falls exclusively within the domain of a state government or when rival state governments settle matters among themselves? *Mia Bibi Razi Toh Kya Karega Qazi?* But the Centre is forced to intervene, positively or negatively, when Mayawati demands President's Rule in UP and CM

Akhilesh Yadav hides behind the Supreme Court's Bommai judgement and the Sarkaria Commission's criteria for action under Article 356. The job of the Union government is not to usurp state functions, as Modi claims was being done, but to be the impartial, benevolent umpire in inter-state disputes. Modi can today earn brownie points by proclaiming state autonomy, but governance from Delhi, he will soon discover, is principally about finding the middle path between states' rights and the Centre's overriding obligation to maintain the Union of India.

He claimed in his speech in the Rajya Sabha to know everything about the requirements of the states as he had served as Chief Minister of Gujarat. But he was far from being the only ex-CM present in the House; had he been less blinded by his own arrogance, he would have seen the scepticism on the faces of such long-experienced former Chief Ministers as the Leader of the Opposition, Ghulam Nabi Azad (J&K), Digvijaya Singh (MP) and AK Antony (Kerala), not to mention Mayawati (UP) and numerous others in the other House (Amrinder Singh of Punjab, Nephiu Rio of Nagaland, and ex-PM Deve Gowda of Karnataka) all of whom have been at loggerheads with neighbouring states and at the receiving end of Central governments not of their hue.

Moreover, while Modi and his colleagues have sworn allegiance to the Constitution but a fortnight ago, they seem to have already forgotten that Dr Ambedkar never talked of "cooperative federalism" (whatever that might mean) but of India as a "Union of States with federal features". That constitutional responsibility can never be abandoned by the Centre lest there be the outbreak in India of the equivalent of the American Civil War (1861-1865) – a precedent to which the Sarkaria Commission on Centre-State relations draws pointed attention.

The President's Address then promises all things to all persons: there is not a section of the population that is not "prioritised" in "Ek Bharat-Shreshta Bharat" – big business, small business, farmers, farm labour, the poor, the rich, the working class, the regions, backward and prosperous, etc, etc – as if Modi were Santa Claus and the President's Address a Christmas gift.

Governance, Modiji, is about making choices. The choices you made in Gujarat were choices explicitly in favour of the mega-rich in land acquisition to the detriment of the hapless tribals; land allotment that grossly discriminated against the MSMEs; massive financial assistance to the fat cats who least needed it; environmental clearance without due diligence – and, in return, all of these billionaires and trillionaires most generously opened their purses for your staggeringly expensive election campaign. Thus, while Gujarat retained its ranking as one of the faster-growing states, a rank it has held ever since its creation in 1960, indeed as a region since pre-Independence days (remember the East India Company established itself in Surat in 1600), Modi's exertions on behalf of the poor have left the state stagnating far below that rank on all human development indices.

Economic policy is about choices and the balancing of competing interests: the poor cannot get all that is promised by Gandhiji's 150th birth anniversary without restraining the access of the rich to a dominant share of the available cake. And it is they and the vested interests they represent that have always loudly resented as "give-aways" whatever is reserved for poverty alleviation (oops, I mean, of course, "poverty elimination", ha, ha) and human resource development.

It is comical for the new government to strut around saying it will consult the states on all matters of policy. When, pray, has this not been done – most conspicuously in the case of the Goods and Services Tax and coal block allocations? Which were the states that objected? Almost always the BJP states.

The problem is that if every state demands "special status" and regards it as grossly discriminatory if that status is not granted, little or nothing remains in the kitty for everyone else. The argument between "stimulus" and "subsidies" cannot be papered over either. Every paisa taken from "subsidies" for the poor augments "stimulus" for the rich, and vice-versa. How can time-bound "poverty elimination" be the priority if stimulated private sector growth is also to be the priority?

To strike the right balance, Nehru established the Planning Commission. Rumour has it that Modi plans to abolish or drastically alter or at least change the name of the Planning Commission, an organ set up by governmental decree, as he appeared to hint at in his reply to the debate in the Rajya Sabha. But that will not resolve the dilemmas that are the stuff of governance in Delhi.

Moreover, as Anand Sharma said, the foreign policy orientation of the President's Address is "fractured", with no mention of ASEAN, Africa, West Asia or Latin America. And even on neighbourhood policy, the government will soon learn that there are dilemmas to be resolved between making impossible demands on Pakistan to end cross-border terrorism as the pre-condition and undertaking dispute resolution through dialogue. He will also discover that "cooperative federalism" gives West Bengal and Tamil Nadu veto powers in regional South Asian policy.

It has been a pathetic beginning. It will lead to a pathetic end.

NDTV.com

A CONSPIRACY OF DENIAL

18 June 2014

I was in Pakistan over the weekend on the invitation of my Cambridge college mate, former Pakistan foreign affairs minister Khurshid Mehmood Kasuri (2002-07), who has started the Regional Peace Institute in Islamabad, under whose aegis he has commenced a series of three "Pakistan-India bilaterals", with part-funding from the Hanns Seidel Foundation of Bavaria. Our team was made up of academics, economists, social sector experts and media personalities rather than the usual suspects – politicians of the "has-been" or "never-will-be" hue, the sole exception (apart from me) being our former Congress Foreign Minister (2012-14), Salman Khurshid. Like Salman himself, most members were first-time visitors to Pakistan or new to track-two exercises. They therefore brought fresh perspectives to bear on well-worn themes. The Pakistani team was, to some extent, similarly constituted, but significantly included two former directors-general of the notorious ISI, Generals Asad Durrani and Ehsan ul-Haq, two former ministers, a phalanx of former Pakistan envoys to India, leading media personalities and a few academics. Besides our exhausting day-long deliberations, opportunities were provided by our hosts and High Commissioner TCA Raghavan for interaction with a broad spectrum of former top armed services personnel, distinguished Pakistani diplomats, ministers and politicians, both defeated and in office (including Sartaj Aziz), and other well-wishers. Since the whole visit lasted under 36 hours, here are a few fleeting impressions.

The attitude to the incoming Modi government may be summarised as a perplexed welcome. The Pakistanis are always better disposed to a non-Congress government for a number of complex reasons. First, the Muslim League-Congress rivalry in the run-up to Partition has left a deep and abiding anti-Congress streak in the Pakistani mindset. Second, while the BJP-Sangh Parivar's Hindutva agenda sparks a certain element of concern and apprehension in Pakistan, subconsciously, the emergence of a Hindu India would finally validate the case for a Muslim Pakistan. The insistence on a secular state on our side of the border has left the Pakistan project incomplete and with little rationale. Third, the Morarji Desai government, in which Atal Bihari Vajpayee was the foreign minister, continues to be seen as the only Indian government that treated Pakistanis as equals and did not involve itself in Pakistan's internal affairs, even as General Zia ul-Haq hanged Zulfikar Ali Bhutto. The legacy of the Vajpayee government, in particular the great "emotional breakthrough" of his visiting the Shaheed Minar to signal his party's definitive acceptance of Pakistan, quite overwhelms any recall of Vajpayee's mobilising a million jawans along the Pakistan border for a whole year or the collapse of the Agra talks. As for Modi, he is seen as a "strong" leader who, unlike Congress prime ministers, is not beholden to even party opinion, leave alone public opinion. Such authoritarianism reverberates well in the Pakistani mind.

At the same time, never before in my 35 years of frequent interaction with Pakistanis, and in the 35 visits (at least) that I have made to Pakistan since I returned from my diplomatic posting in Karachi 32 years ago, have I encountered such a broad spectrum of pessimism about Pakistan's future. This perhaps has much to do with ordinary Pakistani citizens' fury and helplessness at the Tehreek-e-Taliban Pakistan's terrorist attack on the Karachi airport on the eve of our visit, but it has much more to do with the widespread belief that the Nawaz Sharif government just does not have the will or ability to deal firmly with the Islamist menace to the internal security of their Islamic state. One participant frankly stated that the Nawaz government's political base in the critical province of Punjab is founded on its links to Hafiz Saeed's Jamaat-ud-Dawah and, therefore, far from being able to tackle the terrorists, Nawaz depends on them for political survival. This is a view frequently heard in India but, to my ears, it was the first time I had heard it in Pakistani mainstream circles. Another friend, just about as mainline as you can get, warned that Pakistan was on the brink of an "implosion".

I personally find such pessimism exaggerated, but in the face of this build-up of internal security and domestic political pressure, it is unsurprising that many segments of Pakistani opinion, military or civil, political or non-political, media-based or outside the media, are persuaded that a via media with India must be found in Pakistan's own interest. Where there is a kind of subterranean unity is in the view that the ball lies in India's court and it is for India under the new government to make the first move, the key being the dropping of "preconditions" to dialogue, particularly those relating to terror, and the assurance of peace being delivered with "honour". There is little acknowledgement of how unrealistic this is in the face of the BJP's stated position, but the "window of opportunity" was projected as "six months", after which, it was held, any dramatic breakthrough could be ruled out.

Expectations of a breakthrough are, however, hedged in by what is seen as a bad beginning – not the invitation to the swearing-in, which is appreciated, but the briefing on the Modi-Nawaz talks by our foreign secretary, which the Pakistani media have portrayed as Sujata Singh indicating that Nawaz was given a wigging by Modi, to which he failed to adequately respond, and that Nawaz steering away from Kashmir and the Hurriyat amounted to what the BJP used to call "tushtikaran (appeasement)". The morning after my return, I saw headlines about Defence Minister Arun Jaitley having stated in Srinagar that any violation of the Line of Control would jeopardise all progress in Indo-Pak relations. That is going to add fuel to the Pakistani suspicion that the Modi government may be interested in imposing a peace without honour on the northwest corner of our subcontinent but is not in a mood to initiate talks among sovereign equals. The silver lining hoped for is that since Modi's core constituency comprises Gujarati businessmen (including Khojas, Bohras, Ismailis and Memons, the key Muslim business communities), the renamed version of the most favoured nation treatment treaty with Pakistan might furnish him with the excuse for the first bilateral prime ministerial visit by an Indian PM to Pakistan since Rajiv Gandhi went there in July 1989 and Vajpayee a decade later.

But even if such a visit were to take place, it would not succeed unless Modi and Nawaz cease being in denial over the enormous progress made on the back-channel under Pervez Musharraf and

Manmohan Singh, which, for the first time, has been made public by special envoy Satinder Lambah in a speech in Srinagar in May 2014, on the eve of his laying down office. Khurshid Kasuri and Natwar Singh's forthcoming books, slated for publication around the same time in the next few weeks, will significantly augment public knowledge of the back-channel talks. That initiative sputtered over Musharraf's troubles with his judiciary in 2007. But so long as Modi and Nawaz, the latter obsessed with preparing the gallows for Musharraf, engage in a conspiracy of denial over progress in 2004-07, further progress, if any, will be at snail's pace.

Indian Express

THE CRISIS IN IRAQ AND INDIA

20 June 2014

The only time I met Hillary Clinton – or am likely to meet her – was at a small luncheon hosted by Natwar Singh, then our External Affairs minister. I had been specially invited because Natwar knew I had spent two years in our Embassy in Baghdad (1976-78) and was currently Petroleum Minister, a portfolio with a crucial connect to West Asia and Iran who supplied (and continue to supply) the bulk of our massive crude oil imports.

I was startled to find that Ms. Clinton did not seem to have heard of either the Battle of Qadisseyah, where in 637 AD the Arabs drove the Persian Sassanids out of Mesopotamia, nor of Ismail I who from 1501 AD started the progressive transformation of Persia into a Shi'ite state, thus imparting to traditional Arab-Persian ethno-linguistic rivalry the sectarian complexion of a Sunni-Shia confrontation whose historical roots go back to the succession to the Prophet (Peace Be Upon Him).

The emotional consequences of the assassination of the Prophet's son-in-law, Ali, in 661 AD in the Grand Mosque of al-Kufa, and the military defeat of his sons, Hussein and Hassan, at the hands of the Ummayad Caliph, Yazid's army, at the Battle of Karbala, 680 AD, reverberate down to the 21st century, never more strongly than the present when US intervention in Iraq has brought Shia Iran cheek-by-jowl with Sunni-Wahabi Saudi Arabia and the Sunni Emirates of the western coast of the Gulf that they share with Shia Iran on the other side of the same narrow waterway.

Till almost exactly a hundred years ago, Iran's Shi'ism was principally pitted against the Sunni Turkish Empire of the Ottomans and the Sunni Kingdoms of Central Asia. The dismantling of the Ottoman Empire as a result of their defeat in the First World War led to the emergence of a number of Arab nations generally under the Mandate of Britain or France. Britain got Iraq and the modern history of Iraq begins in 1932

41

with King Feisal I being placed on the throne of Harun al-Rashid but as a vassal of the British Empire. (As an aside I cannot resist recalling that under the Mandate, Iraq was administered as a district of the Bombay Presidency. So, when on arrival in Baghdad, I asked my Ambassador, the gracious Romesh Bhandari, what were our "larger goals" in Iraq, he punctured my pompous question by remarking, with a wicked gleam in his eye, that our larger goal was to re-establish that position!)

But to return to our narrative, the Iraqi monarchy was overthrown in 1958 and a decade later the Ba'ath Party under Saddam Hussein established its murderous rule. Murderous it might have been but it was also modernizing and secular. Shia and Sunni both were to be found in high office in the Baghdad where I served, both at the ministerial and civil servant level. The presence of numerous women in universities as unveiled teachers and students, as also in high public sector positions, was truly impressive. Any number of minorities, including the Christian number two to Saddam, Tariq Aziz, even the wretched Armenians, were given respect and security (provided, of course, they hailed the Leader). The Iraqis were especially proud of preserving and pointing out to Indian visitors the precincts where Guru Nanak is said to have meditated on returning from Mecca to India via Baghdad. For Saddam, India was so much the secular exemplar to follow, even as India to him was Indira (which is why he held a mass rally in Baghdad in support of her Emergency!) that when she was defeated in the elections of 1977, I saw several Iraqi officials wearing a black band of mourning on their upper arms in the expectation that in India, as in Iraq, the leader would be hanged when their government fell!

My closest encounter with the secular Iraqi state came from being required from time to time to visit Najf and Karbala on the Euphrates to distribute largesse from a fund set up by the Nawab of Rampur in the thirties to support Indian Shias resident in these holy places. After Independence, the administration of the fund had devolved on the Indian government and through it to the Embassy. That too was when I discovered the extent of Sunni-Shia rivalry for the temperature would be hovering near 50 degrees centigrade but Azmi, our English-Hindi-Arabic interpreter, would drink no water. I asked him discreetly whether he was not thirsty and he solemnly warned that since his name gave him away as a Sunni, he feared the Shias would spit in his glass before they served it to him!

All this changed with the ascendance of Ayatollah Khomeini (who, in fact, had spent 14 years of his exile in Najaf under the benevolent secular protection of Saddam Hussein, the Sunni). By mid-1978, as my posting was drawing to a close, it became clear that the Shah of Iran's days were numbered. At this, Saddam startled the world by inviting the Shah's sister, the notorious Princess Ashrafi, to make a state visit to Baghdad. All stops were pulled out to make the visit a really grand affair (including all private house-owners with villas on the banks of the Tigris being ordered to vacate their homes to make these available to Princess Ashrafi's large suite) in order the better to signal the Ayatollah that the triumph of a clerico-political Shia order in Iran would be fiercely resisted by the Ba'athist regime in neighbouring Iraq. This reflected the millennial paranoia of the Iraqi Sunni that were the Sh'ia Iranians from in front and the Shias of the Euphrates (Farhat) from behind to clamp their jaws together, the Sunnis on the Tigris (Dijla), to whom Saddam and a large part of his cohort belonged, would simply be snapped up as so much carrion.

When the Ayatollah took over, and the US hostage crisis began, the Americans (specifically Donald Rumsfeld) saw in Saddam their surrogate who would win for them their war against the Ayatollah. That is when secular Iraq crumbled. Invoking the Battle of Qadisseyah, Saddam, with massive and unremitting US backing, went in to invade Iran. Meretriciously, he called this the Second Battle of Qadisseyah. While the war with Iran ended in a draw (and the worst blood-letting since the Second World War), the Nineties brought on the first Gulf War, followed a decade later by the second, under respectively the two Bush's, father and son. Iraq as a shared home of Sunni and Shia, and a secular buffer state between Shia Iran and Sunni Saudi Arabia, was destroyed. The latest ISIS capture of almost all of Iraq north of Baghdad definitively smashes the buffer and brings the Shias and Sunnis into eyeball-to-eyeball confrontation over Baghdad. Worse, with US power exposed as hollow and non-sustainable, the field has been cleared for a resumption of the seventh-century Battle of Qadissiyeh, backed respectively by the Sunni Wahabis of Saudi Arabia and the Shia clergy of Iran.

This has been the disastrous long-term outcome of the vacuous American intervention that began with their encouraging Iraq to invade Iran in the Eighties – and all that has since followed. While we might rely on the excellence of our Foreign Service officers to rescue the Indians caught in someone else's war, as they did so magnificently in the two previous Gulf wars and more recently in Libya, what of our political leadership?

From Nehru to Rajiv Gandhi, the careful cultivation of Arab friendships made us the most influential outsider in the Arab world. We began siding with Israel and cozying up to the Americans in Narasimha Rao's time (who, I often think, was perhaps our first BJP Prime Minister). By neglecting our relationship with the Arabs for the better part of the last twenty years, we are now virtually without a voice in a region from where we import 70 per cent of our oil and is host to some 7 million expatriate Indians whose remittances fill our coffers.

What little influence we had left is now reduced to nil by an inaugural President's Address that studiously and insultingly ignores West Asia and a Prime Minister who does not know the difference between Bhutan and Nepal or Ladakh and Thimpu. How then can we expect him to tell between the Farhat and the Dijla? In this gathering darkness, all we have to rely on is the ever-reliable Indian Foreign Service to which I once had the proud honour of belonging. Allah preserve us from the saffronisation of the Indian Foreign Service.

NDTV.com

1914 SERBIA AND 2014 PAKISTAN

28 June 2014

Today, 28 June, exactly one hundred years ago, the Serbian terrorist, Gavrilo Princip, unwittingly started the First and Second World Wars that left more than a hundred million people dead before the madness gave over three terrible decades later. Along with five other young men, all about the same age as Ajmal Kasab and his companions, Princip and his companions lined up under successive lamp-posts along the quay that Archduke Franz Ferdinand, the heir apparent to the throne of the Austro-Hungarian Empire, was to drive down along with his wife, Countess Sophia Chotek, to the Sarajevo Town Hall for a formal welcome reception.

The five terrorists were infuriated because the Archduke and his consort had chosen the precise anniversary of the worst day in Serbia's collective memory, the defeat of the Serbian Tsar, Dusan, by the Turks at the Battle of Kosovo in 1389, more than five centuries earlier, but which rankled as the day when the dream of Greater Serbia was ended for half a millennium. In the eyes of all Serbian nationalists and terrorists, with the Ottoman hold on the Balkans collapsing, the time had now come to avenge that defeat. Just as six centuries of Muslim rule in Delhi, from 1192 AD when Mohammad Ghori established the Sultanate to 1858 when the Last Mughal, Bahadur Shah Zafar, was deposed had reverberated in the minds of the Kasab gang of terrorists as the order to be re-established, so did the Serbian terrorists propose to reverse the 1878 occupation of Bosnia by Austria and its annexation to the Austro-Hungarian Empire in 1908 to pave the way to the re-establishment of Tsar Dusan's Greater Serbian Empire that had perished on the Fields of Kosovo on 28 June 1389.

The K. Subrahmanyam report has indubitably established that plenty of intelligence about what was happening on the other side of the Kargil range was available with the Indian military and civilian authorities even as Prime Minister Atal Bihari Vajpayee was preparing for his "historic" bus-trip to Lahore in February 1999. The establishment brushed all this aside the better to concentrate on making a huge success, in event-management if not substantive terms, of the bus-ride. Not even the Pakistan government's decision to cancel the half-hour bus-ride from Wagah to Lahore for security reasons alerted the Indian government to the fragile nature of the goodwill on display. So also did Oskar Potiorek, the Austro-Hungarian Empire's Governor in Bosnia, ignore numerous intelligence warnings of the security dangers attendant on the Archduke's insistence on visiting Bosnia as the newly appointed Commander-in-Chief of the Bosnian army.

The Archduke's adamant insistence on making the visit was as much a flying in the face of evidence as was Defence Minister George Fernandes being complicit in not passing on with adequate stress the information flowing into military intelligence of unseemly activity in Skardu. And for much the same reason as overtook Governor Potiorek: currying favour with the Boss. In Governor Potiorek's case, there was the personal determination to show his authorities in Vienna how firmly and irreversibly he had consolidated the Empire's annexation of Bosnia; in the case of Vajpayee's cohorts, it was the earnest desire to not play spoil-sport to their hero's race to the Nobel Peace Prize. Anything that would detract from the occasion as evidence of a conspiracy was brushed aside in 1914 by Vienna and Sarajevo just as unwanted evidence was studiously ignored by Delhi and Srinagar in 1999.

But there was an even more touching reason in the case of Archduke Franz Ferdinand and his consort. They had been married on the same 28th day of June fourteen years earlier in 1900. It was a morganatic marriage – that is, Sophia could never become Empress nor her four children succeed their father because court protocol decreed that Countess Sophia did not have adequate blue blood flowing in her veins to have her seated on ceremonial occasions next to the heir apparent and certainly not as Empress after the octogenarian Emperor Franz Joseph passed on. As historian AJP Taylor remarks, the one endearing feature of the heir-apparent's character, for all his faults, was his enduring love for his wife. When he found that, as Commander-in-Chief of the Bosnian army, the same rules of protocol did not apply as in the Emperor's court and, therefore, his consort could accompany him to Sarajevo as an equal, he determined on a second honeymoon and nothing would thwart him from his noble purpose, just as nothing would or could thwart Vajpayee from his.

We now learn from the autobiography of Nawaz Sharif's former (and present) Foreign Minister, Sartaj Aziz, that the Pakistan cabinet was indeed briefed by the army chief, Gen. Pervez Musharraf, in detail at the end of March 1999 – that is, a month after the Vajpayee visit and a few weeks before the Kargil invasion was to begin – and that on being told by Musharraf that his men could possibly be in Srinagar within a week of scaling the Kargil heights, Nawaz Sharif raised his hands and asked, with his Cabinet colleagues, for Allah's *dua*. So also did the Serbian government in Belgrade know that something could go gravely wrong with the Archduke's visit to Sarajevo but as they broadly shared the goals of their terrorists, even if they had nothing to do with this particular plot, the Serbian government played along while covering their tracks, just as Nawaz Sharif did about his government's awareness of Musharraf's Kargil misadventure. Credible denial, not action to halt the plot, was Sharif's leitmotif as it was of the Serbian Prime Minister Nikola Pasic and his Cabinet.

And the reasons for shying away from personal involvement but ensuring that nothing was done to stop the outrage from occurring also weirdly parallel those between the Serbia of yore and the Pakistan of the present. The arch Serbian plotter was Dragutin Dimitrijevic, known by his 'takhalus' of 'Apis' the Bee (the nickname he had acquired as a cadet for always buzzing around earnestly). He had earned his laurels by being the most ruthless of the regicides who in 1903 had assassinated the previous Serbian King Alexandar Obrenovic and his Queen (the two, by sheer coincidence, having been married just three days before Franz Ferdinand and Sophia in the face of similar furious objection from the court and the politico-military establishment – in Queen Draga's case because she was a notorious nymphomaniac, the Interior Minister having lost his job because he protested to King Alexandar that he had himself slept with the incoming Queen!) Apis had gone on to become the chief of intelligence (shades of ISI) and then split off to become the clandestine recruiter and trainer, like Ajmal Kasab's 'Major Iqbal', of an army of subterranean terrorists picked up from the coffee-houses of Belgrade where unemployed but idealistic Serbian youth whiled away their time in useless, unrealistic political dreams – the massacre of *kafir*s to earn a quick passage to Paradise in the case of Kasab and his companions; the realization of Greater Serbia in the case of Princip and his friends.

Apis took care to recruit for the Sarajevo mission boys suffering from terminal tuberculosis who knew they were destined to die young but preferred the glory of death for a noble cause to just wasting away in an infirmary. For the terrorists, of both the 20th and the 21st centuries, death held no fear and cyanide pills were thoughtfully provided in the event of capture. And where young Pakistanis have been fed on dreams of re-establishing global Muslim rule as in the century that followed the Prophet (*pace* Allama Iqbal's *Shikwa*, or Complaint to Allah as to why he had snatched the world from Muslim hands, and his renowned poem on Granada, *Yeh Gumabde Miane*, rendered into immortal song by Malika Pukhraj), Serbian nationalism, and its appendage, Serbian terrorism, also thrived on ballads and epic songs woven around "a mythical pantheon" that included "the celebrated assassin" Milos Obilic who was said to have infiltrated the Turkish camp and slit the Sultan's throat. Matching the revivalist irredentism of Allama Iqbal was the 19th century Serbian writer, Garasanin, and the 1847 epic, *The Mountain Wreath* by the Prince-Bishop of Montenegro, which was to Serbian nationalism what Bankim Chandra Chattopadhyaya's *Ananda Math* was to Indian nationalism. Most significant of all, Apis' Serbian Black Hand organisation operated independent of the Serbian government, but with both immunity and impunity, as does Hafiz Saeed's Lashkar-e-Toiba.

Thus, when the Sarajevo assassination occurred, the Serbian government could carry conviction with most of the world, if not with Vienna, that whatever links anyone might wish to draw between the shadowy Apis and his merry band of terrorists, the Serbian government could not be fairly blamed. Even so, could the Pakistan government credibly distance itself from the 2001 attack on our Parliament and Mumbai 26/11 – at least in the eyes of the world, if not our own. And so also could Pakistan persuade the world to distinguish between the Pakistan government, on the one hand, and "rogue elements" in the ISI and the Lashkar-e-Toiba, on the other. Moreover, the Belgrade government of 1914 could no more dare touch Apis than the Sharif government dare touch Hafiz Saeed.

When, therefore, Vienna laid at the door of Belgrade responsibility for the Sarajevo assassination, the government of Serbia protested that it had nothing to do with the assassination and was quite as keen as the Austro-Hungarian Empire to discover who the assassins were and who were behind them. This cut little ice in Vienna who insisted, as Delhi now does, that the Pakistan government own up, unveil the links between their agencies and the terrorists and demonstratively take action to bring the guilty to book. Belgrade then could no more meet these demands than Islamabad can today.

As the crisis deepened, it seemed to almost all the players that this was no more serious than the several crises that had beset the Balkans in the recent past, all of which had been defused by quiet diplomacy and a little sabre-rattling, most notably the crisis of the previous year, 1913, in which Sir Edward Grey, the British Foreign Secretary, had earned considerable kudos by convening a meeting in London of the envoys concerned and finding an interim solution. He floated a similar proposal in July 1914, but this time there were no takers.

Conscious too that Vienna and Belgrade were not the only players but had Germany behind Austro-Hungary and France behind Serbia, statesmen comforted themselves with the thought that all this was déjà vu, that the first Balkan crisis had been tided over and the much more serious Agadir crisis of 1911 over a German gun-boat, the Panther, having appeared off the Moroccan coast challenging French hegemony in North Africa and British colonial interests in all of Africa, had also been overcome. Why, therefore, could not an amicable solution be found despite Vienna having issued an ultimatum to Belgrade threatening invasion if the Serbian government did not provide satisfaction on a number of conditions put to Belgrade by Vienna that no self-respecting independent nation could possibly accept? Even Churchill thought it was "the most insolent document of its kind ever devised". Yet, Belgrade accepted all the conditionalities but one.

That provided the *casus belli* that Vienna was obliged to follow, at Berlin's urging, even as Belgrade's nerve was being strengthened by Czarist Russia assuring them of Slavic solidarity in the event of Aryan-Magyar aggression by the Austro-Hungarian Empire. France was in two minds, President Poincare sailing to Russia to consolidate the military cooperation arrangements between Russia and France in the event of war, dragging along with him his reluctant pacifist and socialist Premier, Rene Viviani. Britain had its nerve stretched for it wanted no part of any of these quarrels despite the "military conversations" it had had with France which effectively bound it to come to France's help if France were invaded by Germany or Britain's security threatened by Germany violating Belgium's neutrality to gain access to Belgium's Channel ports, principally Antwerp and Ostend.

Despite this tangled skein of alliances, so little was the actual outbreak of war anticipated that in the last week of July the Kaiser went on his annual cruise in the waters of the Baltic, sailing to his favourite summer haunts in Scandinavia; Poincare and Viviani were also on the high seas; the German army commander, Moltke, and the Austrian army commander, Conrad, were both on vacation, as was half the British Cabinet and the Governor of the Bank of England. When Russia issued its 1st August ultimatum to Germany in the wake of the Austro-Hungarian bombardment of Belgrade at the expiry of its ultimatum, almost all the principal players were blissfully unaware that the worst war in human history had started.

On our subcontinent, we are almost as blissfully unaware of what would happen if, as is entirely likely, a similar scenario were to play out between Pakistan and India. There could be a massive terrorist attack on India from a base on Pakistan soil. Knee-jerk, we would, like the Austrians, demand immediate reprisals by the Pakistanis against all non-state and state actors responsible for the outrage. Pakistan, like the Serbian government, would hem and haw, not only because they do not know all that has happened but also because they do know that if they were to find out, all Hell might break loose. If then the armchair generals who are to be seen with their bristling moustaches and beetled eyebrows on our TV sets were to go ballistic, as I bet they would, our government would be forced to reveal its 56-inch chest. Any threat of war, especially between nuclear weapons-armed neighbours, would bring in outside interference. It is not difficult to guess who would play Kaiser's Germany and who Czarist Russia. And even as in 1971, when no one but us was concerned with the merits of our case, so also would no outside power waste time or effort apportioning blame; we would both be held responsible. At this, national pride would triumph over international intervention, and just as Emperor Franz Ferdinand was prevented by the war machine from pulling back from the brink, as he had done on numerous previous occasions, so also would belligerent governments on both sides of our border find it impossible to counsel good sense in the face of the assault led by their respective TV anchors. "The nation wants to know…" And the nation's youth would march off to their deaths and the nation's old would await incineration in a nuclear holocaust.

The lesson for India and Pakistan of "The Sleepwalkers" who led their countries to collective disaster in 1914, a disaster that none wanted but none could prevent, is that menacing mutual brinkmanship must be replaced by pragmatic understanding. We in India need to understand that Pakistani terrorism cannot be ended for talks to begin; and that unless talks begin, there is no handle in the Pakistan government's hands to contain India-specific targeted terrorism. We can climb as many pulpits as we wish, make as many impassioned appeals to the world and Pakistan as we desire, prepare ourselves for the worst and ready ourselves to inflict on Pakistan the worst, but the end result will be an Armageddon worse than anything our imagination can conceive or our mythology grasp, if we do not agree now to an "uninterrupted and uninterruptible" dialogue with Pakistan. What overtook Europe could overtake us – unless we listen to the voice of Gandhi instead of Clausewitz and Nietzsche. It is by engaging with our opponents that we can turn them from friend to enemy; by confronting them, we could potentially turn our millions of Pakistani friends into implacable enemies. We cannot afford to sleepwalk our way to war. We must seize whatever opportunity presents itself, or which we ourselves can create, to make the 21st century the Asian century instead of repeating in Asia in the 21st century the horrors of Europe's 20th century. Then perhaps the two World Wars might not have been fought in vain.

The Hindu, an expanded version later in The Equator Line

'NO ENGLISH. NO HINDI. HOW?'

28 June 2014

The title is the immortal response of K Kamraj, President of the Indian National Congress in January 1966, when his colleagues begged him to succeed Lal Bahadur Shastri as Prime Minister of India after Shastri died suddenly in Tashkent. It comes to mind now when, in conformity with its hidden, ulterior, Sangh-driven agenda, the Modi government has floated a feeler designed eventually to abolish English and establish Hindi as the sole official language of the Indian government: "No English. Only Hindi. Now!"

For the moment, the howl from Tamil Nadu has stalled the effort, but Moditva still has 4 years and eleven months to run. Without the utmost vigilance, we may be left with Jammu and Kashmir in the North seceding over the deletion of Article 370 and Tamil Nadu in the far south doing the same over the imposition of Hindi. Nothing less than the continued unity and integrity of the nation is at stake.

Given that not more that 10-15 per cent of our population was adult when the language issue last reared its ugly head in 1959-67, it is perhaps necessary to revisit those days to see how the extremists at both ends of the spectrum were thwarted by the wisdom and patriotism of Nehru and Indira Gandhi, while the principal protagonists of the two opposite views, Atal Bihari Vajpayee and CN Annadurai, allowed logic, good sense and moderation to inform reasoned debate in and outside Parliament in the midst of anger and violence in the streets. There is little historical recall and even less imagination in the current corridors of power. Hence this little historical recap by one who was moving from his late teens to his early twenties as the drama played out.

In the first flush of freedom, the Constituent Assembly had agreed that English would be phased out over what then seemed a long period of fifteen years, that is, by 1965, but subject to flexibility over the time-line as the successful propagation of Hindi would, as a practical matter, have to precede any total switchover from English. Therefore, Parliament, said the Constitution, would by law decide when to effect the switch. With the deadline approaching, the pro-Hindi lobby stepped up its pressure to the growing alarm of the non-Hindi speaking peoples. Following the submission of a number of reports by high-level Commissions composed of very eminent persons, debate was initiated in both Houses of Parliament in September 1959. To read those debates today is to be filled with profound sorrow. For the extraordinarily high level of debate, and the dignity and decorum on display, have quite disappeared as the House now is adjourned day after day in the midst of bedlam, sometimes for an entire session. But then it was different. The records show Parliament conducting itself as a forum for discussion, not demonstration.

The submission of a Joint Parliamentary Committee report on the issue in 1959 kicked off a major and heated public debate on the issue. It appeared to have been settled when the Prime Minister, Jawaharlal Nehru, intervened in the Lok Saba on 7 August 1959 to make a three-part suggestion. One, there must be no "imposition" of Hindi. Two, English might continue as an associated additional or alternate language "for an indefinite period". Third, that he would leave the decision on when to give up English "not to the Hindi-knowing people, but to the non-Hindi-knowing people".

This assurance was then incorporated in the Official Languages Act, 1963, but did not satisfy the upcoming DMK led by the redoubtable CN Annadurai, known universally as 'Anna' or 'Elder Brother'. In May 1963, Anna had stressed in Parliament, "I speak for English not because I am enamoured of it, but because it is the most convenient tool, it is the most convenient medium which distributes advantages or disadvantages evenly." He added, "If the British were to remain here and say, take it (English), then we will have to resist it. But now there is no question of imposition of English by the British." Instead, in independent India, "the consequence of the imposition of Hindi as the official language will create a definite, permanent and sickening advantage to the Hindi-speaking States." Moreover, he wanted Nehru's three-part assurance to be incorporated in the Constitution, holding that a mere law passed by a majority vote in a Parliament heavily dominated by the Congress could just as easily be changed.

Nor, at the other end of the spectrum, was there satisfaction that Hindi-speaking provinces were obliged indefinitely to receive and respond in English to correspondence from the Centre or other states. As Vajpayee put it, "English will not be forced on (the) Hindi provinces" and added, "We do not want to impose Hindi but we will not allow English to be imposed" (Rajya Sabha, 22/2/65). Later, he argued, "If Tamil is used in Madras, Marathi in Bombay, Bengali in Calcutta, will English keep hanging on in New Delhi like Trishanku?" (RS, 12/12/67).

For the first fifteen years of the Republic, argument was heated in Parliament and the media but the streets were spared agitation and violence. Then, since the DMK felt that Hindi "zealots" were determined to use the fifteenth year of the Republic to ram through Hindi as the sole official language, they declared Republic Day, 1965 as a "Day of Mourning". The Congress government in Madras cracked down on the DMK leadership. Arresting one and all, it opened the way to a student takeover of the movement, with two young men resorting to the hitherto unknown tactic of setting themselves on fire in protest. The situation was defused only by Indira Gandhi courageously rushing to the middle of the melee in Madras, much to the annoyance of Lal Bahadur Shastri, but with that one move, and the reassuring words she spoke to the Tamils, raging violence was ended and the debate brought back to the floor of the Houses of Parliament.

When Parliament reconvened for the Budget session in February 1965, just as the riots were petering out in consequence of Indira Gandhi's bold initiative, Vajpayee clarified that he was "against forcing Hindi on any non-Hindi province" and added, "The decision to bring Indian languages is a revolutionary decision, but if it endangers the national unity the non-Hindi States may continue English." (Modi, please note). That set the stage for reflecting on further amending the 1963 Act to respond to continuing Tamil concerns. (Cooperative federalism at its best: will Modi please take note?) the government brought the required amendment to the House in December 1967, with Indira Gandhi intervening to warn, "Language is becoming a wall dividing people from each other, a source of conflict. If this debate creates discord, then neither Hindi nor any other language will be promoted." (Modi, please also note!) Underlining that "there are seven states that do not want Hindi to be imposed on them," she urged that "the passage of this Bill [Official Languages (Amendment) Act, 1967] is necessary to remove all apprehensions from the minds of the people of the South and of the non-Hindi-speaking regions" (LS, 5/12/67).

Thus, was a compromise reached that has endured for the better part of four decades. To unravel that concord, as the Modi government's blunder in its first month in office indicated, is, indeed, to endanger national unity. Moreover, it will not do for the Moditva Union government to concentrate on propagating Hindi alone. It will have to answer the question posed by Era Sezhiyan to Vajpayee in 1967 when Vajpayee argued that there were Hindi Prachar Sabhas in all South Indian states: "Is there one Tamil Prachar Sabha in UP? Is there one Malayalam Prachar Sabha in Madhya Pradesh?" Answer!

NDTV.com

WHAT ABOUT ACHHI RAATEIN?

28 June 2014

"Stumble, stumble/Mumble and bumble" succinctly sums up the first month of the Narendra Modi government. A sampling:

Having raved and ranted at the UPA for its Ordinance Raj, Act No.1 of Modi's good governance model is to issue an ordinance to overcome the legal ban on his appointing as his principal secretary a man notorious for having so bungled the order he issued as chairman of Telecom Regulatory Authority of India, that the ambiguity of that order was at the root of the 2G scam.

On the morrow of the swearing-in, the minister of state in the Prime Minister's Office stirs a hornet's nest by asserting the primacy in the BJP's scheme of things of abolishing Article 370 of the Constitution. Omar Abdullah warns that any such attempt could lead to Jammu and Kashmir seceding from the Union of India.

On the same day, a howl of protest is unleashed in the Pakistan media as the Indian foreign secretary's briefing on the Modi-Nawaz Sharif talks indicates that Modi had given a wigging to Sharif, who took it lying down. Modi is still to show that Sharif's gift of a white sari to Modi's mother is not a white flag of craven surrender.

Delhi is plunged in darkness, which only deepens the darkness metaphorically resident in Race Course Road. As the citizenry sweats it out in airless nights, it anxiously inquire: *achhe din toh aaye hain, lekin achhe raat kab aayegi?*

Forty Indians are kidnapped in Iraq and a government that does not even acknowledge West Asia in its first policy statement, the President's Address, is left without any friends in the region.

Oil prices shoot through the roof and threaten to breach the $150/barrel mark, but the Modi government does not even have a cabinet minister to handle the looming threat.

Meanwhile, prices of essential commodities soar to unprecedented heights and apart from blaming the previous government, Modi has only vacuous excuses to offer.

While the self-appointed BJP mentor, Herr Doktor Professor Subramanian Swamy, threatens Reserve Bank of India Governor Raghuram Rajan with instant dismissal for failing to lower the interest rates, price rise compels Finance Minister Arun Jaitley to retain the UPA-appointed governor. Then, passenger fares on the railways go up by 14 per cent and freight charges by more than 6 per cent even as the Modi government claims that it is not their fault.

To distract attention from the government's inability to handle the nation's economic woes, a needless controversy is stirred on the Uniform Civil Code, alarming the minorities, especially the Muslims, and alerting secularists to the hidden, ulterior agenda of the forces of Hindutva.

The government is trying to muzzle civil society activism by targeting NGOs like Greenpeace for foreign funding, forgetting that the Sangh Parivar is the biggest beneficiary of foreign, specifically NRI, funding.

A Special Investigation Team is established to recover the black money stashed away abroad by Indians but no special team is formed to plug the channels through which the money is funnelled out of the country.

Moreover, there is no disclosure of information already obtained from Switzerland because, as the UPA government pleaded, the Swiss and the Germans disclose names and account numbers only against iron-clad guarantees of non-disclosure.

Sparking Bonapartism in the Indian Armed Forces, the BJP not only gave a ticket to former General VK Singh but also made him a minister even after he launched a vicious attack against a brother-officer destined for the high office of the Chief of Army Staff.

Zero tolerance to violence against women is proved by clinging on to Nihal Chand Meghwal (Meghwal who?) as an indispensable minister of state in the Modi dispensation.

At this rate, Rahul Gandhi can start stitching his curtains for an early return to Race Course Road!

The Week

DO HINDUS WANT A UNIFORM CIVIL CODE?

4 July 2014

My Sikh wife and I were married 41 years ago under the Special Marriage Act, 1954. But for a slight hiccup when I had to suppress a giggle reading the prescribed oath, swearing that I was not married to anyone else "to the best of my knowledge and belief", the event went off smoothly. If, however, we had contracted a civil marriage before 1954, we would have first had to relinquish our respective religions before the knot could be tied. A Uniform Civil Code was available before 1954 only to agnostics and atheists who had proved their credentials by foreswearing the religion of their ancestors.

This changed in 1954. The Special Marriage Act, read with the Indian Succession Act, 1925 (note the non-denominational adjective "Indian"), constitutes the voluntary Uniform Civil Code we gave ourselves sixty years ago. Yet the very Moditvists who have pledged to impose a compulsory Uniform Civil Code on our minorities have not deigned to explain why they themselves have not availed of the Uniform Civil Code that has been on our statutes for six decades. No, they prefer to get married under the Hindu code and regulate their personal lives in terms of Hindu Personal Law, embodied in a series of four laws enacted in 1955 and 1956 – that is, well after the voluntary Uniform Civil Code was bestowed on the country – while sneering at the minorities who baulk at their respective Personal Laws being substituted by a compulsory Uniform Civil Code.

Why this hypocrisy? Only to mock at Muslims, to claim that the Muslims are reactionary while the majority is progressive. There is no Personal Law more progressive than the laws under which I got married. That was a decision I made reluctantly and only because the priests at the temple my father had built refused to perform the rites since the girl I wanted to marry was not a Brahmin. They offered instead a whisky priest who would do what was required for a small fee. Furious, I rejected the offer outright and opted instead, with her consent, for us to be married under a modern, secular law.

That modern, secular law being readily available, why did the majority community opt instead for their own Personal Law? Only because Hindu Personal Law is precious to Hindus. In which case, why should their respective Personal Laws not also be precious to other communities?

True, Hindu Law has been codified by Parliament while the other Personal Laws have not. But that is only because Mahatma Gandhi had ensured that our Freedom Movement was not only about ridding ourselves of foreign rule but also of shedding horrendous malpractices that had adhered to the religion and culture of the Hindus to the shame of the Hindu community. Codification had proved possible because it was the unfinished business of the struggle for Independence.

Indeed, long before Independence, in 1941, the British Indian government set up a Hindu Law Committee under B.N. Rau that took 6 years to complete its toils and reported to the Constituent Assembly on the eve of Independence. Another eight years were taken in getting the Hindu Marriage Act passed in 1955; the Hindu Succession Act in 1956; the Hindu Adoption and Maintenance Act, also 1956; and the Hindu Minority and Guardianship Act, also of 1956. Numerous amendments have since been brought to these laws, and this will doubtless continue. It could be regarded as a 'work in progress'. To expect other communities to act any sooner to reform their own laws would be invidious.

It may also be noted that in the many debates in Parliament on the legislation that derived from the Rau committee's Hindu Code Bill, it was only Hindu MPs who took part; there was little or no Muslim, Christian or Parsi participation – for the non-Hindus felt, quite correctly, that it was for the Hindus, not others, to reform and codify their law. Then why should non-Muslims tell Muslims or other non-Hindus how to reform themselves?

Reform is not easy. Hindu conservatives, from the President, Dr. Rajendra Prasad, down fought a rearguard battle to fend off reform as long as they could. And introduced so many loopholes in the code that there are more bigamous and polygamous marriages among Hindus than Muslims

(1961 Census and 1974 Committee on the Status of Women). Besides, as a result of an amendment brought in 1964 to the Hindu Marriage Act, now, under Hindu divorce law, Hindu wives can be "simply expelled from the matrimonial home when the husband state(s) that, as far as he is concerned, the marriage ha(s) broken down." Triple *talaq* anyone? (I am not quoting myself, but an eminent jurist, Prof. Ajay Kumar, Dean of the Faculty of Law, Ambedkar University, Lucknow in his magnum opus, *Uniform Civil Code: Challenges and Constraints*, 2012). He goes on to quote another authority on Hindu law, Dr. JDM Derret, as saying the subsequent Marriage Laws (Amendment) Act, 1976 has led to "still more amazingly gender-insensitive case law". Flavio Agnes' celebrated article in *The Economic and Political Weekly*, 16 December 1995, documents a whole sheaf of such vicious case law.

Moreover, as Vice-Chancellor Farzana Mustafa of NALSAR University of Law, Hyderabad asks with regard to reformed Hindu law, "Has it resulted in the upliftment of Hindu women? How many Hindu women get a share in property? The amount of land actually inherited by Hindu women is only a small fraction of the amount of land they are entitled to under the reformed Hindu law. Changes in law do not bring about necessary social reform." And she concludes, "Normative changes in law certainly do not bring about necessary social reform." (*The Hindu*, 2 July 2014).

Which leads us to the key point, that is, reform must come from within a community if law is to translate into social changes on the ground. That is precisely what the Bharatiya Mahila Muslim Andolan (BMMA) is engaged in doing. Noorjehan Safia Niaz, co-founder of BMMA has been quoted in *The Hindu* magazine section of 29 June 2014 as saying that after consulting with a wide cross-section of mostly poor Muslim women, running to thousands in 10 states over a period of seven years, they have drafted a new "Muslim Marriage and Divorce Act". She says, "Let the community debate our draft first."

As several Muslim countries, including Pakistan, have shown, reform of Muslim Personal Law is certainly as feasible as the reform of Hindu Personal Law – but, as in the case of Hindus, only when the pressure for reform comes from within the community. Imposition from the outside, especially when the community is in a minority, cannot but be resisted. That is why Begum Safia Niaz states categorically, "We oppose the Uniform Civil Code." They want the Personal Law of their community to continue but believe they can reform it from within. Surely any patriotic Indian would laud that initiative.

It is argued, among others in obiter dicta pronounced from the Supreme Court, that a Uniform Civil Code would strengthen national integration. Quite to the contrary, attempts to precipitate legislation without general consensus will only provoke communal tension, even as denigratory remarks about another community's beliefs and practices only result in national disintegration. If, impatiently, we move to reform Muslim Personal Law by Parliamentary decree in a Parliament where Muslims are woefully under-represented, and before a consensus evolves within the Muslim community on the nature and details of reform, we would be in danger of transgressing the Constitution's "country-specific and situation-sensitive method of handling complex socio-legal issues." Kumar hits the nail on the head when he argues that because the Constitution "is typically Indian, full of the recognition of differences between various groups of people and respectful of diversity at many levels," it has succeeded in promoting "the existing plurality of laws, with the Personal Law system as a central element re-anchored within the over-arching framework of the Indian Constitution." At the same time, says Kumar, "The Indian State has acted purposefully, albeit silently, surreptitiously, cautiously and gradually (in) harmonizing various Indian personal laws along similar lines without challenging their status as separate personal laws." He cites, by way of example, the Prohibition of Child Marriage Act, 2006. That is the intelligent way forward.

So, while putting any Uniform Civil Code on hold, the Modi government might like to make a beginning towards giving the country a Uniform Fiscal Code. Why tax concessions for only Hindu Undivided Families (HUF)? Why not for any Undivided Family whatever the community? One expects Finance Minister Arun Jaitley to respond to that googly in his Budget speech next week.

NDTV.com

TWO LITTLE WORDS MISSING FROM MODI BUDGET

12 July 2014

For all the bumph in the BJP manifesto and the President's Address about Moditva intending to prioritize the poor, there is nothing – literally nothing – in Arun Jaitley's first budget to bring cheer to any rural household. The only silver lining is that Jaitley has not fiddled over much with the slew of pro-poor programmes initiated by the previous government. Perhaps one should thank the Lord for small mercies.

Yet, Modi has the gall to describe the budget as an "arunodaya". It's not. It's just Arun Jaitley. The Finance Minister deserves an award for being the first FM ever to talk for two-and-a-half hours without once mentioning Panchayat Raj – a feat possible only by someone so far removed from the rural poor as to leave them not even entering his reckoning of whom the budget is for. For Jaitley, the only constituency to whom the budget is addressed is the pink papers and his patrons on Dalal Street. (Yet, Dalal Street was so unimpressed, Sensex and Nifty actually fell as he droned on!) In this, he is at one with *The Economic Times* which has devoted all 23 pages of its main edition on the morrow to the budget without once referring to the hundreds of millions of the rural poor who are most in need. Fortunately for them, the UPA government lasted ten years before the "arunoday". Arun Jaitley was thus able to re-circulate all the UPA programmes with nary a change to claim them as the BJP's own. If one is relieved at that, that is only because during these self-same ten years, Jaitley & Co. have torn into these programmes as a waste of money, a drain on resources, schemes, as Modi claimed during his infamous campaign, that have no aim other than "filling the pockets of the Congress netas". Well, perhaps they have been left untouched the better to fill the pockets of the BJP's netas.

If there is at least a little hope for the really poor it comes from two sources. One is the long list of 29 token schemes announced by Jaitley each with a token allocation of ₹100 crore, which is North Block-speak for saying, "Don't worry we won't actually implement any of these schemes but will work on them in the coming year to see what is feasible and how much it will cost." Other FMs have done the same – but for one or two schemes. Jaitley has topped them all with a wish-list (or deception list) of 29. My apprehension is not that these schemes will fall by the wayside but that it will all amount to tinkering with the machine without addressing the fundamental question of why compared to financial allocations, outcomes are so poor, be it education, health, drinking water, sanitation or any of the 29 subjects illustratively listed in the Eleventh Schedule as the Constitutionally-proposed domain for Panchayat Raj Institutions (PRIs).

Moditva seems not to understand that panchayats are the forum for "Jan Shakti" and "Jan Bhagidari" – people's empowerment and people's participation that Modi has claimed for Jaitley's budget. But if the two little words "Panchayat Raj" are not even mentioned in a 150-minute oration, and no note is taken of the five-volume report on leveraging Panchayat Raj Institutions for the more effective delivery of public goods and services that was submitted over a year ago by an expert committee I chaired, then I fear that all this business of jan shakti and jan bhagidari is just empty rhetoric of the kind that befooled the electorate in the first half of this year and which the country will soon learn is what Modi means when he incessantly mouths the words "good governance".

Modinomics has never, not in Gujarat, not since, ever understood the needs of the poor. That is why Modi's Gujarat has so pathetically lagged behind almost half the states of the Union on the Human Development Index despite being fourth on the growth rate measure (after Bihar, Maharashtra and Tamil Nadu). This is principally because Modi does not understand or empathize with Panchayat Raj.

In an investigative article in *The Economic and Political Weekly* of 31 May 2014, a fortnight after Modi rode to power, which got drowned in the media euphoria of Modi's election, Atulan Guha of the Institute of Rural Management Anand, in Gujarat, has detailed how the Gujarat government under the Samras Gram Yojana has forestalled elections to Panchayats by incentivizing panchayats with monetary grants to not hold elections. This has insulated panchayats in Gujarat from the people they are supposed to serve, reducing these panchayats to political agents of the party in power in Gandhinagar instead of letting them evolve as forums for the ventilation of people's concerns and the redressal of people's grievances.

If there is no people's involvement in the delivery of public goods and services, that is, no jan bhagidari, how can there be any jan shakti? And if in twelve years of ruling Gujarat with an iron hand, Modi has devolved precisely nothing to the panchayats, then what hope is there of his ensuring this will happen through his one innovation – central assistance programmes rather than centrally-sponsored schemes? Where local politicians and the local lower bureaucracy alone are entrusted with performance, outcomes will inevitably be sub-optimal. As Guha observes after quoting the official justification for not encouraging elections to panchayats, "power structures have remained unchanged and continue to favour traditionally powerful communities...(R)epresentatives, including the sarpanch, have to be acceptable to the dominant family or group of families in the village." Moreover, "there are no district planning committees formed" – a key requirement of the Constitution – and "there is no formula for the devolution of funds from the state government to the PRIs." In a word, "fiscal federalism within Gujarat is non-existent." State Finance Commissions in the state have been consistently crippled. No wonder "(a)ccording to the reports of the Thirteenth Finance Commission, Gujarat has scored 'zero' in the index of devolution."

For the better part of a decade I have wondered why Modi, almost alone among the Chief Ministers of India, refused to invite me as Union Minister of Panchayat Raj (2004-09) to his state to review Panchayat Raj and sign an MoU about how to improve matters like 21 other CMs had done. I suspected he did not want anyone to uncover his sins of omission and commission. I now have the definitive explanation. He knew I would rip off the mask and expose him to the public gaze as Enemy No. 1 of Panchayat Raj. That is no longer needed. He has indicted himself through this Budget.

NDTV.com

A BAD WEEK FOR FOREIGN POLICY

18 July 2014

The BJP had, of course, threatened us in their manifesto with "rebooting and reorienting" foreign policy, but one had rather hoped that was just one of the usual simplistic alliterative phrases in which Narendra Modi likes to couch what passes for his "thoughts". But the week that has passed seems to indicate that they mean it. Take two events, the BRICS summit in Brazil and the Palestine crisis.

Dropping bricks at BRICS

This was Modi's first outing as Prime Minister at an international forum and one would have expected Protocol to be tickety-boo. Apparently, while the rest of the world was glued to football, Protocol did not know that Germany was the favourite. And so dinner with Angela Merkel was scheduled in Berlin even as dear Angela was telling everyone within earshot that she intended to skip out of Berlin to be present when her team would prove to be uber alles (above all others).

So even as Modi descended on Berlin, she hopped off to Brazil. This left Modi with only himself to feed, rendering the stop at Berlin wholly infructuous (except for the aircraft that was re-fuelled). True, on the return flight, he managed to refuel his aircraft at Frankfurt to give himself the opportunity of a telephone chat with Merkel. But he had nothing to say that, as a social media aficionado, he could not have tweeted or asked Merkel, "What's Up?" by WhatsApp. All he achieved was annoying Japan which had been promised Modi's first visit out of the subcontinent.

That, alas, was not the last protocol bloomer. Modi had arranged to meet Putin on arrival. But Putin had more important business talking to the Brazilian President in Brasilia, 1600 km from Fortaleza. So, accidentally or with deliberate intent to show Modi that he disapproved of our less than vocal stance on the happenings in Ukraine, Putin fetched up in Fortaleza a good two hours after his scheduled meeting with Modi.

Another get-together was cobbled at the last moment but it was a hurried encounter instead of the leisurely conversation that was to be expected between India and her oldest and closest friend. The most charitable explanation that I can cook up is that perhaps Putin got held up because he knew Modi was going to suggest a gas pipeline from Russia to India and Putin was checking on how the line was to cross the Pamirs and the Hindukush to keep Modi khush!

The main outcome of the sixth BRICS summit was the agreement to establish a New Development Bank, the BRICS Bank. But that had been in the works since long before Modi became PM. The NDB was agreed at the Fourth BRICS summit (in 2010, at New Delhi, under Dr. Manmohan Singh's chairmanship, please note) and taken forward at the Fifth Summit into a "direction" to their Finance Ministers to complete the work before the next Summit. Our Foreign Service and Finance Ministry sherpas having toiled mightily to the summit, all that remained was for Modi to affix his signature and claim the credit. And, boy, did he claim the credit!

The magic of the man is that he positions himself at the right place at the right time to do none of the work and get all of the credit. We saw that in 2001 when he came to office as Chief Minister in the very year that the Sardar Sarovar Dam was commissioned, thereby garnering to himself all the bonus points for converting arid Gujarat into a green field. In fact, had it not been for Rajiv Gandhi clearing the project and PV Narasimha Rao stepping in with the financing when the World Bank withdrew, there would have been no scope for Modi to point with pride to his rate of agricultural growth. Of course, he exaggerated, which is why his bogus claims of +10 per cent agricultural growth has now been shown to be not much more than 6 per cent.

So also, with the BRICS Bank. The idea was Dr. Manmohan Singh's; the hard work was that of the UPA government; and Modi arrives just in time to climb the victors' stand and claim the cup as all his own!

And much the same applies to China having invited us as an Observer to the Asia-Pacific Economic Cooperation (APEC) meeting: that too was in the works aeons before Modi moved to Race Course Road, as was the decision now secured to have an Indian presence in the Shanghai Cooperation Council that battles regional terrorism. Nothing Modivian to this beyond affixing his seal on someone else's draft.

This is the way the world used to hail Dr. Manmohan Singh:

• President Obama at the G-20 Summit in 2010: "I can tell you here at G-20, when the Prime Minister speaks, people listen."

• At BRICS 2013, Chinese President Xi Jinping "was all praise for Dr. Singh for his statesmanship".

• President Putin at his farewell meeting with him in October 2013 attributed to Dr. Manmohan Singh "most of our mutual achievements have been achieved under your leadership."

And yet the BJP has the gall to say that it is they who will ensure that India's "voice is heard in the international fora". Ha! Ha! Worse, they go on to say, "India's relations with traditional allies have turned cold." And this in the face of the encomiums showered on the last PM. Please note: It was not Manmohan Singh whom Putin stood up at their first date - it was Modi!

Shilly-shallying over Palestine

The External Affairs Minister spent the entire week ducking out of a discussion in Parliament on Palestine. Here is a country of whom Gandhiji said in 1938, "Palestine belongs to the Palestinians as England to the English and France to the French." That has been the theme song of our relationship with Palestine through all the turbulence of the last seven decades – which Nehru alone, of all statesmen in the world, foresaw – when in November 1947 India became the only non-Arab, non-Muslim country to vote against the partition of Palestine, urging instead a one-State solution with an autonomous area for the Jews and an autonomous area for the Arabs functioning under a democratically elected Union Government of Palestine.

The Palestinians have never forgotten our solidarity with them – until now, when we have the distressing spectacle of the Palestine Embassy in Delhi and its charge d'affairs pleading that India not equate the air bombing of 200 innocent Palestinian civilians with Hamas rocket attacks that have killed no one in Israel.

I never dreamed it would come to this – that we would forsake our Arab brethren at the moment of their greatest need. Despite all Arab countries and Iran being Muslim, and despite Pakistan's nefarious attempts to swing the Arabs and Iranians to their side on grounds of religion, all Arab and Iranian regimes – monarchist or republican, revolutionary or Islamist – have always stood by us, played host to eight million of our expatriate workers, furnish more than 70 per cent of our crude oil requirements, and constitute a key destination for our exports.

All this is being jeopardized by a BJP that cannot look beyond its communally prejudiced eyes. We have got back our nurses thanks principally to the goodwill built up with all the Arab countries and Iran over the last seven decades. We are at risk of wrecking that with the one-eyed focus that the BJP has on anti-Arab, anti-Muslim Israel. That is a tragedy all patriotic, secular Indians must resist.

NDTV.com

RIGHT TURN TO WRONG

18 July 2014

While it would be churlish not to recognise that External Affairs Minister Sushma Swaraj has come out well from her first foreign policy crisis, it would be more than churlish not to recognise that our nurses returned safe because of the goodwill that India has built in the Arab world over the decades. That goodwill stands in danger of being dissipated if the BJP remains unwilling to nuance its pro-Israel, anti-Muslim approach to West Asia.

That is putting it bluntly, but the fact is that, perhaps for the first time ever, the President's Address on June 9 – the new government's first policy statement – did not even mention West Asia and aggravated the omission by waxing eloquent on defence ties with Israel.

Then came Prime Minister Narendra Modi's reply to the debate on the motion of thanks, in which he thundered about how India had suffered not just 200 years of British rule but "1200 years of mental slavery". The first thousand of those years were the ones in which India had interacted closely with the Muslim world.

Contrast Modi's vituperation with Indira Gandhi at Baghdad University (January 1975): "Arab civilisation dazzled the world with its brilliance"; the friendship between India and Iraq "is one of the oldest in history"; and how "during the high noon of the Arab renaissance, there was fruitful exchange between the philosophers and scientists of our two countries."

If the new government continues to treat the Arabs as slave-drivers who only oppressed us for a millennium – which is the standard Sangh Parivar perspective – our relations with the Arab world will plummet.

The tone of the India-Arab relationship was set when Mahatma Gandhi wrote in the 1930s, "Palestine belongs to the Palestinians just as England belongs to the English and France to the French."

In March 1947, Jawaharlal Nehru convened the first Asian Relations Conference. It was there, writes Shankar Sharan in an article commemorating 50 years of the conference, where the delegates from Egypt and the Arab League "disputed some of the statements made by the Jewish delegation. Pandit Jawaharlal Nehru, with tact and patience, controlled the situation and the whole assembly gave a thundering applause when the leader of the Jewish delegation shook hands with the Arab delegates."

The following month, India was named in a UN committee to resolve the Palestine issue. India, herself recovering from Partition, took the principled stand that Palestine must not be partitioned. With pressure from the West and the Soviet Union, many UN members changed their views. But not India. We were the only non-Muslim country to vote against Palestine's partition.

Solidarity with Palestinians has been but one aspect of our relationship with the Arab world. When, in 1956, the British, French and Israelis declared war on Egypt over Colonel Nasser's nationalisation of the Suez Canal, we were in the forefront to condemn the aggression. Along with us, Egypt became a founding member of the Non-Aligned Movement.

Pakistan's attempts to portray itself as the wronged party in the Islamic forums were thwarted by a phalanx of our Arab friends. And, as various Arab countries attained liberation, India was seen by them as a champion of their causes.

While the Arab world is in turmoil at present, whoever emerges victorious, India's friendship will be valued. This has everything to do with the policy expounded by Rajiv Gandhi at the tenth Non-Aligned Summit in Belgrade on September 5, 1989: "The people of Palestine are denied a state of their own in their homeland and subjected to unspeakable cruelties.... The Intifada is an authentic revolution of our times. We welcome the proclamation of the State of Palestine."

And in return for such support, the Arabs of West Asia and North Africa have become host to 70 lakh Indian expatriates, and been our principal oil suppliers.

It would be a folly to leach that relationship of its significance to our national interests. Yet, there is the danger of that happening if the Sangh Parivar's ideology is going to permeate our relations with the Muslim world. It is a tragedy that must be forestalled.

The Week

GAZA CONFLICT – MODI, LEARN FROM NEHRU

21 July 2014

The BJP government in its first foreign policy outing disgraced itself today in the Rajya Sabha debate on Palestine. It showed itself to be communal, biased, and careless of the country's vital interests.

Sushma Swaraj claimed that her foreign policy was not founded on religion, but the first speaker on her side, Anil Madhavan Dave, had already revealed the communal angle by invoking "namaz" and "jannat" in a debate on Palestine, adding that he had a Muslim friend who desisted from saying his namaz when Dave told him that the mosque which he was preparing to enter was a "vivadhit dhancha" (disputed structure – the old Babri Masjid terminology). What a comical definition of a "good Muslim"!

Worse was the assertion outside the House by the Parliamentary Affairs minister, Venkaiah Naidu, who declared to the media that for the Opposition this was "an issue of the minorities" (*The Economic Times,* 16 July 2014). This was of a piece with Jaswant Singh's ridiculous assertion when he was Foreign Minister that India had held back from according full diplomatic recognition to Israel only because the Congress was "appeasing" the Muslims. Sushma's protestations notwithstanding, Dave was only echoing the views of his seniors and, more generally, the Sangh Parivar that controls the BJP like a puppet on a string.

It is because of this communal line that the BJP is so utterly biased in its treatment of Israel's current invasion of Palestine. They equate Israel's blistering bombing of the Gaza strip with the rocket attacks of Hamas. The Israeli blitz has claimed nearly 500 innocent lives thus far, including women, children and the aged. Thousands more have been seriously injured, few with any hope of surviving as Gaza just does

72

not have enough hospitals, medicines or doctors to attend to all of them. Thousands more have been rendered homeless. Hospitals have not been spared; nor schools; not even old-age homes. Yet, the BJP blatantly equates the aggressor with the victim, forgetting that Israel has the most sophisticated arsenal and nuclear bombs as well, while Palestine does not have, and is not permitted to have, an army, an air force or a navy. Gaza's port is blockaded; its air strip closed down. It has no way out of the siege other than underground tunnels. To get at these, the Israelis are mercilessly killing and maiming the innocents who live overground. The BJP is blinded to all this by sheer bias and prejudice.

Leave alone poor Sushma, take Modi himself. His three-sentence statement on the Israel-Palestine situation at the BRICS summit is a classic of obfuscation. He begins by expressing "concern" over the on-going "conflict". Concern? What about condemnation? Moreover, how can there be equal concern over the victim whose casualties run to thousands, and an aggressor who is behaving like a school bully because he knows there can be no equivalent retaliation from the Palestinians?

He then goes on to say, "We support a negotiated solution." What he fails to mention is that negotiations cannot be restarted until Israel stops its massacre of unarmed, innocent Palestinians. He also fails to recognize that it was not the Palestinians but the Israelis who broke off the negotiations last year just as they seemed about to succeed. Why? Because Hamas, which had been democratically elected by the people of Gaza, had decided to bury their differences with Al-Fatah and the two together were presenting a joint front to the Israelis. In a classic case of divide and rule, the Israelis objected to the two factions coming together and insisted that it is only when they split apart that Israel would return to the negotiating table. How can Modi talk of "negotiations" without recognizing who is responsible for sabotaging them?

Modi's final sentence was that if a negotiated solution were found, this would "inspire hope and confidence round the world". Of course, it would. But who is responsible for stalling negotiations? Should they not cease fire, accept the delegation the Palestinians send to the talks and thus "inspire hope and confidence", Certainly, Modi inspires neither hope nor confidence. We have been nakedly revealed to the world as a country with no conviction in our foreign policy, no principles, no long-term vision, and with nothing to contribute to world peace.

One can only recall in growing despair Jawaharlal Nehru's wise counsel to Parliament when it first discussed the Palestine issue on 4 December 1947, just after Palestine was partitioned. Referring to our independent and principled stand against the partitioning of Palestine, he said, "Inevitably that means...we have to plough a lonely furrow in the United Nations or in international conferences of this type." And went on to add: "Nonetheless, that is the only honourable and right position by which we shall ultimately gain national and international prestige."

Modi forgot that lesson at Fortaleza. He meekly went along with paragraph 38 of the BRICS Declaration which neither condemns Israel nor calls for a ceasefire. We are back at November 1947 when other powers tried to make us change our mind. They succeeded with several weaker powers but failed with us. Eventually, it was India that gained international prestige that went with our founding and leading the Movement of Nonaligned Countries (NAM). Nehru's prophecy was fulfilled. We did gain "national and international prestige" that is now being betrayed by Modi and his government. Alas, alas, alas!

NDTV.com

THE GAZA EVASION

23 July 2014

Next only to South Asia, West Asia matters most to us in foreign policy. It is where nearly eight lakh expatriate workers are making their living. It is from their remittances, constituting more than half of our total foreign exchange earnings, that we get the wherewithal to buy arms from Israel. Their safety is crucially dependent on the Arab goodwill that we have patiently built with Arab and Iranian regimes, monarchist or republican, revolutionary or Islamist. The region is the second or third most important destination for our exports. And it is from there that we source 70 per cent of our oil imports.

The issue that most unites the otherwise fractious nations of West Asia and Iran is Israel. It is in this respect that, owing to the immense foresight and sheer goodness of Jawaharlal Nehru, we made what till recently was an indelible mark on the West Asian and Iranian consciousness. Gandhiji set the tone with his celebrated remark in 1938, "Palestine belongs to the Palestinians as England belongs to the English and France to the French."

In keeping with that, but recognising that Palestine was also home to a large and growing number of Jews, Nehru invited both Palestinian and Zionist representatives to the Asian Relations Conference in March 1947.

Inevitably, the two clashed, and it was left to Nehru to bring them together. The audience burst into thunderous applause when the heads of the two delegations shook hands.

In keeping with that spirit, India played a leading role in the two committees set up by the UN to consider the future of Palestine at the termination of the British mandate. While the West and the Soviet Union were united in their demand that Palestine be partitioned to create a sovereign homeland for the Jews, India, itself under the shadow of a looming, blood-soaked Partition, took the lead in arguing for a single federal state in which there would be two autonomous Jewish and Arab regions, but with a common central government democratically elected by all the citizens of a common state. To begin with, it looked as if the Indian formula would work as a compromise between the two diametrically opposed positions taken by the Arab states and the Zionists, but slowly, as pressure on the smaller states mounted from the major powers, they moved to the other side and Palestine was ultimately partitioned. The consequences have been more far-reaching and far more prolonged than was the case with the partitioning of India. But every dire prophecy of the Indian delegation has been more than tragically fulfilled, with terrible human consequences over the last 67 years.

The alternative two-state solution has been proposed but is far from being realised. Israel, with all the cards in its hands, has encroached so far into Palestinian territory as to have reversed the shares originally intended, from 95 per cent for the Arabs and 5 per cent for the Jews to 95 per cent for Israel and 5 per cent for Palestine, that too a Palestine split into a series of Bantustans and divided by Israeli territory between the West Bank and the Gaza strip, besides being peppered with illegal Israeli settlements. For a moment in 1992, the Palestinians (but not the brilliant chief negotiator, Hanan Ashrawi) were befooled into believing that the Oslo process had handed them the state of Palestine on a platter. When I then argued that it was not a state but merely panchayati raj in Gaza, I was accused of trying to be more Arab than the Arabs. But ultimately the truth dawned, and the Palestinians realised they had been tricked into returning from Tunisia to Gaza, where they were locked up and effectively isolated from the world.

Not wishing to be more Arab than the Arabs, PV Narasimha Rao decided the moment had come to upgrade relations with Israel to full diplomatic level. Since then, and particularly after Israel supplied the shells we needed to fire our Bofors guns in the Kargil war, relations with Israel have boomed while those with the Arab world have slid to now hit rock bottom.

How rock bottom was revealed in Narendra Modi's performance at Fortaleza. His intervention on the merciless aerial bombing and ground assault by the Israelis on Gaza was limited to three sentences. First, he said, he was "concerned" at the ongoing "conflict". Concerned, not outraged? Earlier, his foreign office spokesman had equated Israel with Hamas, overlooking hundreds of Palestinian innocents that were and are being killed, whereas the retaliatory Hamas rocket attacks have killed much fewer Israelis. Moreover, Hamas has no army, navy or air force. Its port has been blockaded, its solitary airport dismantled. The only way out is underground tunnels; so the Israelis slaughter those who live above the tunnels. How can Hamas's military capabilities be compared to those of Israel? Yet, from Modi, no condemnation, no harsh words, just mere "concern" over the one-sided ongoing massacre.

His second sentence is brief to the point of abruptness, "We support a negotiated solution." But who broke off negotiations last year just when they were coming to fruition? Israel. And why? Because Hamas and Fatah had buried their differences and come together. In a classic divide and rule manoeuvre, Israel walked out of the peace talks and refuses to come back so long as Hamas sits at the table. Surely, therefore, the line on "negotiated solutions" should be addressed to Israel first. And for negotiations to commence, surely aggression and the killing of the lambs has to stop. Who is presiding over this slaughterhouse? Israel, of course. And therefore, whose responsibility is it that the butchery be ended? Israel's, of course. But Modi has nothing to say about a ceasefire as the necessary precondition for negotiations to be resumed.

Third, Modi said a negotiated solution would "inspire hope and confidence" the world over. That's all very well, but surely the cat to be belled is Israel. Let them cease fire on the condition that talks are resumed – and the talks will be resumed. But a ceasefire without talks is the road to nowhere. And although Israel claims to be prepared to cease fire, it is not ready to negotiate unless Fatah dissolves its new found ties with Hamas.

Finally, what of the BRICS? Paragraph 38 of the Fortaleza Declaration blabbers on and on about Palestine, but it neither condemns Israel nor calls for a ceasefire. Modi and External Affairs Minister Sushma Swaraj take convenient cover behind that. In doing so, they forget Nehru who, referring to the problems we had had in the

Palestine committees, said in the Constituent Assembly on December 4, 1947: "Inevitably that means we have to plough a lonely furrow." But he added, "Nonetheless, that is the only honourable and right position by which we shall ultimately gain national and international prestige." Modi and Swaraj cowering behind the BRICS position is not an edifying sight. The BJP has betrayed its own clarion call in its manifesto of giving us an independent voice in international fora.

Indian Express

SILENCE FROM MODI, GREAT SOCIAL MEDIA MOGUL

28 July 2014

Eleven Shiv Sainiks go on the rampage in New Maharashtra Sadan, stuffing chapattis down the gullet of a Muslim canteen-wallah protesting that he is keeping the roza in the middle of Ramzan – and the Great Communicator keeps his mouth shut and his Twitter account on silent mode. An innocent Muslim techie in Maharashtra is murdered in Pune for the sin of wearing a skullcap and growing a beard – and the Social Media Mogul has nothing, absolutely nothing to say on his Facebook page – even in Hindi. 19 boys – all Muslims – are hauled up by the police in Kerala for a spoof on Modi, and Modi has nothing to say about Fundamental Freedoms. His supporters cover his tracks by saying that all three incidents took place in Congress-run states and the Prime Minister is only being discreet in the interest of "cooperative federalism". The same argument is trotted out for his silence over the outrageous remarks of Trinamool MP, Tapas Pal. There too the Government is not the BJP's. In which case, why has he spoken out only on the rapes and murders in Badayun, where the Samajwadi Party, not the BJP, is in power? Only because 'Maulana' Mulayam is a soft target?

A minister in Modi's government is accused of rape – and with a mulishness more becoming of a worthier cause, the Prime Minister refuses to sack or even suspend the man. And even when a BJP member of the Telangana Assembly utters scandalous, defamatory remarks against a youth and women's icon like Sania Mirza, thundering is the silence from the PMO. Is it only incidental that Sania is a Muslim – and does he share his MLA's view that she is to be deleted because she has had the temerity to marry a Pakistani? Is it no surprise then that the massacre of 700 Palestinians does not evoke even a simper of sympathy for the innocent victims? The same person who thundered from every election platform about the venality of the Congress, and furiously tweeted away about this, now silences his mobile and locks

79

up his laptop? Is this because, as his defenders claim, he is suddenly overwhelmed by his official duties? Or is this the Silence of the Lambs?

Much as he would like everyone to forget the past and move on to the future (as he pleaded in the Rajya Sabha in his reply to the debate on the Motion of Thanks), the past will not cease to haunt 7 Race Course Road until he owns up to his responsibility – at least his constructive responsibility – for the 2002 massacre. This is not a stick to beat him with but an empathetic reflection of the widows who still cry and the mothers who will never see their sons again, and the newly-married girl whose womb was sliced open and the foetus tossed into the sky. For any reconciliation to begin, there has to be humble acceptance of at least constructive responsibility, an expression of genuine compassion for all those who suffered and are still suffering, massive rehabilitation for those who lost their homes and livelihood, a reaching out to them, and retribution for those who caused and undertook the carnage. Begum Jaffri needs to be comforted for what her husband told her was the response when he called the Chief Minister – "What, they haven't got you yet?" Those are scars that will not heal merely by forgetting and asking others to forget. Forgiveness requires genuine repentance, not mocking the victims as puppy dogs.

Modi's apologists will, of course, point to his "exoneration" by the courts. He has not been exonerated. A local court has held that proceedings cannot go forward because the Special Investigation Team set up by the Supreme Court has said they have not been able to find any "prosecutable evidence" against him. They have not said there is no evidence against him; they have only said they have not been able to unearth any prosecutable evidence.

The amicus curiae, on the other hand, has reported in a quite different vein to the same Supreme Court that appointed both him and the Special Investigating Team (SIT). He has held that there is damaging, even damning evidence of both omission and commission against Modi. There are two levels at which culpability might be established: one is the legal level; the other is the moral level. While at higher levels of the judiciary, a quite different verdict of legal responsibility might be returned, at the moral level, the argument is crystal clear: the dreadful pogrom occurred on his watch; ergo, some responsibility must attach to the Chief Minister.

A moral man would unhesitatingly accept moral responsibility; a moral man would at least not appoint as minister one of his closest colleagues who has since been pronounced guilty and sentenced to a virtual lifetime in prison. But Modi takes no responsibility, not even moral responsibility. Indeed, for a month after the massacre began, he refused even to deal with relief and rehabilitation of the victims. It is only when he was almost bullied by the then PM that he began taking some desultory action. It is this dereliction of moral duty that has led to such a sharp division in Gujarati society that Muslim areas of cities like Ahmedabad and Vadodra are routinely referred to as "Pakistan".

The communal divide has paid Modi huge electoral dividends, first in Gujarat, now in the country as a whole. But the nation has suffered. The suffering continues. That is the price that a want of morality in the leadership extracts.

NDTV.com

MODIJI, GANDHIJI ONCE SAID THIS ABOUT ENGLISH

3 August 2014

After I joined the Indian Foreign Service in 1963, I was sent to the Free University of Brussels to learn my "compulsory foreign language" – French. It so happened that my class were the guinea pigs for the first audio-visual teaching course. A linguistic psychologist was, therefore, attached to the class to see how different nationalities – Syrian, Turkish, German, Italian, Peruvian, Cuban, Japanese, American – who were all thrown together with an exclusively French-speaking teacher to swim or sink were picking up the language. It quickly became evident that the two Indians – KP Balakrishnan and I – were top of the class, picking up the rudiments of the language within a few weeks. I asked the psychologist how this was happening – was it because we were brighter than the rest or was there something in our background that made it easier for us than the others to learn a foreign language. She said our racing ahead of the rest of the class had a simple explanation. Linguistic psychology had long established that anyone who could speak two languages would in adulthood (the cut-off age was 35) easily acquire much more fluency in a third language than someone who had reached adulthood with only one language. My batch-mate, Balakrishnan's mother tongue was Malayalam and mine was Tamil; we both also had a fairly firm grasp of Hindi, and, of course, both of us knew English; so, French was our fourth language, which accounted for us being so far ahead of everyone else, particularly the Americans (who did not even know proper English, they having been brought up on a ghastly nasal dialect called 'American'!)

All those who make it to the IFS have to learn enough of their compulsory foreign language to pass an oral and written exam before they can be confirmed in the Service. Even before leaving the first phase of our training in Mussoorie, we also had to compulsorily pass written and oral tests in Hindi. So, even though all of us had passed the Civil

Services exam in English, before we really embarked on our careers post-confirmation, we had to have a fair command of at least three languages – English, Hindi and a foreign language. Moreover, although it is now nearly 40 years since I had the opportunity of speaking and listening to French on a daily basis, when I am interviewed in French or meet a French-speaking person, I am amazed at how smoothly my French returns to my tongue.

Similarly, our IAS colleagues had to pass the compulsory Hindi exam and if they were posted outside their home State (as nearly two-thirds of IAS officers are) they had to learn the language of their State of posting before being confirmed. When I think that two of the most successful Chief Secretaries of Uttar Pradesh that I have known are Kalyanakrishnan and TSR Subramaniam, it is clear that learning a State language is the sine qua non for the advancement of one's career as a civil servant. Certainly, of the numerous SDMs and Collectors I have encountered in my Tamil Nadu constituency, several from Hindi-speaking states had passable or even commendable Tamil (an extraordinarily difficult language for most Indians to learn because, unlike other Indian languages, Tamil has evolved without any Sanskrit roots and little Sanskrit influence).

It seems to me that here we have the seeds of a formula to deal with the CSAT problem from practical experience. Why should the aptitude test be conducted in English only? If we prescribe that the aptitude test will test linguistic skills in any two Indian languages (of which English might be one) and the 200 CSAT marks are evenly divided between comprehension in each of these languages, it would be a common platform for testing all students, whatever their language. Clearly all would be fluent in one of these two languages and somewhat less so in the second language. So, no one would be particularly advantaged in testing linguistic skills. And if the two languages could exclude English, then too there would be a level playing field because every candidate would have language proficiency, and, therefore, language-learning skills, in at least two languages, neither of which need necessarily be English. This would, in fact, encourage Hindi speakers to attempt Tamil or Malayalam, or Bengali or Odiya, or Mizo or Assamese, thus deepening national integration. In an earlier article, I had quoted a great Tamil parliamentarian, Era Sezhiyan, responding to Atal Bihari Vajpayee who had said there was a Hindi Prachar Sabha in every southern state, by asking: "And how many Tamil Prachar Sabhas do you have in UP? How many Malayalam Prachar Sabhas in Madhya Pradesh?" If the CSAT aptitude test required some proficiency in a second modern Indian language, not necessarily in English, those who regard English as an Imperialist language would be free to learn any other modern Indian language – Telugu, perhaps, Konkani, Kannada, Urdu?

But what, it may be asked, would we do about a Tamil who chose Malayalam as his second language for CSAT? Who outside Tamil Nadu and Kerala speaks these languages? How would he or she communicate with their northern, eastern, western and northeastern colleagues? The answer is simple. For being confirmed in the Service, that candidate would have to pass the compulsory Hindi exam and, if he gets posted to, say, Maharashtra or Gujarat would have to have a duly tested working knowledge of Marathi or Gujarati, as the case may be.

Linguistic ability fitted to the administrative task is an indispensable requirement for an administrator. It is no use his knowing his TS Eliot if he has to work in Arunachal Pradesh. This is not a question of Hindi and English. If it were, we could get rid of English. But those who do not speak Hindi as their mother tongue are apprehensive that if some 42 per cent Indians who speak Hindi as their mother tongue are advantaged over 58 per cent of Indians for whom Hindi is not a mother tongue but a "learned" language, then permanent linguistic dominance will be established by the Hindi speaker over the non-Hindi speaker – and we would be put in the position of pre-1971 Pakistan where the Urdu-speaking minority tried to establish linguistic dominance over the Bengali-speaking majority. That is why the non-Hindi states prefer the equal disadvantage of English over the built-in disadvantage they would suffer if the mother tongue of the minority is made the sole official language for the non-Hindi speaking majority.

Similar equality through inequality might be achieved by allowing the CSAT aptitude test to be conducted, if the candidate so desires, in any two modern Indian languages to the exclusion of English as compulsorily the second. Any attempt to overthrow the Angrezi-bhashi by making Hindi or even the recognized scheduled languages as the only qualifying language would be firmly resisted in the northeastern states (e.g. English is the state language in Nagaland, which otherwise has 16 tribal dialects) and by many others who would insist that an India with winners of the Nobel and Man Booker Prizes in English literature has Indianized English, whatever the place of origin of the language. Indian English is as much a language native to India as American is the US version of British English. (Indeed, even in the UK, English is murdered in a hundred different ways – "Oh! why can't the English teach their children how to speak?": Prof Higgins in *My Fair Lady* – and anti-English linguistic patriotism lies at the bottom of the Scottish and Welsh movements for independence – in the 21st century!)

For the rest, let us please note that ALL the other papers (the only ones whose marks count towards the final result) can be written in English, Hindi or any of our scheduled languages. In any case, even if we remove the "compulsory" aptitude test for English, we will be benefiting candidates by only 70 marks out of 200 because anyone who scores 70 out of 200 is eligible to appear in the mains where no knowledge of English is required. But if even 70 marks sticks in the throats of students who neither know nor wish to know any English, then let the 70 marks go, but, remember, before they are confirmed, they will have to learn at least two more languages if they are Hindi-speakers and, if they are non-Hindi speakers, three more languages (English, Hindi and the state or foreign language). Yet, if that is all it takes to end the despair of the students on strike in Mukherji Nagar, so be it. But if Modi sticks to his campaign promise of Hindi-izing everything, this country will disintegrate on his watch. This time round he looks stymied. If he thinks he can break the impasse by giving in to linguistic chauvinism, it will be, as the Old Testament says, "No more water/ The Fire Next Time."

Modiji, once upon a time, there was a Gujarati who said: "English is the language of international commerce; it is the language of diplomacy, and it contains many a rich literary treasure, it gives us an introduction to Western thought and culture. For a few of us, therefore, a knowledge of English is necessary."

That Gujarati was called Mahatma Gandhi. He was quite right in saying that "for a few" – but only a few – a knowledge of English is necessary. For it is those very few who are precisely the ones in the higher civil services. The rest have no need of knowing English and no one will begrudge them their right to refuse to learn that language or be tested in its skills. Gandhiji added that "to get rid of the infatuation for English is one of the essentials of Swaraj." We have achieved that in the Civil Services exams by providing for the papers on which marks are taken into account for determining ranking to be in English or Hindi or any one of our scheduled languages. It is only for 70 marks that thus far English is indispensable. Let us get rid of that but not of the need for civil servants to have language skills by insisting that some competence, amounting to 70 marks in any two modern Indian languages, would suffice for passing the first Part of the exam (prelims) – but insist that linguistic capacity in English, Hindi and a third language is indispensable for confirmation before being put to the hard and demanding work of a Class I or Class II government officer. That is the real challenge, and the one way of sorting out the present UPSC-CSAT imbroglio.

NDTV.com

THE FALL AND FALL OF NARENDRA MODI

9 August 2014

The first straw in the wind has been the result of the three Uttara-khand by-polls that the Congress won in July 2014. The Modi wave that had swept the country in May suddenly collapsed in Uttarakhand, leaving the BJP licking its wounds in precisely the places they had inflicted these wounds on the Congress. Modi's fall has been quite as precipitate as his rise. Is the Modi wave over?

It is far too early to say, but when a candidate raises expectations sky-high, the electorate expects him to deliver something spectacular, almost immediately. At a similar stage in the rise of Rajiv Gandhi, he had said he found the expectations "scary". But in what was to prove the enduring honeymoon of his PM-ship, he delivered such a shower of stunning outcomes that he was applauded as perhaps no other PM has been at the outset of his term of office. Having risen to the highest number of seats ever in the elections of December 1984, he rose still further in popular esteem all through the Golden Year of 1985, climaxed by his renowned speech at the Congress centenary – a radical oration that passed muster only because he had over his first year pulled off the Punjab accord; brought around the Assamese students to a peace agreement; thrilled the nation's imagination with his visits to the remotest parts of the country; took his place on the world stage with his bold advocacy of nuclear disarmament through the Six-Nation Five-Continent initiative; and wowed the US Congress with the most rousing speech they had heard till then or since from any Indian leader. In Parliament, he electrified the voters with legislation that ended the era of *aaya Ram-gaya Ram*.

Compared with that record, what has Modi to show for his 60 days? Dither, yes, and bewilderment, too. Where has good governance gone? Reduced to a slogan that has everyone tittering: *acche din aaye hain*. Oh, really? Instead of seeing decisive governance, the aam janta is moving from amusement to anger over Modi's penchant for wandering the world instead of dealing with pressing problems at home. Remember, Rajiv took six months to make his first series of foreign visits. Of course, all prime ministers are their own foreign ministers. But they have to give primacy to the domestic scene.

Buzzing around the neighbourhood has been good PR but wholly wanting in substance. Has Jaya moved on Sri Lanka? Has Mamata on Teesta or the land boundary? Is Nepal anywhere nearer a Constitution? Has Pakistan stopped firing across the ceasefire line or arrested Hafiz Saeed? Is there any new thinking on Afghanistan?

On Palestine — although the death toll there has now breached Modi's performance post-Godhra — not one meaningful word has been uttered. And, little further action on rescuing our expats from hard spots in West Asia, after the government exhausted the entire stock of Arab goodwill built over decades by previous — principally Congress — governments in getting the 46 nurses out of Tikrit. And Fortaleza showed how low we have sunk even in the eyes of BRICS; there was not one phrase in more than 90 paragraphs that could be shown to be a distinctive Indian contribution.

The Modi government's first policy statement — the President's Address — was the least inspiring document of its kind ever produced. I challenge readers to remember even one telling sentence from that litany of boredom. And my brother, Swaminathan, has memorably dismissed the Modi government's first budget as "Chidambaram's budget with saffron lipstick"!

On domestic issues, Modi's report card has nothing of significance to show, unless you count as "governance" cleaning the corridors of government offices to lend cover to sweeping inconvenient files out of sight. All domestic issues are in abeyance or, as in Belgaum, flaring up anew. Yes, the Union government is adept at taking potshots at Akhilesh Yadav (this is called "cooperative" federalism!), but has done nothing to rein in its goons in Saharanpur or allaying the apprehensions of Muslims in Maharashtra after the killing of the techie or the arrest of 19 Muslim students in Kerala who mocked Modi in a college rag. The only action taken is to appoint Dinanath Batra (good God!) to a place of prominence in the nation's "education" – if that is any longer the right word – and a known saffronite as the head of the national body for historical research. Are you still surprised that, as far as the *aam aadmi* is concerned, the Modi wave is over?

The Week

FROM RED FORT WITHOUT VAJPAYEE'S GENTLE HUMOUR

16 August 2014

The Roman Emperor Nero decreed, "Give them bread and give them circuses." All authoritarians since then have combined demagoguery with drama, none so pointedly in India as Narendra Modi with his flamboyant red turban blowing in the wind, his arms flailing, his oratory swirling, and giant screens and other gewgaws carrying the spectacle far and wide.

But what of the substance? His Independence Day address amounted to no more than old wine in old bottles with new labeling. Much is being made of his invoking toilets from a public platform to a prudish public. What, however, had he to add to the Nirmal Bharat Abhiyan, successor to the Total Sanitation Programme, announced last year by his predecessor, Dr. Manmohan Singh, from exactly the same platform? Nothing. For dealing with sanitation has been a principal preoccupation of our enlightened leaders' programme ever since Mahatma Gandhi picked up the jhadu and asked Kasturba in South Africa to clean up her own mess. "Cleanliness," said Gandhiji, "is next to Godliness." But he did not proclaim it from the ramparts of the Red Fort. He set a personal example, beginning with himself and his family, without ostentation but inner humility. Indeed, his entire "constructive programme" was built around personal and community hygiene.

We did not have to wait till Modi to be told about the importance of toilets. What we needed to be told was the degree of progress achieved in attaining total sanitation and the hurdles faced by the decades-old Nirmal Gram Abhiyan. Had Modi cared to study the subject instead of merely inventing slogans, as is his wont, he would have found that the problem of constructing public toilets from MPLADS funds, as I was doing when Modi was running around in khaki knickers doing prachar and pravachan, is that it is easy enough to construct public toilets; the problem is to ensure maintenance. When these public toilets are first built, they are celebrated as if they are the Taj Mahals. Within a week, they are rendered unusable because there is no proper arrangement for maintenance. And if Modi had the time or inclination to read recent surveys, he would have found that even when toilets are provided in private homes, there is inadequate motivation to regularly use them.

Social motivation being the principal challenge, the Gram Sabha is the obvious place for the Panches and Sarpanches to propagate the importance of sanitation. But to go by Modi's Independence Day address, he has not even heard of his fellow-Gujarati, Mohandas Karamchand Gandhi's Panchayat Raj. Obviously. How can an authoritarian be kindly disposed to the devolution and dispersal of power? Not that we had not been warned. Modi's Gujarat has been among the poorest performers in Panchayat Raj. That is proved again in the absurd proposal for a "Sansad Adarsh Gram Yojana" which MPs are to promote through their MPLADS funds. First, how can 700 "sansad adarsh" villages make a difference to the horrendous hurdles faced by 7 lakh villages? Second, and more importantly, why a "Sansad" programme; why not a Panchayat Adarsh Gram Yojana? That would instantly reach every village of India, provided – and this is a big proviso – the villages are effectively empowered under the Constitution through the devolution of the required Functions, Finances and Functionaries. Alas, Modi's "re-imagined" India does not incorporate the empowerment of the people but the canonization of NaMo.

The same goes for his sententious and ultimately meaningless remarks about preventing rape and the sexual harassment of women by parents subjecting sons and daughters alike to the same restrictions. It would have been a much greater contribution on his part to have sacked Nihal Chand Meghwal from his council of ministers, laying out practical steps (other than hanging 16-year-olds) for superior law and order to protect women in public places and stringent, timely judicial action against offenders. But it wouldn't be Modi if there were to be a practical road-map. He just exhorts but does nothing. Gandhi both exhorted and set a personal example of high ethical rectitude. He said and did. Modi merely alliterates with silly, childish slogans.

The latest in this series of Moditvisms is "Make in India". What else is 'swavlamban' and 'swadeshi' than 'Make in India'? And if the point Modi were trying to make to foreigners in ungrammatical English was that they should invest in manufacturing, what again is new about the concept? We have been rampantly seducing foreign investors ever since economic reforms began under PV Narasimha Rao and his Finance Minister, Dr. Manmohan Singh. Success has largely eluded us although hot money inflows into our stock market, particularly through the notorious Mauritius route, have escalated manifold. If foreign direct investment in manufacturing has been pathetic despite reforms, it is not because the UPA government was deficient in coining ungrammatical slogans but because there are very real constraints – political, social and economic – on freeing up the rules and regulations that govern foreign investment. If Modi had the guts (or the foolishness) to dismantle all these restrictions, he would not have needed empty slogans to woo the foreigner. But because he knows his own saffron brigade will not let him run riot, instead of meaningful policy changes, all the potential foreign investor got from Modi was yet another slogan. No wonder, on the eve of Independence Day, *The New York Times* described Modi as "a cipher".

The cipher proved it once more with yet another slogan – that of calling for a moratorium on communalism for ten years. The question – why only ten years, why not forever? – has been asked by others, so I will desist. What would have been far more telling would have been Modi apologizing for the massacre of Muslims in Gujarat on his watch and publicly pledging to rein in all the Bhagwats, Togadias and Kodnanis with whom he surrounds himself and who played such a crucial role in bringing him to 7 Race Course Road. Can he disavow them? Does he wish to disavow them? Is he ready to promise on the eve of the UP polls that every knicker-wallah involved in pre-poll communal violence will be thrown out of the Sangh Parivar? No. Because if he did, the Sangh Parivar would first throw him out. Modi is like Lady Macbeth. "Here's the smell of the blood still: All the perfumes of Arabia will not sweeten this little hand."

Lastly, the Planning Commission. There could be an argument for abolishing the Planning Commission. Only Modi did not make it. All we got was the petulance of his attempt to overthrow one of the greatest legacies of the Nehruvian era. Exactly like the iconoclastic Delhi Sultans smashing every idol they could find but being unable to cogently explain such vandalism, to destroy the Planning Commission without spelling out in detail what is to come in its place is like a child wantonly destroying its playthings only because it is such fun to do so.

What we need is a return to adult behaviour from the Red Fort. We need a Jawaharlal Nehru announcing the nation's fulfilling ("not wholly, nor in full measure") its "Tryst with Destiny". We need a Lal Bahadur Shastri proclaiming, "Jai Jawan! Jai Kisan!" We need an Indira Gandhi rallying the nation to liquidating the pogrom in neighbouring East Pakistan. We need a Rajiv Gandhi announcing the Assam accord, carrying forward the Punjab accord, presaging the Mizo accord. We need a Narasimha Rao unfurling the roadmap to a new prosperity. We need the gentle humour of Atal Bihari Vajpayee. We need the sober, sombre tones of Dr. Manmohan Singh. To expect any of this over the next five years (minus 70 days) is, alas, to ask for the moon.

NDTV.com

BEING A BULLY

20 August 2014

There was nothing to be gained from making an issue of such a trivial matter.

Working out a viable relationship with Pakistan is in India's vital national interest. But the wholly bogus nature of the Narendra Modi-Nawaz Sharif bonhomie on the occasion of Modi's republican coronation now stands revealed in all its nakedness. In a childish display of extreme petulance, the India-Pakistan foreign secretary-level talks have been called off. The excuse proffered is that the Pakistan envoy had met with, and was scheduled to meet again with, Kashmiri "separatist" leaders on the eve of the talks. He had been warned after Round 1 of his interaction with them that if Round 2 took place, India would spurn dialogue and revert to the two-year-long stand-off.

The excuse is wholly misplaced. The Simla Agreement of 1972 removed Jammu and Kashmir from the international agenda and effectively placed it in the ambit of bilateral discussion and resolution: "a final settlement of Jammu and Kashmir". The trade-off was simple. India recognised that there were issues relating to J&K that needed to be resolved and Pakistan agreed to secure the resolution of these issues bilaterally instead of in an international forum. In actual fact, India, much more than Pakistan, especially in recent decades, has shied away from bilateral dialogue, while Pakistan has attempted from time to time, but without success, to revert to the UN. But the basic position today continues as it was four decades ago at Simla – India accepts that there is an external dimension to J&K, and Pakistan that dealing with these issues is strictly remitted to the bilateral, not multilateral, sphere of diplomatic interaction.

On the domestic front in India, the principle of "the sky is the limit" has long been instituted for determining the parameters of "autonomy" for J&K; autonomy that must, however, fall short of challenging the integrity of India or the finality of J&K's accession to India. All else is negotiable. On the external front, it is recognised as legitimate for Pakistan to raise issues relating to "a final settlement of Jammu and Kashmir".

It was in pursuance of this legitimacy granted to Pakistan by the Simla Agreement of 1972 that, just under two decades ago, the PV Narasimha Rao government recognised the legitimacy of Pakistani envoys and political leaders including Kashmiri "separatists" (under the umbrella of the Hurriyat) in their consultations in preparation for successive phases of the ongoing dialogue process. There has thus been a bipartisan, indeed, multipartisan understanding within India (at least till now) that such interaction falls in a class by itself and so does not constitute a casus belli or even a casus diplomati to break off the bilateral dialogue to which both are pledged.

Had Modi any new objection to this, he was duty-bound to make it clear to Nawaz Sharif when he met him in New Delhi and they discussed the resumption of the dialogue. The Pakistan desk of the Ministry of External Affairs knows full well that Nawaz Sharif was attacked on his return to Pakistan from New Delhi for his failure to meet with the Hurriyat, as his predecessors had done. This became such a big issue that when I was in Pakistan days later (in the august company of Ved Pratap Vaidik), both formally and informally, this was stressed. Thus, the consequences of warning High Commissioner Abdul Basit against maintaining his scheduled meeting with the "separatists" should have been clear to the meanest intelligence in the MEA. If the meeting with the Hurriyat leaders were called off, the howls of protest in Pakistan would have drowned all attempts at dialogue. There was nothing to be gained from making an issue of such a trivial matter.

I say "trivial" because nothing earth-shattering, either for us or the Pakistanis, has resulted from earlier meetings of the Hurriyat with the Pakistanis, including visits of Hurriyat leaders to Pakistan that we ourselves had permitted. From a Pakistani point of view, meeting the Hurriyat is an excellent way of selling to the Pakistani public the explanation that "Kashmiri" wishes are not being ignored or bypassed in the dialogue process. From the Indian point of view, the "separatists", who are Indian citizens, whatever their view, are of such significance as to have warranted our "interlocutors" talking to them. What harm, then, can come of Geelani et al letting off steam in Pakistan House – the same steam they let off on a daily basis in the Valley?

Then there is the question of sovereignty. Pakistan may be weaker than India in every respect but there is at least one in which Pakistan is our equal and will remain so, and that is in the dimension of sovereignty. If India as a sovereign country refuses to buckle under Pakistani pressure, it is only natural that Pakistanis will not countenance infringement by India of their sovereignty. That is why the imposition of new conditionalities, flying in the face of precedents, will be seen as infringing on Pakistan's sovereignty. The parallel being drawn in some quarters with India snubbing Pakistan by talking to Baloch separatists is as misbegotten as it is misplaced, for Balochistan is not an issue between India and Pakistan. We have neither had nor sustain any claims on Balochistan. On Kashmir, the Pakistanis do — and that has been acknowledged by India, even if India is (rightly) adamant that there can be no compromise on its sovereignty over the whole of J&K, as a result of the Instrument of Accession and Article I of the J&K constitution.

Such are the subtleties of diplomacy. They go ill with foreign policy strutting on a 56-inch chest. I am sure the MEA as an institution knows all this but is helpless because all power is being increasingly concentrated in one authoritarian. We stand warned that whimsicality and bullying are going to characterise our relations with Pakistan over the next five years; exactly the kind of whimsicality and bullying that led to the Austro-Hungarian Empire attacking Serbia a hundred years ago, leading to the devastation of the two world wars.

Indian Express

PM'S INCOMPETENT HANDLING
OF PAKISTAN

25 August 2014

When Narendra Modi so peevishly cancelled the Indo-Pak Foreign Secretary-level talks that were scheduled to commence 25 August, did he take into account the possible repercussions in the Valley of Kashmir of proffering Pakistani contacts with the Hurriyat as the proximate cause for the breakdown? If he did not, that was irresponsible. And if he did, then it was even more irresponsible.

For, as a long-time non-Kashmiri resident of Srinagar texted me, "So unfortunate. Now the Hurriyat are heroes in the Valley. Inept beyond belief!" I have just spent half a day in Srinagar. I was amazed at the way in which a cross-section of academics at Kashmir University, students, ordinary policemen and drivers greeted me and hugged me as if I were a long-lost friend – in fact, I was seeing most of them for the first time. The warmth of their welcome was entirely owing to my having aggressively opposed on the media – particularly on television – the whimsical, childish decision of the government to cancel the talks merely because the Hurriyat was talking, as it has done for the past19 years, to Pakistan.

After front-paging rival statements by the Pak High Commissioner and the Indian spokesman, *Greater Kashmir* also front-paged Hurriyat chairman Geelani's demand to Pakistan that they "give preference to the resolution of the Kashmir dispute than trade ties and other issues with India". We have long settled with Pakistan that our dialogue will be comprehensive and composite – that any issue of interest to either side may be raised and discussed. Why give the Kashmir separatists an opportunity to highlight their alternative Kashmir-centric view of how the dialogue might be structured? Their view had few Kashmiri takers over the years. Now, Modi has made Geelani sound reasonable to many

Kashmiri ears. What monumental incompetence!

Geelani's spokesman added that, "Geelani *sahib* conveyed his gratitude to Pakistan Prime Minister Nawaz Sharif for taking a stand on meeting with separatists." Had the Hurriyat been allowed to meet the Pakistan High Commissioner, those thanks would have been directed to our government.

Instead, Nawaz Sharif scores brownie points while our guy is portrayed as a petulant, truculent obstructionist. Again, monumental incompetence!

Yasin Malik argues, "Due to the unresolved dispute, over 80 per cent Kashmiris are suffering with depression. Trade and other issues can wait but there is an urgent need to resolve the Kashmir dispute as it is taking a heavy toll on Kashmiris." Where Hurriyat is a grouping of factions locked in internecine conflict, Modi has brought them together, sinking their differences. Is this what he intended to do? If not, does he realize that this is what he has in fact done?

And Shabir Shah has seized the opportunity to "pitch for unity among like-minded separatists" – a goal far distant thus far, and entirely to India's advantage. Meanwhile, Mirwaiz Umar Farooq has twisted the dagger further into the Indian side, arguing that, "Terming Kashmir a bilateral issue won't change its dispute nature!"

Such voices are by no means confined to the separatist Hurriyat. The J&K Bar Association have expressed their "dismay" over the cancellation of the talks and denounced India for having "never been sincere in holding talks with Pakistan or Kashmiri pro-freedom leadership... it is only to hoodwink the world community that it occasionally agrees to hold talks with Pakistan, but thereafter backtracks." The local state Aam Aadmi Party leader, Dr. Raja Muzaffar Bhat, goes further, "When a senior Indian journalist, Dr. Ved Pratap Vaidik, can meet Hafiz Saeed in Pakistan, why cannot Kashmiri leaders meet Pakistani officials, as Kashmiris are the major stakeholders in Kashmir?" The Jammu Kashmir Salvation Movement chairman, Zaffar Akbar Bhat, says, "If Kashmiris aren't stakeholders of Kashmir dispute, then why the BJP government in 2000 held talks with Hizb-ul-Mujahideen leaders and commanders?" And, to top it all, a Hindu leader in the Valley, Pandit Bhushan Bazaz, "calls upon the Government of India to take serious and effective steps for resolution of the Kashmir issue in accordance with the wishes and aspirations of Kashmiri people."

Even mainline Kashmiri politicians like the National Conference MP, Mohd Shafi, are saying, "Dialogue is the only way out to address the issues. Any break-off in the dialogue process has a direct bearing on the people of Kashmir besides the two countries. There is need for holding talks so that the Kashmir issue is resolved amicably."

Whew! It takes some doing to unite disparate, quarreling Kashmiri groups across the spectrum to articulate their positions in a more or less unanimous voice. Modi's done it! Why?

The widespread belief is that the imbroglio over the Hurriyat encounter with the Pakistan High Commissioner was a "ploy" to call off the India-Pak talks. Naeem Akhtar of the PDP has said, "If New Delhi wanted to have talks with Pakistan, they could have stopped the separatists in Srinagar itself. But it allowed them to go to Delhi and then used it as an alibi for cancelling the talks." Adds Shabir Shah: "Our presence in Delhi was used to flare up nationalist passions through news channels and then they called off the talks."

He asks why they were not imprisoned in their houses in Kashmir except to trot out an excuse to cancel talks the government did not want. And why did they not want talks with Pakistan at this stage? Because, argues Shabir Shah, "The BJP again is appealing to the Hindu votebank for upcoming Assembly elections by first allowing us to reach Delhi and then calling off the talks." He recalled that there were several instances in the past when Hurriyat leaders were detained in Srinagar rather than allowed to visit Delhi for interaction with Pakistani leaders: in 2011, when Foreign Minister Hina Rabbani Khar was in Delhi and again in 2013, when National Security Adviser Sartaj Aziz came visiting. On both occasions, Shabir Shah was kept under house arrest.

Moreover, why did the government, which knew of the High Commissioner's invitation to the Hurriyat on 10 August, wait for eight full days till the separatists were in Delhi to meretriciously state its objection to the consultation knowing full well that Pakistan would severely lose face if they meekly fell in with this new conditionality? I spy the nefarious hand of Amit Shah. He is in charge of the forthcoming J&K elections. With the Kashmiri Pandits being mobilized to send in postal votes, Amit Shah clearly guesses that Modi being shown as a dragon with teeth by bullying the Pakistanis is an excellent tactic for drumming up the Pandit support.

Fair enough. But if relations with a key neighbour are going to be made a cat's paw in domestic electoral politics, it reveals even more nakedly the naivete and irresponsibility that characterizes Modi's foreign policy.

The consequences of such irresponsibility are summed up tellingly by the Srinagar daily, *Greater Kashmir*: "There is surprise and disbelief over New Delhi's dramatic cancellation of Foreign Secretary level talks over the Pakistan envoy's invite to separatists... The NDA government has run itself out of options as far as the dialogue with Pakistan is concerned. There is now no immediate possibility that an engagement could be resurrected in the near future. And this is a tragedy. In the absence of any contact, the regional atmosphere will grow more tense with an attendant possibility of an escalation of the conflict." Is this what Modi wants?

NDTV.com

UNDOING PLANNING

29 August 2014

In all the brouhaha over winding up the Planning Commission, the key unanswered question remains: what are they going to provide in its place?

Narendra Modi is not the first to reflect on the relevance of planning to the economic life of the nation. Indeed, my first crossing of swords with Dr Manmohan Singh on the subject occurred at the Pachmarhi chintan shivir in 1998. I was required to draft the principal conclusions of the *shivir* for the consideration of the Congress Working Committee. While the CWC luminaries foregathered on the verandah of a bungalow on the other side of the road, on this side I was provided a computer to hammer out the draft. As each page was finished, it was sent off to the Big Bosses. The first page contained a cliché from previous Congress communiqués about "planned development". Doctor sahib had scored out "planned" and written "balanced" in the margin. I rewrote the phrase to read "planned and balanced development", and sent it back for final approval.

After finishing the draft, I went across the road to receive the congratulations that were invariably showered on me for writing a few paragraphs of recycled trite. I was, however, faced with an incensed Dr Singh, who demanded to know how I had dared retain "planned" after he had crossed it out. I began protesting when he thundered that if I did not remove it, he would take it up in the formal meeting of the CWC, and if there, too, it were retained he would have to consider resigning. At this point, I felt my kurta being tugged from behind. I turned. It was Natwar [Singh]. He whispered, "*Chhodo, yaar.*" In some heat, I whispered back, "But, sir, planning has been the Congress credo since the Karachi Congress of 1931." "I know," he said. "But what difference does that make?" "If it makes no difference to you," I muttered, "why should it to me?" and stormed off to delete the offending word.

So, through the two UPA governments, the Planning Commission was run by people who did not believe in planning. No wonder, Montek Ahluwalia's last act reportedly was to write a long note suggesting drastic reform, or even winding up, of the Planning Commission.

But before we move in haste, a word of caution. Of course, the economy has changed so significantly since 1931, or even 1947, as to warrant rethinking, particularly as we now have a more broad-based entrepreneurial class that goes beyond the pre-Independence triad of Tata-Birla-Dalmia. They can look after themselves – the coda being that the state must not intervene to bail them out as our government has been doing at an average of 15 lakh crore stimulus a year since the global meltdown, additional to our banks running up mammoth "non-performing assets" – unpaid loans – to keep the most prosperous Indians in champagne and caviar, however much of a mess they might have made of their businesses. That lot can, and should be, left to look after their own.

The real task of a reformed Planning Commission, following Dr Singh's outburst, should have been to look after the unsuccessful Indian, amounting to 77 per cent of the Indian population, according to Dr Arjun Sengupta (a figure since reprised by Rahul Gandhi). They are the ones in need of subsidies, technological innovation, skill development and all the other necessaries for poverty and "vulnerability" (Sengupta's phrase) to move to self-reliance and, perhaps eventually, towards prosperity.

Let us, however, end the Planning Commission's massive stimuli for the AAP – the Ambani Adani Party – and concentrate on the disadvantaged. Their advancement requires the social, political and, above all, administrative empowerment to enable them to access their entitlements and thus to combine empowerment with entitlements to attain, as the nascent middle-class has done, a measure of enrichment. We need a Devolution Commission, if not a Planning Commission. Without that, the rich will swim and the poor will sink.

The Week

LESSONS FOR INDIA FROM WORLD WAR I

2 September 2014

My wife and I have been traipsing around the Warmia district of Poland this last week visiting the sites of the Battle of Tannenberg on precisely the dates, 26-30 August, the opening engagement of the First World War between Russia and Germany, in 1914 on the soil of Poland.

The German plan, drafted two decades earlier by a military genius, von Schlieffen, provided for the German army to enter Paris within 33 days of D-Day. It was the expectation that even if Russia came into the war against Germany, she would need at least 30 days to mobilize. So, Germany would wrap up France well in time to turn the full force of its wrath on the Russians. But to the astonishment of most, Russia completed its mobilization within 15 days while Germany was still caught up in Belgium and northern France.

The Russian plan was to push their First Army under General Rennenkampf through the north of Warmia to cut off any German attempt to flee to the Baltic Sea through the principal Warmian port of Danzig. Rennenkampf was then to wheel left to link up with the Russian Second Army under Gen Samsonov coming up from the south to envelope the Germans in a pincer movement before the Germans fell back westwards to the River Vistula.

After wrapping up the German army before the Vistula, the Russians would then be able to cross the river and position themselves for a week's march to Berlin. Once Berlin was captured, it could be traded for Paris, and the war would end within six weeks. Had this happened, nearly 15 million lives would have been saved before WWI actually ended in 1918. And had WWI ended in September 1914, there would neither have been a World War, nor, therefore, a Second, and close to a hundred million lives would have been saved. That is how crucial the Battle of

Tannenberg looks a hundred years later in retrospect.

However, to get back to what actually happened, as against what was expected to happen...

Unable to spare the troops from the Western Front to confront Russia on the Eastern Front, the German army in Prussia, under the charge of a most incompetent general, von Prittwitz, decided to withdraw west to the river Vistula to fight off the Russians at the river or perhaps even from behind it. The Russian First Army, coming in under Genral Rennenkampf, were thus astonished to find themselves marching through miles and miles of abandoned villages. But one disobedient German corps commander, Gen Francois, unable to countenance the German High Command abandoning Prussia, decided to not retreat and instead challenged Rennenkampf head on at Gumbinnen. He lost heavily on the right and left flanks of the Russian army but smashed through the Russian centre with his cavalry.

To Gen Francois' amazement, instead of being encouraged to consolidate his victory, he was ordered to withdraw and regroup in the far south-west to confront Samsonov's Second Army. To Francois' further amazement, his counterpart Russian general, Rennenkampf, broke contact and did not harry the retreating German troops. At the same time, the defeated Russian cavalry corps, under a really weak and cowardly commander, simply disintegrated, with the remnants running back to, and even behind, the Russian frontier.

The fact is that Rennenkampf and Samsonov hated each other, and Samsonov was also despised by General Zilinsky who was to coordinate the two armies from his rear base in Warsaw. Unlike Rennenkampf and Samsonov, who had some, indeed, considerable experience of warfare, Zilinsky, like our own Gen. BM Kaul, appointed commander of the ill-fated IV Corps at the start of the 1962 India-China war, was a *chamcha* who had risen by Court favour rather than any merit. Zilinsky was mis-promoted by the Russian Foreign Minister, Sukhomlinov, much as Kaul was mis-promoted by VK Krishna Menon – and for much the same reason: Zilinsky was reputed to be close to the Czarina through Rasputin, just as Kaul was supposed to be related to Teen Murti House!

Consequently, instead of berating the First Army commander, Rennenkampf, for not pursuing the retreating Germans, or cashiering the cavalry commander who had fled, and urging Rennekampf to position himself to wheel to the left to link up with the Second Army, Zilinsky ordered Gen Samsonov's Second Army to force march forward to the Vistula without adequate supplies. The Russian pincer, so beautifully planned on paper, never got off the ground.

Meanwhile, the Germans decided to replace their useless commander and bring in the combination of Hindenburg and Ludendorff who were to become the most famous twin commanders in German military history, reinforced by two corps rushed from the Western to the Eastern Front. But not even this formidable combo could have succeeded but for the bone-headedness of the same corps commander, Gen Francois, who had won at least a partial victory at Gumbinnen by disobeying orders. He insisted on not attacking until his heavy artillery caught up with him. (I thought of Brigadier John Dalvi at the Namka-chu who, if only he had similarly refused the stupid order to attack coming to him from Army HQ, might still have survived the humiliation of the total rout of Dhola Post that signalled the start of the 1962 war).

Notwithstanding Hindenburg and Ludendorff driving down to Francois' base to order him to attack earlier than he planned, Francois stood his ground. He might have been dismissed for insubordination the same evening but for two extraordinary intercepts that changed the face of the battle. Since the Russians were transmitting their orders "en clair", that is, not in code, the Germans, stopping off at a local telegraph office, received copies of Russian orders showing that Rennenkampf had decided not to link up with Samsonov and listing the precise dispositions of Samsonov's corps for the next day (just like the IPKF revealing to Prabhakaran through 'en clair' transmissions its plans for air dropping paratroopers into Jaffna University, and consequently being picked off the skies as at a duck shoot). So when next morning, Francois opened up with his heavy artillery, Samsonov's Second Army was decimated, except for one Russian commander, Gen Martos, who routed his German counterpart at Hohenstein, a few miles north of Francois' devastation, but in the process lost 4000 men and most of his officers, much like Brig

Hoshiar Singh against overwhelming Chinese might at Sela.

Meanwhile, instead of coming to Samsonov's rescue, as per the original plans, Rennenkampf contented himself with sending to Samsonov a single regiment, who, despite brave fighting, were mowed down at Deureten by the Germans in a narrow defile between two great lakes.

Samsonov was thus left with no alternative but a shameful retreat. This brought on a nervous breakdown (remember Kaul tottering sick off the Tawang battlefield?). And at the edge of a forest near the Russian frontier, unable to face up to the humiliation of telling the Czar he had lost an entire army, Samsonov shot himself, the final victim of a stunning and unforeseen defeat, which ensured that a hundred million would die after him.

My mind goes back to a meeting at the India International Centre in 1983 just after the Sri Lanka crisis erupted where a very, very senior general of the Indian Army – with a very, very propah British accent – insisted that if only our government would let the Army do so, they would slice through Sri Lanka "like a knife through buttah!" We know what happened. The Battle of Tannenberg classically illustrates that between the plans of mere men and the workings of Destiny falls a shadow that cannot be foreseen.

So, if we allow ourselves to be swayed by retired militarymen on TV sporting handlebar moustaches, as most are wont to do, South Asia might find itself caught in the 21st century in the same mincing machine that in the 20th century made keema of the lives of millions and millions of young men in their prime.

I went to Poland not in search of war but to learn why we must give peace a chance. Nothing is more terrible than war. War is not Glory. War is Hell!

NDTV.com

MODI'S IMPOSSIBLE CHOICES ON PETROLEUM FRONT

18 September 2014

When Mukesh Ambani declined at the last moment to join the business delegation that accompanied Modi to Japan, quite a few jaws dropped. Was he signalling his displeasure at the new government having completed 100 days in office without taking a decision on the pricing of natural gas? The previous government had indicated that the minimum price of natural gas, of which Reliance is the principal private sector producer, would be approximately doubled in April, then said the elections were on so a decision would be deferred till after the elections.

In view of the close nexus between Big Business and the funding of Modi's extravagantly expensive campaign, the assumption was that a decision in favour of Reliance, perhaps well in excess of what was being rumoured as the direction in which the UPA was tending, was likely. In the event, the present government seems to be caught in the same set of dilemmas that bound the previous one.

After the New Exploration Licensing Policy (NELP) was announced in 1997, Reliance, along with its Japanese partner, was among the first private enterprise entities to be awarded a mining license after signing a Production Sharing Contract (PSC) with the government.

The PSC stipulated that any gas found by Reliance and its partner in the Krishna-Godavari basin off-shore would be marketed by Reliance at a price to be determined in a transparent manner through what is technically called "price discovery at arms' length," which means the price has to be what the market is willing to bear, subject to its not being a collusive price reached on non-market factors by agreement between buyer and seller.

This general principle was particularly relevant to the marketing contract that Reliance entered into with a sister enterprise of the

Reliance Group for the bulk of the gas it had discovered. This was a contract between the two Ambani brothers, Mukesh running the gas business and Anil embarking on the electricity business. The contracted price of $2.34 per unit being similar to that signed between an ONGC subsidiary and the public sector NTPC, all was considered straightforward and above board.

As Minister of Petroleum & Natural Gas (May 2004-January 2006) I trumpeted the Reliance discovery as the world's largest off-shore discovery of the year 2003 as I travelled the world drumming up bids for the 2005 NELP round. It was a national achievement which, if it fulfilled the expectations roused by Reliance's own announcements, would have sharply reduced demand for gas from abroad, perhaps even making us self-sufficient, and that too at a most affordable price.

Two things happened in 2004-05 to rock the boat. First, the price of crude oil rocketed to $100 and at one time even touched $140. Second, the two brothers fell out with each other. The selling brother reckoned that he stood to lose a great deal if he persisted with the contracted price. The buying brother insisted on his pound of flesh. The dispute went to the Bombay High Court that ruled in favour of Anil Ambani.

Meanwhile, even as the case was on, the government impleaded itself and was, therefore, a party to the appeal to the Supreme Court that followed. The argument made by the government in the Supreme Court was that since natural resources like natural gas belong to the nation and its people, and the KG basin had only been leased not sold to Reliance, the government must have the final say in determining the price at which KG gas would be marketed. The Supreme Court agreed. And the government eventually raised the price by almost double to $4.20 (leaving some wits to point out that 420 translates into "char sau bees"!)

The consequence of this sequence of events was that the earlier Reliance contract between the two brothers was, in effect, torn up, and the arms' length market discovery of price, written into the PSC, put aside. The new policy reverted to the administered pricing of gas, with the government, not the market, becoming the determinant of gas pricing.

Alarmed at the government becoming the price determiner, foreign firms, who had been flocking in droves to India's burgeoning petroleum sector in my time, shied away from NELP rounds after 2006. Meanwhile, Reliance, notwithstanding its tie-up with the global oil major, BP, has been unable to maintain its production commitments. Gas output from KG is at a fraction of what it was drummed up to be. Our energy security, at present and into the future, stands in jeopardy, as does our foreign exchange and fiscal balance. For the extent to which domestic gas production does not match expectations generated earlier, our foreign exchange outgo rises to import the balance requirement; and the extent to which government intervention raises gas prices, it increases the subsidy to be paid out on account of fertilizer and power (the two principal consumers of gas) as well as cooking gas (LPG). That, of course, impacts the fiscal balance.

But worst of all, administered prices drive away the very foreign oil majors who, a decade ago, were looking on India as an emerging petroleum giant. And, of course, Reliance has shown that not even India's biggest entrepreneur has the technical expertise or deep enough pockets to confidently meet the enormous risks involved in petroleum exploration. We desperately require the foreigner to realize our petroleum potential.

While we wrestle with our domestic issues, the world of petroleum is being transformed beyond recognition. High oil prices have led to Western producers and consumers shifting to shale oil and shale gas, breaking the nexus between oil and gas prices. Result: Indian gas prices are rising while international gas prices are declining. We appear to have landed ourselves in the worst of all worlds.

The easiest way for the Modi government to distance itself from the previous government would be to give up the administered pricing system reintroduced by the previous government and go for market pricing hell-for-leather. This is what the Kelkar committee has recommended. But Modi is hesitant because that might drive up his subsidies to unmanageable levels or drive up consumer prices to levels that would be politically unmanageable.

Achhe din aaye ya nahi, burre din toh aa hi gaye hain! One answer might lie in reviving the Iran-Pakistan-India gas pipeline that I fostered. But that requires a minimum of understanding with Pakistan that the government is loath to extend.

So Modi dithers. He is now discovering that "good governance" is not about alliterative slogans and rhetorical bombast. It is about making impossible choices where there are no win-win solutions. How delightful to watch them twisting slowly, slowly in the wind!

NDTV.com

IF OTHERS HAVE PMs,
WE HAVE AN EM

7 October 2014

Other countries have PMs We have an EM – an Events Manager. Having returned from his rocking visit to the US (Madison Square Garden, venue of boxing matches and pop concerts, forsooth!), where he achieved little of substance but much adulation from his fan club of NRGs (Non-Resident Gujaratis), Modi sought out yet another photo-op by picking up a broom and positioning himself, most photogenically, in front of a mound of garbage in a Valmiki Colony, an ersatz version of a 21st century Gandhi. There he proclaimed the commencement of his Swachh Bharat Abhiyan, tokenism run riot as we already have a Nirmal Bharat Abhiyan that he has usurped wholesale, pausing only to slap a saffron label on an old Congress bottle. Indeed, the Nirmal Bharat Abhiyan was preceded by the Total Sanitation Campaign, 1999, of the previous Vajpayee-led NDA government, but our Modi does not scruple even at pinching his own party predecessor's programmes.

Such patent pinching would be OK provided Modi would at least study the lacunae of the past and the immense volume of research that has gone into the conception and implementation of the TSC and NBA with a view to making the course corrections essential to ensure the attainment of these noble objectives. Alas, he has no use or time for administrative detail. What he concentrates on is the colour of his waistcoat, admirable in a fashion model, deplorable in a Prime Minister.

Had he a head for anything other than the trivial, Modi would not have been looking for film stars (and comprador Congressmen) as "brand ambassadors", but summoning the hard working authors of the SQUAT survey to learn what has gone right and how much has gone wrong with the sanitation programmes we already have and what we need to do to get the strategy right. SQUAT, incidentally, stands for Sanitation Quality, Use, Access and Trends. The survey has been undertaken by New Delhi's Research Institute for Compassionate Economics, and the two young authors, Aashish Gupta and Payal Hathi, have summarised their findings in an article published the day after the launch in the *Indian Express*. Their survey finds that over 600 million Indians defecate in the open every day. Indeed, *The Daily Mail* of 7 August 2014 says 70,000 Gujaratis in Ahmedabad still defecate in the open; *The Hindu* of 17 September 2013 reports that 40 to 50 per cent of Gujarat's population defecate in the open; and a blog by VB Rawat of 2 March 2013 in Countercurrent.org says that even now 2500 households in Gujarat have been forced into manual scavenging. Ending this "will require a shift in mindsets, because without addressing the attitudes that shape people's distaste for latrine use", the mere building of household toilets will not scratch even the surface of the problem.

They have found that more than half the mothers they interviewed do not even believe that in-house toilets are safer for their children's health than the consequences of outside defecation. They have found also that even in households where toilets are used, one or more of the family members prefers to go outside. It is such mindsets and misinformation that have to be patiently and diligently transformed. Does the PM intend to sweep Race Course Road every morning, noon and night to change the Indian mindset? Or does he think one snapshot of him in a heliotrope jacket and – voila! – 600 million Indians will swear never again to go to the fields and the roadside?

TR Raghunandan of Accountability Initiative put the same point in a more colourful light. He describes a road journey at twilight from Bhubaneswar to Kandhamal in Orissa, watching the spectacle of villagers squatting on the roadside, their behinds picked up by the headlights as their jeep tears down the road. Raghu asks the Orissa government official, who has been trumpeting statistics about toilets built, toilets planned and toilets to be built, why the people are not using the thousands of toilets that they have already been provided. The official replies: "Well, people believe it is unhygienic to relieve themselves at home because God lives in the home." Raghu wryly adds: "Quite clearly, government-constructed roads have reached the appropriate level of Godlessness!"

It is such mindsets that have to be changed – village by village, home by home, across 700,000 villages and uncounted, but possibly lakhs of urban slums. It is not by handing joint secretaries brooms to sweep out their offices once a year that Modi is going to achieve that objective. We need an army of Swachh Sevaks, handsomely paid and well-equipped, going from village to village morning after morning, to ensure the repeated and perpetual removal of what Gandhiji called the village "dungheaps", under the supervision of the Panchayat Swachhta Samiti and the local Gram Sabha. But Modi had nothing to say – on Gandhi Jayanti, of all days – on the Gandhian conception of the critical role of Panchayats in ensuring village sanitation. Local government has been ignored altogether, notwithstanding the Constitutional injunction that village panchayats and municipalities be entrusted the duties of "sanitation". So too has been the detailed analysis of the issues, based on diligent academic research, and the model Activity Map provided in the 1500-page Report of an Expert Committee I chaired last year. Modi's Swachh Tokenism Abhiyan would have left the Mahatma weeping.

I live on a lane inhabited by two BJP ministers and one of their senior MPs. None of the three was in sight this morning as I took my daily morning walk. But poor little Pappu was there as usual, sweeping the street and carefully stacking the plastic wrappings abandoned by the cohort of BJP aspirants who haunt the lane through the day and throw their detritus everywhere, besides irrigating the sidewalks at will, not to mention the unmentionable left behind by stray dogs and infants who are encouraged by their poor parents to do it on the pavement running outside the ministerial bungalows.

Municipal cleanliness is only going to be assured by recruiting an army of safai karmacharis and ensuring priority to their unbearable working conditions, inadequate equipment and pathetic remuneration. Municipal cleanliness is a function of well-organized municipal services responsible to local ward sabhas and residents' welfare associations

(RWAs) in towns and efficient panchayats responsible to the gram/ward sabhas in rural areas. Gandhi Jayanti should have marked a major drive to vastly expand and ensure much higher levels of income, perks and welfare for the safai sewaks and safai karmacharis in both rural and urban areas to lend dignity and pride to their occupation, and thus involve the populace at large. Their work can never be replicated by PMs and Governors inexpertly waving an occasional broom. Instead, municipal services are increasingly being outsourced, depriving lakhs of safai karmacharis of their daily roti.

Worse, such outsourcing to private enterprises not obliged to observe reservation quotas means the source of living for millions of those entitled to employment quotas is being snatched from their mouths. Gandhi Jayanti would have been rendered meaningful if it had been celebrated as Safai Karmachari Day, with special emphasis on the lowest category of municipal karmacharis who live and work in the filthiest conditions imaginable in what ought to be the most enlightened metropolises of Mumbai, Chennai, Kolkata and Delhi. Instead, the educated middle classes pinch their noses as these municipal workers, sitting atop the filth they've picked up for disposal, roll by and close their eyes to the terrible issues that plague the lives of these "scavengers", as these municipal workers still insist on describing themselves in all honesty. All this has been brilliantly documented by Milind Ranade of Mumbai and the experts on safai karmacharis whom he has assembled and among whom he works, with sweat and tears, day after day after day. The urban middle class wants clean cities but has no time for Ranade and his ilk. No wonder, therefore that when Gandhiji was asked what he despaired of most in India, he replied that it was "the hard-heartedness of the educated Indian".

But Modi, and his hard-hearted urban middle class following, know none of this – and care less. What Modi wants is a TV slot - and gets it from a fawning media that is even more trivial than he is. *He' Ram!*

NDTV.com

PAKISTAN'S JAW STILL INTACT

14 October 2014

Arun Jaitley thumps his chest and proclaims that we have given the Pakistanis a "jaw-breaking reply" (*munh tod jawab*). Oh yeah? The Pakistanis are still there – with their jaw quite intact and a nuclear arsenal nestling in their pockets. Rajnath Singh adds that the Pakistanis had best understand that "a new era has dawned". How? Is retaliatory fire a BJP innovation? Or is it that we have ceased being peace-loving and become a war-mongering nation? And Modi thunders that his guns will do the talking (*boli nahin, goli*). Yes – and for how long?

The government struts around as if it has silenced the Pakistani guns. Nothing could be a more dangerous illusion. If the guns have ceased for the present to bark, it is because the Pakistan army has silenced its own guns, even as the Indian Army has silenced ours. The idea that we have terrified the Pakistanis into submission by shelling a few homes and killing a few soldiers and several innocents might be a myth that washes here but it is far, far from the truth. The danger is that we will forget the limits that divide peace from war.

If losing half their country in 1971 and leaving 90,000 prisoners of war in Indian hands has not dimmed Pakistan's zeal to protect itself, big words from our end are not going to make them grovel at Modi's feet. Pakistan is a sovereign nation. It makes its own assessment of the threats to its security. And the kind of talk they have heard in recent days from our governmental chiefs only persuades them that they are right in regarding India as the biggest threat to their security. This marginalizes the sane voices across the border and brings Pakistanis of all hues and colours together in the defence of their homeland. The language of the *akhara* is not the language of statesmen. And war is not a continuation of diplomacy by other means; it is a confession of the breakdown of diplomacy.

Dr. Manmohan Singh showed, especially during the first three years of his government, how much could be achieved by talking to Pakistan instead of shooting at them. Even Kashmir was tackled on the back-channel. It was agreed that territories could not be changed nor populations exchanged. What was needed was fostering exchanges of all kinds between Kashmiris on both sides of the LoC – the restoration of Kashmiriyat by fostering exchanges between people, relatives, friends, media, goods and services across the LoC in a two-way traffic. Pakistan has repeatedly – even with the change of regime in India – shown that it is ready to talk with India. It is we who are stalling the dialogue. But as the history of the last 20 years has shown, proxy war in Kashmir did not come in the way of Vajpayee's bus journey to the Shaheed Minar in Lahore; Kargil and the Parliament attack did not stop the invitation to Musharraf to come to Agra; nor did it prevent Vajpayee from going to Islamabad to sign a joint declaration that presaged the resumption of dialogue. 26/11 certainly threw the spanner in the works but was not enough to forestall the invitation to Nawaz Sharif to the forecourt of the Rashtrapati Bhavan. So, a "munh thod jawab" is for domestic consumption, a pathetic attempt at proving the breadth of the Prime Minister's chest.

The bigger danger is that overblown rhetoric can tip the subcontinent over the precipice. That is what we must remind ourselves in this centenary year of the commencement of the First World War. The parallels between the events that sparked WWI and the contemporary India-Pakistan situation are striking. The Austro-Hungarian Empire and Serbia were neighbours, much as India and Pakistan are neighbours. There was no comparison between the military power, the economic strength and the political clout of the two neighbours: Austro-Hungary, like India vis-a-vis Pakistan, was undoubtedly superior. Nevertheless, tension between the two neighbours was rife, as in the case of India and Pakistan. Serbia-based non-State actors were secretly readying for a major terrorist strike against the Empire, backed by powerful forces within Serbia but out of government control, much as Pakistan-based non-State terrorists are constantly preparing for terror strikes against key Indian targets, backed by powerful forces within Pakistan, but outside government control.

When a young band of Serbian terrorists slipped into Bosnia to kill Archduke Franz Ferdinand, the Government of Serbia did not know, even as it is entirely likely that the Government of Pakistan did not know that Ajmal Kasab and his gang had slipped into Mumbai to target the iconic Taj Hotel.

But, as in India, so in Austria, there was a strong suspicion that rogue elements in the Serbian establishment were backing the terrorists, no proof needed: suspicion amounted to conviction.

Therefore, when the Serbian terrorists struck, assassinating the heir-apparent to the Austro-Hungarian throne, the Empire needed no conclusive proof that the Serbian government was behind the assassination. It knew, as India "knew", that 26/11 was master-minded by the Government of Pakistan. And even as the Pakistan government denied any involvement in such cross-border terrorism and undertook to set in train an investigation into the dastardly terrorist attack, so also, a hundred years earlier, did Serbia condemn the assassination and offer to investigate and bring to justice those responsible.

But Vienna would not be appeased. An eight-point ultimatum was sent to Serbia demanding full acceptance of the eight conditions within a month. Eventually, after much hemming and hawing, Belgrade accepted seven of the conditions but baulked at the eighth – that a joint Austrian-Serbian investigation be launched into the assassination. That was enough for Vienna to insist that if all conditions were not fulfilled, the far more powerful Austro-Hungarian forces would reduce Serbia to rubble in a matter of days.

The threat was meant to cow the Serbians. The Serbians went as far as they could, but baulked at abject surrender. In consequence, military plans began to roll – to the alarm of both Emperor Franz Joseph of Austro-Hungary as well as the German Kaiser whose belligerence was pushing Vienna further and further down the road to disaster. Their political misgivings were entirely understandable. For Russia had declared that any military action against her Slav cousin would invite Russian retaliation against both Austria and Germany. At the same time, Germany had made it clear that her first target was France. Treaty obligations made it incumbent for France to come to Russia's rescue and vice versa in the event of war. Britain was committed to entering the war in these circumstances. The very balance of power that was supposed to have kept the peace in Europe for a hundred years was now pushing the world to the brink.

To prevent this catastrophe, the two Emperors who had been the loudest in proclaiming a *"muh tod jawaab"* to Serbia tried at the last moment to stop the guns from booming, but were overruled by their respective military hierarchies. War was launched. The mighty Austro-Hungarian Empire conquered Serbia but ended up losing the War and disappearing from the map of the world. Germany won the opening rounds but ended in humiliating defeat. Defeat on the battle-field led to the Peace Treaty but contained the seeds of resentment that resulted in WWII breaking out 20 years later. It did not end till nearly a hundred million people – mostly unarmed non-combatant civilians - had been killed the world over. That was the outcome of Vienna saying *"Boli nahin, goli."*

Let us remind ourselves that it was the Father of the Nation who taught us that "taking an eye for an eye would leave the whole world blind." *Shanti! Shanti! Shanti!*

NDTV.com

MODI'S TWO SELF-GOALS
IN ONE WEEK

21 October 2014

When Narendra Modi steals other people's schemes and re-launches them as his own initiatives, this purloining of the heritage of others is but a reflection of the absence of anything in his heritage to proclaim as his own. But such larceny is nothing compared to the havoc he wreaks when he begins to think for himself. Two examples of Modi's self-goals have struck this benighted nation in the week of 11-18 October.

The first was his *Sansad Adarsh Gram Yojana* (MPs' Model Village Programme). Pray, what business is it of MPs to establish model villages? Is that not the domain of the Panchayats? Launched on 11 October, the birth anniversary of Loknayak Jayaprakash Narayan, it mocks everything that JP stood for in wishing to insulate Panchayats from higher echelons of government, including interfering MPs and MLAs. I know Modi has little knowledge of what went before him but, had he cared to ask, someone might have handed him JP's "Swaraj for the People", priced at one rupee and published in 1961 by the Akhil Bharat Sarva Seva Sangh, Rajghat, Varanasi.

He would have read JP's passionate plea for empowering Panchayats far more effectively than had been achieved by Jawaharlal Nehru on the basis of the 1957 Balvantray Mehta Study Group recommendations. Clarifying that he was "indebted" to many but "most of all to Gandhiji", JP stressed his view, the same as the Mahatma's, "that as you proceed from the bottom level of government to the top, each higher level should have less and less functions and powers." Instead, he bemoaned, we had created an "inverted pyramid" from which it was necessary that the "broad upper levels" be "sawed off (and) brought down to earth so that the pyramid of democracy becomes a real pyramid – narrow at the top and broad at the bottom." In such a system, he said, "the people at each level would have the full opportunity to manage all those affairs that might pertain to that level."

So, what is an MP doing setting up "model villages" at the Panchayat level? At the level of the village panchayat, who more needs the "full opportunity to manage all those affairs that pertain to that level" than the Panchayats themselves? Had Modi been a JP follower, he would have started a *Panchayat Adarsh Gram Yojana*, ensuring that at least 50 lakhs a year is made available to every village in every panchayat so that within ten, perhaps even five years, every one of our 7,00,000 villages is made an "adarsh gram". Launching such a scheme on JP's birthday would have then been highly appropriate.

But to go against the grain of JP's thinking in asking legislators to do the executive's job of facilitating model villages, and that too by leaving it to MPs to decide which three of the 600 plus village panchayats in each constituency he is going to choose, is such a gross violation of everything that JP stood for that it adds insult to injury – that too on his birthday of all days – and amounts to transgressing the most dearly cherished principles that JP stood for. This is what happens when lesser human beings try to steal the clothes of the truly greater ones.

I also pity the MPs. At three villages every year over a five-year period, they would be left explaining to 585 of their 600 Panchayats why they were not chosen, and the privilege extended only to 15 others. And how will the MP choose the 15 "adarsh grams"? In all probability, as a reward for votes cast for the MP. This will ensure the MP's defeat at the next election in all the other infuriated panchayats. If, on the other hand, he chooses to please three villages that did not vote for him, the fury of those who supported him last time but, in turn, were not supported by him, will lead to a stern reckoning at the next elections. Thus, both from the Panchayats' point of view, and from the MPs', this is truly a lose-lose scheme.

As JP said, "Swaraj from Below" means not a "procedural reform" but bringing "swaraj to the people" by ensuring "a real devolution of power and not a make-belief. It is possible," he warned, "to construct the outward structures of Panchayati Raj and to give it no substance.

That would be like a body without a soul, dead from the start, a still-born child." Modi has made a "still-born child" of Panchayati Raj, "dead from the start," by devolving powers and funds to MPs and not Panchayats for the building of model villages.

Worse, to this farcical inauguration in Vigyan Bhavan, he had invited thousands of Panchayat representatives, but instead of listening to what they had to say (as Dr. Manmohan Singh and Soniaji had done on a previous occasion when we celebrated the 15th anniversary of Panchayati Raj under my chairmanship in 2008), Modi rudely left the meeting immediately after making his speech and Minister Nitin Gadkari promptly dissolved the proceedings, abandoning the Panchayat participants who came to me to complain bitterly about the treatment they had received at the hands of the Modi dispensation.

Next, we have the *draft labour legislation* tabled in the last session and procedural reforms announced on 16 October. The intended labour reforms signal Modi's payback time to the giant corporates who funded his hugely expensive election campaign. They have so infuriated organized labour that even the RSS-affiliated Bharatiya Mazdoor Sangh has joined its comrades in the trade-union movement to issue a joint statement on 15 September 2014 decrying the failure of the Central Government to "push through" amendments to the relevant laws "without any consultations with them".

The joint statement explains painstakingly how "liberalizing the provisions of the Factories Act will imperil safety at the workplace (and) push the majority of factories out of its coverage". Further, the amendments proposed will result in "the principal employer and the contractor becoming unaccountable for service conditions of the workers in a large number of enterprises". Moreover, the amendments proposed for the Apprentices Act "will pave the way for the replacement of contract/casual/temporary workers, and even regular workers, by comparatively low-paid apprentices". And the endgame will be the empowerment of employers to "retrench/lay off workers at will (and) resort to mass-scale contractorisation."

Is this how Modi proposes to promote industrialisation – as growth without jobs and decent employment? To secure an answer to these and other connected questions, the country's entire trade union movement is calling National Protest Day on 5 December. Modi has stirred the hornet's nest – and the country will have to pay the price in widespread industrial unrest.

With regard to Modi's "Shrameva Jayate Karyakram", trade unionist Gurudas Dasgupta has accused the government of catering to the corporates so that "they can play hell". The moves are "anti-worker and pro-corporates". The CPM, for its part, has both pointed out that the Universal Account Number for EPF, which Modi is touting as his achievement, is no more than the finalisation of a programme that has long been in the works, but added that the new norms for implementation of labour laws "will only worsen the situation and encourage further violations by employers".

Prof. KR Shyam Sundar of the Xavier Labour Research Institute, Jamshedpur, adds that the new procedures violate ILO's Labour Inspection Convention No. 81 by "centralizing inspections" and "controlling inspection visits from above" and regulating "inspection timings". We are likely to be hauled up in an international forum for Modi's rush to embrace his principal backers.

NDTV.com

NIGHT OF THE LONG TRIDENTS

24 October 2014

This text message is doing the rounds: "The Congress brought Modi to power. It is the BJP that will kick him out!"

Modi is a great believer in centralisation and authoritarianism. He is not running the Modi government. He is the Modi government. The administrative dictatorship is best exemplified in the official orders issued by the cabinet secretariat pertaining to the allocation of business among the ministers. In addition to usual departments always held by the prime minister-atomic energy, space, personnel – the orders add that "all important policy matters" also fall in Modi's exclusive domain. Thus, the hallowed principle of the prime minister being no more than the first among equals is given the go-by and all that matters is assigned to one man. A man who distinguished himself in Gujarat by being a law unto himself.

Also consider that virtually every economic ministry has been put in the charge of a minister of state, not a cabinet minister. Thus, by default, the Prime Minister becomes minister for planning, minister for commerce and industry, minister of environment and forests and a sheaf of other such portfolios. His trusted coterie of Jaitley (his most ardent supporter over the Gujarat pogrom), Gadkari and (the late) Gopinath Munde got their due, as did some others like Ashok Gajapathi Raju, the civil aviation minister. The latter got so because he was a key alliance partner. Everything else is concentrated in one pair of hands. And even when it is not, as in the case of external affairs, the sidelining of Sushma Swaraj for and on the foreign jaunts of our peripatetic prime minister has become downright embarrassing.

The greats of the BJP past are left to nurse their grievances on the margin. The saddest of these is Lal Krishna Advani, founder member of the Bharatiya Jana Sangh, deputy prime minister and BJP candidate for prime minister in 2009. In astonishing good health at his advanced age, Advani saved Modi's neck in the aftermath of the post-Godhra riots, but has not survived Modi's ire at allowing a discussion on his failings in Parliament in order to facilitate the budget being discussed. Murli Manohar Joshi is out for the sin of having been a past president of the BJP and liable to have views of his own. Others paying the price for having riled Modi at the time of Gujarat 2002 include Vajpayee, for having compelled Modi to pay his first-ever visit to a Muslim refugee camp one month after the riots broke out; Arun Shourie, for having emerged as Vajpayee's principal confidant over Gujarat, and Jaswant Singh, for having hinted that there might, after all, be some good to Jinnah. All pushed into the outer darkness so that they might not dim the sun of Modi.

Now, the state leaderships are being shown their place. By not naming in advance the BJP's candidates for Chief Minister of Maharashtra or Haryana, and taking upon himself the mantle of chief campaigner, Modi intends to ensure that if the BJP does come to power in these states, the chief ministers will not become independent poles of authority like Shivraj Chouhan or Raman Singh. While underplaying the role of these two stalwarts in the 2014 elections, Modi is now on track to show that after three successive setbacks in polls after the triumph of May 2014, Maharashtra and Haryana have fallen into the BJP lap because of Modi and Modi alone. Only Vimal. Remember the old commercial jingle?

Therefore, the sharpening of the knives that you hear in the background is not that of the Congress. It is of all those BJP aspirants who see the ground slipping from under their feet. They fear that their political future is being robbed from them and no rewards await them for the years they spent honing the party when they were in opposition. And, of course, those who have the taste of office on their lips live in mortal fear that they will be the *Eid ka bakra* when the Night of the Long Knives arrives, as it must.

For Modi, a terrible reckoning is in the offing.

The Week

HOW MODI GOVERNMENT IS WRECKING MGNREGA

28 October 2014

To the insult he inflicted on Gandhiji's name by launching his Swachh Bharat Abhiyan without even mentioning the Mahatma's principled insistence on Panchayats as the medium of the message, Modi has now added injury by tinkering with the National Rural Employment Programme being run in the name of Mahatma Gandhi (MGNREGA).

There is a great deal that is right with MGNREGA. Hunger is the single worst bane in the life of the poor, especially the destitute. MGNREGA directly attacks hunger by providing the supplementary income that bridges the gap between destitution and poverty. The latest Global Hunger Index shows that India has slashed malnutrition rates by nearly 15 per cent since MGNREGA was launched – the improvement in nutrition levels among mothers has translated, as it would, into better nutrition levels for their children.

Other social indicators have also shown improvement. This is essentially because women are the prime beneficiaries of the programme, and the substantial increase in their own disposable income has bettered indices across a wide range of measures. Moreover, by providing employment opportunities to women when the family is stalked by economic uncertainty, MGNREGA has enhanced the dignity and role of women as the principal providers for the family. Above all, as MGNREGA is the most important programme run by the Panchayats, inclusive growth has been secured through a participative model that, ideally, runs from the sarpanch to the ward members of the Panchayat and the community as a whole in their gram sabhas and ward sabhas.

Yet, there are many shortcomings. Foremost is that the average number of days for which employment is provided is under half the prescribed number of 100 days, principally because, by a fiscal sleight of hand, less than half the required funds are provided through the budget. This gaping lacuna in implementation is covered up by claiming that the programme is "demand-based" – that is, additional funds will be made available in keeping with additional "demand" for employment. But as no simple and transparent method has been devised of communicating the pent-up demand, particularly from an individual in need, there is no practical avenue for people to demand further employment. Therefore, the availability of funds determines the amount of work offered, rather than the other way round, and those in further need are unable to press their demand for work. In other words, instead of being a "rights-based" programme, where anyone needing work is immediately given work (within the ceiling of one hundred days), the programme is run as a "scheme" in which the available budget translates into the work-days available and when that quota of work-days is exhausted, generally at well below a hundred days, there is no automatic enhancement of the budget.

Moreover, while the Central legislation provides for the payment of a dole if employment is not made available within 15 days of work being demanded, the burden of paying the dole has been devolved on state governments, almost none of which have been prepared to bear the burden, with the result that this key provision has remained a dead letter. There is no incentive to ensure that all who ask for 100 days of work are given work. Combined with poor administration in several of the states where MGNREGA work is most needed, such as UP, Bihar, MP and Orissa, the percentage share of households actually securing 100 days' work is as low as 6 to 10, when it is intuitively obvious that these are precisely the states where work is most needed but not being provided.

There are other specific issues. Notwithstanding the provisions of the legislation, in many states, particularly poor performers such as Uttar Pradesh, Panchayats are not being involved, only the sarpanch is, thus setting up a nefarious nexus between the lower bureaucracy and the sarpanch to the detriment of the community. Rotation of work between sites often makes employment location-specific instead of being available to anyone in the Panchayat, irrespective of the locality in the Panchayat where the person lives. Community involvement in planning projects for execution under MGNREGA is provided for in the legislation, but is often not reflected in practice, making MGNREGA bureaucracy – planned and bureaucracy – implemented, in blatant violation of both the letter and the spirit of the legislation.

Moreover, MGNREGA is an "employment-creation" programme, not an "asset-creation" programme. For asset creation, there are several other schemes. That is why the success or otherwise of MGNREGA must be measured in terms of employment opportunities offered, not in terms of assets created. Alternatively, MGNREGA could be deployed for the labour component of asset-creation programmes. Why, it should even be possible to link private asset-creation, especially in the fields of small and marginal farmers, with MGNREGA.

Instead of dealing with these real issues of MGNREGA, the Modi government has gone off on a tangent. First, it wants to change the ratio of labour to materials to increase the use of machinery and supplies without realizing that every rupee taken from employment to pay for materials reduces the funds available for employment – and this further cuts the already low level of employment being offered under the programme. To emphasise asset-creation at the expense of employment-creation is to undermine the very logic of this hugely popular and desperately needed programme. Yet, mindlessly, this is precisely what the Modi government is contemplating.

Worse, the Modi government plans to restrict the programme to designated "backward" areas, constituting about a third of the country. This is ridiculous. For one thing, there is already a pretty successful Backward Regions Grant Fund. It requires strengthening. Additional funds for backward areas development should be made available to this Fund. Why shift the burden to MGNREGA?

More fundamentally, the programme in Gandhi's name is targeted at the individual in need, not the place of his or her residence. There is no part of India where the destitute and the poor do not live. The proportion may be higher in some places than in others. But those in need are everywhere. To deprive people of employment merely because they happen to live in the wrong place is to inflict the gravest injustice on them for no fault of their own.

Finally, the beauty of MGNREGA has lain in the self-identification of the beneficiaries. Anyone willing to undertake the hard, backbreaking, unskilled work involved in MGNREA, toiling in the boiling sun for the pittance required to keep body and soul together, has been the only criterion for making work available. There are no tiresome, discriminatory identification procedures pockmarked with corruption and nepotism. The Modi innovation will re-introduce patronage networks to run the programme.

No wonder a concerned group of over 20 top economists and social activists led by Jean Dreze has written to Modi begging him to reconsider. Their views are backed by international experts like Martin Ravallion. Behind them is a phalanx of those like me who have been involved with the programme since its conception. Instead of consulting those in the know about what changes to make, Modi has shot off on his own, to the detriment of the poor and the destitute and the dismay of poor women all over rural India. Modi must be stopped in his tracks before he wreaks further havoc. Let us not forget that, under his watch, Gujarat was among the worst-performing MGNREGA states.

NDTV.com

SAVE INDIA FROM MODI'S GUJARAT MODEL

4 November 2014

The twin pillars of Modi's "Gujarat development model" were unrestrained environmental damage and massive displacement of tribals to help the capitalist fat cats reap undreamt-of windfall profits to then fund Modi's revoltingly expensive election campaigns.

The symbol of that outrage is Vapi, the industrial city in south Gujarat that is the most horrendously polluted cluster in the whole country. In his 12 years in power in the state, Modi did nothing to clean up Vapi. He now threatens the whole country with a similar ecological disaster.

Moreover, over the period of his Chief Ministership, as many as 76 per cent of those displaced by so-called "development" were tribals. To comprehend the scale of callousness that goes into the mindset of the Gujarat development model, one has to set this figure against the share of tribals in Gujarat's total population: a mere 8 per cent. Thus, a mere 8 per cent of the population has had to bear 76 per cent of the burden of displacement. The poorest and the least empowered are pushed to the side to enable private sector barons to lord it over ordinary people. This is not even capitalism. It is feudalism in industry.

This too is now being replicated all over the country. Already, the Minister of State for Environment, Prakash Javadekar, has announced with pride (!) that he has cleared 240 projects in three months. How is that possible except by sweeping under the carpet the laws, regulations and procedures carefully devised to protect the environment and give tribal people a fair deal? He has also delinked forest clearance from clearance by the National Board of Wild Life and halved NBWL clearance requirements from 10 km to 5 km around forest reserves, besides emasculating the Board by replacing eminent experts and concerned NGOs with rubber stamps. He has also relaxed procedures for the application of the Forest Conservation Act in precisely those areas where FCA is most required: Naxal-affected areas; linear projects in forest areas; and in eco-sensitive areas along the international border.

Relaxations have also been introduced in regard to public hearings for coal mines; irrigation projects; and even the moratorium on clearances for the 43 "critically polluted clusters" identified by his own ministry.

All this is capped by undermining the National Green Tribunal and considering doing away with the gram sabha consent for forestland diversion for minerals' prospecting. The Modi government has further threatened to heavily dilute the landmark Land Acquisition Act that they themselves voted for but a year ago, and amend with a view to diluting a whole raft of environmental protection legislation ranging across the gamut of the Environment Protection Act, the Wildlife Protection Act, the Forest Conservation Act, and the Water and Air Pollution Act, while preserving as it is the highly discriminatory colonial legislation that is the Mother of all forest Acts – the Indian Forests Act, 1927.

Ashish Kothari, to whom this column owes most of the previous paragraph, has summed up the consequences of the development model with which the country is threatened, as follows: "Employment in the formal sector has hardly grown; undernourishment and malnourishment are at an all-time high; India ranks among the worst in social indicators of various kinds; inequalities between the rich and the poor are growing significantly; and ecological un-sustainability has already set in. "O tempora o mores"! ("Oh, what times, what ways," as Cicero exclaimed).

What is being done to the tribals is even worse. The root cause for the spread of Naxalism is tribal unrest. 65 million tribals have been displaced since Independence, most of whom have received neither rehabilitation nor resettlement. It has been no "Independence" for them. They do not see "development" as desirable; they see it as disruptive. The bureaucracy and police they deal with are unbelievably oppressive (as detailed in the 2007 Bandyopadhyay Committee report).

The oppressive forest guard, the bullying *thanedar* and the exploitative *patwari* are the instruments of state they encounter. No wonder they are seduced by the Maoist talk of revolutionary change.

We can only integrate our tribals in nation-building by making them part of the national mainstream. That means empowering them to control their own lives and habitat, and manage their lives as they wish, according to their norms and their traditions, not in terms of imposed and alien value systems. The Maoists live among them, share their food, their homes and their ways of life. The State merely bares its ferocious teeth at them. Hence the tribal revolt that, by Home Ministry accounts, has affected nearly a third of India, including a wide swathe across the breadth of the country at its widest, from Odisha to Gujarat.

Modi has sought to stamp out that tribal revolt in his home state by stamping out the tribals. They have reacted by over three-fourths of them not voting for Modi even at the height of the Modi wave. Being but less than a tenth of the population, their voice is barely heard in Gujarat. But as we move eastwards, the tribal voice grows stronger. It has to be heard. Indira and Rajiv Gandhi were among the first to hear it in the country, but the credit must go to the Deve Gowda government for passing in 1996 the most important pro-tribal legislation that independent India has seen – the Provisions of the Panchayats (Extension to Scheduled Areas) Act, 1996 – usually known by its acronym, PESA.

This is the only legislation mandated by the Constitution. As a Congress back-bencher and former Minister of Panchayati Raj, I regard the failure to secure universal compliance with PESA as the single biggest failure of ten years of UPA governance, but worse is imminently in store – the dilution of PESA by the Modi government.

We must resist it. We will resist it. However brute Modi's majority might be in the Lok Sabha, in the Rajya Sabha he is in a minority. There, we will hold up reactionary amendments for as long as we can.

NDTV.com

MODI THE CENTRALIZER

10 November 2014

Through his 12 years as Chief Minister of Gujarat, Panchayat Raj in the state stagnated under Modi Raj. That is principally why his performance on growth rates – worse than Maharashtra, Tamil Nadu and even Bihar, but better than several others – was not matched by any improvement in human development. Going by the Human Development Index ranking, Gujarat never rose above the 15th position out of some 30 states and Union Territories.

In respect of devolution to Panchayat Raj Institutions (PRIs), Modi the Centraliser could not bring himself to allow decentralization to get any headway. Hence, notwithstanding Gujarat having been the home state of the three Great Pioneers of Panchayat Raj – Gandhiji, Balvantray Mehta and Ashoka Mehta – Modi failed to build on the strong foundations laid by these great predecessors.

Not only Kerala and Karnataka, but a whole raft of relative newcomers ranging from Maharashtra to Haryana to Rajasthan and recent performers like Tripura, Sikkim and Himachal Pradesh far outdistanced Gujarat in moving along the path of participative democracy. Modi was too busy being authoritarian to push his economic agenda to care for the inclusion in development of the garib and the aam aadmi. (And no wonder either that he consistently refused me permission to visit Gujarat as Union Minister of Panchayati Raj – he was too scared that he would stand exposed).

Without waiting for wisdom to dawn on Modi, the Congress government in Karnataka under Chief Minister Siddaramaiah has taken a giant step to restore the state to the prime position in the country in Panchayat Raj and to take the lead over Kerala and Maharashtra who have in the past decade and a half stolen a march over Karnataka.

A committee on amendments to the Karnataka Panchayat Raj Act, chaired by former Speaker KR Ramesh Kumar, last week submitted its report to the state government titled *The Path to Gram Swaraj in Karnataka*, containing radical proposals for course corrections based on the accumulated ground-level experience of the last 20 years, indeed, the last 30 years if one takes into account, as one should, the pioneering innovations in the 1980s of Chief Minister Ramakrishna Hegde and his unforgettable Panchayat Minister, Abdul Nazeer Sab.

The proposals include giving statutory powers of supervision and control over the Panchayats to Gram Sabhas defined radically as representative assemblies of each habitation, in addition to ward-level consultations and Panchayat-level consolidation. In one stroke, the biggest conundrum of effective Panchayat Raj has been solved – namely, the need to reconcile the imperative of effective staff support, possible only for larger basic units, with smaller and more homogeneous units which would facilitate effective participation by the people.

This legal empowerment of the Panchayat with a careful spelling out of their duties and responsibilities is significantly reinforced by vesting in the Gram Sabhas the authorization of the issue of "utilization certificates", which means that no payment to contractors is validated till the Gram Sabha by consensus agrees that the work has been undertaken economically and completed satisfactorily. Thus, not only is the community satisfied but the scope for corruption and malfeasance is sharply reduced.

Besides, the proposals tend in the direction of establishing a District Panchayat Service, supervised by a Panchayat Seva Pradhikar, to ensure adequate staffing at the bureaucratic, accounting and technical level for each level of Panchayat, thus compensating for the want of experience and training of panches and presidents of Panchayat units.

If Karnataka takes up the offer of the Institute of Public Accountants of India for the provision of a trained chartered accountant for every 10 Panchayats at a highly affordable fee, the demands of modern, computerized, online administration can be easily married to the indispensability of representative local government to ensure responsible local governance and, therefore, responsiveness to local demand.

The menace of Sarpanch Raj is countered by ensuring the collegiate functioning of the Panchayats by statutorily ensuring that all Panchayat work is done through subjects committees and decisions are taken with all Panchayat members present. To mitigate money-and-muscle power in Panchayat elections, the Committee has recommended State funding of elections, to the exclusion of any private or party funding, combined with statutory autonomy for the State Election Commission to decide everything election-related, from delimitation to disqualifying candidates who break the code or the law, without any interference from the political authority.

But by far the most exciting recommendation of the Report relates to the process and ambit of endowing powers and authority to the Panchayats. Resting on a detailed parsing of Article 243G of the Constitution, the Report delineates the procedure and content of the kind of devolution required for rendering the Panchayats as "institutions of local self-government". Annexed to the report are detailed Activity Maps (Responsibility Maps) for each of the 29 subjects listed in the Eleventh Schedule (plus four more) regarding the methodology for the simultaneous devolution of the 3 Fs – Functions, Finances and Functionaries – which would ensure the effective empowerment of the Panchayats in their legally designated spheres to have control and supervision over the planning and implementation of plans, programmes, and projects of economic development and social justice.

This is reinforced by the proposal that the State Finance Commission recommendations should have the same automacity of acceptance and implementation as has been the practice for the recommendations of the (central) Finance Commission.

Karnataka does not need Central permission to go ahead with these revolutionary proposals. They can decide all the issues in Bengaluru, of course with legislative support. If the state government acts quickly, it will sweep the Panchayat polls due in April 2015 – and perhaps that would teach the anti-Panchayat Modi government that you can fool all of the people some of the time, and some of the people all of the time, but you cannot fool all of the people all of the time!

THE BLACK RED HERRING

13 November 2014

There is a delightful short story by Jeffrey Archer, "Clean Sweep Ignatius", which sums up the ethos of the Swiss banking industry. A whistle-clean new finance minister joins the Nigerian government and embarks on a much-publicised drive to end corruption, and, much like Arun Jaitley, to retrieve for his nation's treasury the vast quantities of illegal money stashed away in foreign havens. He reaches Geneva unannounced and proceeds, with an attaché case in his hand, to the office of the head of Switzerland's biggest banking corporation. Once inside, he demands the bank account number of his predecessor. The president of the bank politely refuses citing confidentiality laws. The Nigerian insists. There is an ugly impasse. At this, the finance minister pulls out a pistol and, pressing it against the president's temple, threatens to shoot if the account number is not revealed. The president breaks into a cold sweat but is unable to bring himself to revealing the number. At that, the finance minister puts his pistol back into his pocket and, flipping open the attaché case, says he was looking for a reliable banker!

That is the Switzerland (and *hamshakal* Liechtenstein) from where Jaitley nurses his fraudulently obtained lists of Indian account holders. Fraudulent because they were obtained without authorisation and have to be authenticated before any action can be taken. To get the lists authenticated, India has had to resort to its Double Taxation Avoidance Agreements with France and Germany. The principal condition is that the lists will not be publicly revealed until India starts the process of prosecuting specified account holders for violation of Indian laws. Holding an account abroad is not in itself a crime under Indian law. Hence, the transgression has to be specified before a particular account can be publicly identified.

There lies the rub. The UPA government had received the lists under DTAAs. Wrongdoing has to be asserted in a court of law by the Finance

135

Ministry's Enforcement Directorate and charges framed by the court for the name and number of the account holder to be revealed. This slow and demanding work was being patiently undertaken by the UPA government when Modi and his cohort unleashed their irresponsible election tirade, promising to put the lists in the public domain on the morrow of their election and within 100 days bring back home the money parked abroad all of which was assumed to be "black". That this claim was rubbish has now been proved, which is why Jaitley and Modi are hoist with their own petard and twisting slowly in the wind.

I have little sympathy for them. I am, however, concerned about India's international standing and the future prospects of continuing to secure such information. Both are under threat. Under intense international pressure centred on the "war on terrorism" and the drug menace in developed countries, G20 has initiated a "global war against tax invasion". The governments of the Western tax havens have agreed within the framework of G20 to enter into a binding international agreement among themselves to reveal some information to each other, but under strict safeguards that will protect their legitimate banking interests. The agreement was concluded when the UPA was in power. All Jaitley needed to do was send a plenipotentiary to Berlin last week to sign the agreement. But Modi's lot have botched it. The agreement has gone into effect without India's signature. And, therefore, we are shut out of its benefits. Why?

For three reasons. Onlooking at the list, Jaitley, to his deep embarrassment, found that there was nothing in it to indict the Congress or its leaders. Second, he discovered that he could not release the lists at will. Third, when under Supreme Court orders he submitted the lists in a sealed envelope, some names started coming out. Worse, the most detailed recounting of the lists is in *Indian Express* by a gossip writer whose husband is Jaitley's best friend. No G20 government is ever again going to trust us. The Enforcement Directorate should investigate their own minister.

The Week

THE DANGER OF A RISING BJP IN KASHMIR

26 November 2014

Early polls indicate that the Congress and the National Conference have lost a great deal of support in Jammu and Kashmir. They also indicate that the PDP is likely to be the overwhelming winner in the Valley and the BJP the big winner in Jammu and, possibly, Ladakh.

Poll findings are notoriously unreliable and as the campaign progresses, the picture will become clearer. But as of now, it would appear that, unlike in the past, when the NC-Congress alliance ensured that the ruling coalition would have a joint presence in all parts of the state, this time round, there might be a dividing line along the Chenab, in effect dividing the Hindu-majority Jammu from Muslim-majority Kashmir, with Ladakh standing helplessly on the sidelines.

While the NC-Congress alliance will take defeat, as they have victory, in their stride as part and parcel of the ups and downs of the democratic process, all Indians, including voters in the state, need to ponder the consequences of splitting the state politically on religious lines. Mehbooba Mufti has made it clear that she intends to have no truck with the BJP within the State. In an interview to *The Hindu* (23 November) she said the BJP "is trying to convey to a particular group of people that they are going to handle things in Kashmir differently and teach Kashmiris a lesson." She adds that the BJP's aim is to "disempower them (the Kashmiris) because when they talk of Article 370 it means disempowerment of the state." She also draws attention to "the communalization they [the BJP] are fostering". This, she says, is an attempt to pit "Jammu vs. Kashmir and then Kashmir vs. the rest of India." She describes this as "a very, very dangerous game." She has also strongly condemned the language ("loot") with which Modi began his Kashmir campaign in Kishtwar.

It is difficult not to agree with her. Pakistani interlocutors, in particular

Niaz Naik, who once served as Pakistan's High Commissioner to India, have long propounded the theory that if all of J&K cannot become part of Pakistan-Occupied Kashmir, at least allow the Valley to be merged into Pakistan, leaving Jammu and Ladakh with India – for the sole reason that there is a Muslim majority in the Valley, but not in the other parts of the state under Indian sovereignty and control. We have consistently rejected such mischief-mongering and defended the integrity of the state, and the integration of all of J&K (including Pak-Occupied Kashmir) with the Indian Union.

But if the forthcoming Assembly elections result in the state getting politically divided along religious lines, pro-Pak elements in the Valley, and Pakistan itself, are bound to get incentivized into demanding integration with Pakistan. Happily, Mehbooba adds that "we will not allow it to happen" and one can only hope she is right.

However, the waters are in danger of being muddied because of the BJP's stated position on Article 370. After the PM's own MoS, Jitendra Singh, who is a Jammu MP, stirred an angry controversy within hours of being sworn in by raising Article 370, the BJP have tried to moderate their stand by saying they want no more than "a public discussion" on the continuation of the Article. Even a discussion of the continuing validity of the Article is bound to cause disquiet and unease in the Valley.

Of course, the Article is in the "temporary and transient" section of the Constitution but the fundamental reason for persisting with it is that the original reason given by Law Minister Gopalaswamy Ayyangar in the Constituent Assembly continues to hold good – namely, the continued forcible and illegal occupation of a part of the state by Pakistan. The vacation of Article 370 can only follow, and not precede, the vacation of Pak aggression. Were there to be that "final settlement" of issues related to J&K envisaged in the Simla agreement of 1972, there might be cause to reconsider 370 but short of that, it is the height of irresponsibility on the part of Modi to talk, on the one hand, in terms of reconciliation with the people of Kashmir and, on the other, provoke tension by starting a public debate on 370, and that too in the midst of a tension-filled election.

Moreover, it is historical illiteracy (of the kind we often get from Modi) to delink Article 370 of the country's Constitution from Article 1 of the J&K constitution. The latter clarifies and confirms that J&K is an integral part of the India Union. If 370 is prematurely thrown in doubt, integration will also be questioned by a swathe of public opinion in the Valley, including those Kashmiris who regard 370 as the condition precedent for Article 1 of the J&K constitution. Finally, what happens to PV Narasimha Rao's promise of the sky as the limit for Kashmiri autonomy, which broke the back of Kashmiri insurgency, if even 370 is brought into question?

Actually, the BJP is hoist with its own petard. Since even before Syama Prasad Mookerjee's ill-fated 1953 visit to the Valley, where he fell terminally ill and died, the Jan Sangh-RSS combine has challenged the validity of 370. Now that they are in power at the Centre, their past stand on 370 hangs like an albatross around their neck. Neither can they shrug off their past nor can they continue to assert it with the stridency of the past now that power in the state is a distant possibility.

The minute they revert even tangentially to the idiom of the past, they will be sure of losing every seat in the Valley and possibly the Muslim-majority seats in the shadow of the Chenab in Jammu as well. So, while it is always a pleasure to watch Modi twisting slowly, slowly in the wind, in the present context, this spectacle gives no comfort because we are not talking polemics, we are talking of the unity and integrity of the Indian Union. Only a categorical repudiation of the long-held saffron position on 370 will reassure public opinion in the Valley and, therefore, lend substance to the BJP's dreams of dominating the state. This, Nagpur will never permit Modi to do.

Of course, it is for the people of Kashmir to decide who to vote for, but this time – they have to think through their vote more carefully than ever before, for if the result is as foretold by the polls – a straightforward politico-religious divide along the Chenab – the only ones to derive any satisfaction from the outcome would be the very Hurriyat whom Modi forestalled from meeting the Pak High Commissioner.

NDTV.com

RAMLILA RALLIES IN NEW YORK

29 November 2014

Are Modi's partisan political rallies abroad doing any good to India? To Indians abroad? To India's relations with the host countries? In the first flush of their unexpected but overwhelmingly decisive election victory, it is, of course, to be expected that the BJP supporters of Indian origin would want to celebrate their hero's achievement. But the manner in which they did so in New York and now in Sydney, and which they threaten to repeat in other capitals, does not augur well for anyone.

For one thing, it lacks decorum and dignity. Every democratic country ensures that domestic differences are left behind when the head of government or even humble MPs travel abroad.

The continuation of the election campaign into the kind of tamasha we have been seeing is a violation of that unwritten code. For at these rallies, Modi openly raises issues of domestic contention. Moreover, he makes a spectacle of himself choosing venues associated with pop concerts and boxing contests. What, after all, would one make of Obama visiting India for the Republic Day and holding a 'Democrats only' convention in the Jawaharlal Nehru Stadium to the exclusion of all US Republicans resident in the city?

And what would happen if the Indian Overseas Congress decides to retaliate and holds counter-rallies at the same time? Would that not show India to be a divided house? Should we be washing dirty linen at another's doorstep? And is not Modi provoking such action by holding these provocative partisan rallies?

One has known of opponents of the government holding rallies against the visitor when they have a point to make. For instance, when Rajiv Gandhi went to Washington in 1985, a group of Khalistanis protested. They were entitled to do so.

Equally standard is for prime ministers, and even ordinary run-of-the-mill ministers, to meet the Indian community when they travel overseas. But there is a certain protocol and etiquette to such meetings with the issues being raised relating to the problems of the community as a whole not degenerating into a slanging match on domestic issues.

Yes, press conferences are held, sometimes questions about domestic politics are raised, but, as a general rule, party politics is kept out of answers at press conferences abroad. That is why the PM talks to the Indian media accompanying him on the way back. Of course, brand new PMs can change the rules but not at the cost of the dignity of the nation.

Then there is the question of what Modi will do if he were to visit the Gulf countries, host to millions of Indians, mostly working class, and overwhelmingly from Kerala, a state not particularly well-disposed to him and the BJP. Will he defy local regulations that sternly prevent any overt political activity? And, if the millions of Indians in the Gulf are to be left out of these jamborees, then what is proved by middle-class NRIs, mostly Gujarati, fetching up at these partisan shows of strength?

There is also the question of community solidarity. Do we not want to see the overseas Indian community standing strong and united? Also, what of the reaction in the host country? They want the Indian community to behave as good citizens of their adopted country. They do not want to see these communities ghettoised and divided. Yet, that is precisely the consequence of Modi's cohorts mobilising BJP workers to convert a visit to the host country into a homeland rally.

Modi proved his point in May 2014 when he was elected PM. He will be doing a great favour to the country, to Indians abroad and to host countries if he stops this tasteless circus and gets on with giving substance to foreign policy. Or, does he have to prove himself to himself again and again because he knows that the Holy Grail will slip from his hands at any time?

The Week

WE NEED TO TALK WITH PAKISTAN, URGENTLY

1 December 2014

Apart from the Hurriyat, there are at least four fundamental issues that, from the Indian point of view, need to be overcome, if progress in Indo-Pak relations is to be sincere and genuine.

First, resolving Kashmir. Both governments appear to be in denial about what was achieved between them in the years that followed the Islamabad Declaration when Vajpayee visited Islamabad in January 2004 and the Satinder Lambah-Tariq Aziz back-channel was opened later that year. The record shows that the negotiators were able to agree that "the final settlement of issues related to Jammu & Kashmir" must eschew exchange of territories and people, and concentrate on facilitating the movement of friends and family across the Line of Control (LoC), as well as trade and cultural contacts between the two halves of Kashmir, along with the "joint management" of the region to render the LoC irrelevant to the lives of those living on either side of it.

True, the back-channel agreement was never brought to either government for ratification, but as the negotiators were negotiating at the behest of their respective governments, at least it could be said that dialogue could show the way to some form of resolution.

Second, firing across the LoC (and even sometimes the international border), accompanied on occasion by barbarity, leading to the death of not only combat troops but also civilians, besides the destruction of property and the displacement of peoples. Such deplorable incidents cause general outrage on both sides of the border, and the outrage is aggravated by the media. The factual position is that there is an inverse relationship between dialogue and border incidents. There was a palpable reduction in cross-border firing and killings between 2004 and 2008 when the dialogue process was on; the number and gravity of such incidents has been inexorably rising ever since the dialogue process was effectively ended by 26/11. Thus, if the aim is to end the needless loss of life, destruction of property and cruel displacement involved in cross-border firing, it needs to be recognized that a resumption of contacts leads to a diminution of tension which, in turn, reduces and all but eliminates such regrettable incidents. If we do not talk, the cost in life and limb will be considerable.

Third, there is the question of action to be taken by and in Pakistan to fulfil their Islamabad Declaration (2004) commitment to prevent cross-border terrorism and bring to justice those who perpetrate such heinous acts. Putting Pakistan in the dock does not appear a very fruitful way of proceeding – although undoubtedly they have much to account for. But India can hold them to their word only through a process of dialogue. Should the ending of terrorism based on Pakistani soil be the pre-condition for initiating talks – or the object of the dialogue? Moreover, given the problems of ending terrorism directed by Indians against Indian nationals in several parts of India, should India be more sympathetic to the fact of Pakistan itself being the most terrorist-affected state in the world, with some 40,000 Pakistani lives lost to terrorism and the US-Pak war on terrorism in Pakistan, especially in the far northwest of the country? Should not India take note of several key establishments having been the object of terrorist attacks, among them the ISI HQ in Lahore, the Army GHQ in Rawalpindi, and the Mehran naval establishment on the outskirts of Karachi? Would not India-Pakistan cooperation, both bilaterally and within the SAARC framework, offer a more productive approach to carrying forward a common front against all forms of terrorism?

Fourth, the vexed question of whom to deal with in Pakistan. It has been an oft-repeated argument in Indian circles that as democracy is a fragile plant in Pakistan, it is not, in fact, the civilian government but the armed forces, the intelligence community, powerful clerics, and gun-toting 'jihadis' who control the levers of decision-making. Whom then is one to talk to? And what is the point of talking to those who are not really in charge? Apart from recognizing that Pakistan is a sovereign nation and, therefore, there is no alternative to talking to the government, the fact is that India has been negotiating – often with a measure of success – through the usual government channels.

To bring in the other entities might constitute recognition of ground realities, but cannot be the basis for denying any role to the elected civilian government in negotiating with India. Would, for example, the Indian government be ready to permit Pakistani negotiators to talk directly to our Army chief given that India's armed forces are the ones most reluctant to give in on Siachen? The civil government in Pakistan will, of course, have to take all domestic players into account – as, indeed, will India – but to portray the democratically – elected government as a helpless puppet of stronger non-state forces (and their collaborators in the armed forces and intelligence community) is to undermine democracy in Pakistan, which India has always regarded as crucial to the improvement of India-Pakistan relations.

Therefore, all things considered, there appear to be only two alternative ways forward. One would be to neglect Pakistan – benign or malignant neglect. There is a school of thought in India (and perhaps also in Pakistan) that despairs of any progress being made on any substantial point and, therefore, thinks it wisest to just ignore Pakistan and get on with other dimensions of foreign policy. Superficially feasible though this line of thinking may appear to be, it assumes that issues with Pakistan can be swept under the carpet. Can India ignore firing across the LoC? Can Pakistan ignore water shortages in the Indus basin? Can India ignore infiltration across the LoC? Can Pakistan shut its eyes to smuggling across its borders? Can India shrug off cross-border terrorists? Can Pakistan wash its hands of Kashmir without "a final settlement"? Is Pakistan going to give up indefinitely its claims on Siachen, Sir Creek, Wullar-Tulbul? Are we? Can we give up transit routes through Pakistan to and from Afghanistan? Can either country forego trade opportunities with the other? Will the world let matters drift? Will the rattling of our nuclear sabres not cause world-wide concern? No, mutual neglect is not an option. It is, at best, a pipe-dream. Whether we want it or not, Pakistan impinges on India, as India does on Pakistan – not just politically but in everyday life, from divided families to a shared love of Bollywood.

Hence, if both mutual neglect and mutual engagement are ruled out, is there then any way out of the impasse? Only one, for the present. That would be for the India-Pak dialogue to be put on the backburner, but 'talks about talks' to be initiated to explore avenues of returning to the negotiating table. Such talks-about-talks could be undertaken quietly through diplomatic channels (or even clandestine back-channels) so that, if and when the heat subsides and face-saving devices for resumption are settled, the dialogue could be resumed, preferably as an "uninterrupted and uninterruptible" process.

NDTV.com

MODI, ARE WE NOT
A NATION ANYMORE?

9 December 2014

Modi has dismantled the Planning Commission but, as yet, not put anything in its place. But does he know why the Planning Commission was set up in the first place? And do we not need an institution to serve those goals and objectives anymore?

The 1950 Government of India resolution establishing the Planning Commission (PC) laid down its purposes. It said the PC should "make an assessment of the material, capital and human resources of the country." Is that no longer required? Does the nation not need to know what its resources are? Second, said the resolution, the PC should "investigate the possibilities of augmenting deficient resources."

Have we become so flush with resources that there are deficits and deficiencies no more? Do we not still need to expand and deepen our resources? As Jawaharlal Nehru said a year after he had established the Planning Commission: "The Plan is in essence a realistic survey of what it is possible to do with the resources likely to be available within the framework of our Constitution and without a marked break from our existing social and economic framework. The Plan has done a valuable service by saying in a realistic way what we can do and what we cannot do in existing circumstances."

Why is Modi scared of such realism?

Third, said the resolution, the PC should "formulate a Plan for the most effective and balanced utilization of resources". Have we reached the stage where we do not need a nationwide Plan at all? Are we no longer a nation, just a congeries of states? Are there to be no national goals, no national purpose? Should we be leaving it to each state and each enterprise to decide what it wants – and get what it wants, whatever its purpose, national or partisan, and without reference to an overarching national architecture? After all, resources are limited and someone has to see how to share limited available resources among competing ends. If we do not, then the fat cats will get everything they want and the deprived and disadvantaged will be left with nothing or, at best, the dregs.

Is that the India the BJP wants, where those with access to resources (rich industrialists close to the administration) rule the roost while 70 per cent of India's poor and vulnerable get little or no share of the national cake because they cannot grab their share except from the grasping hands of the richer and more powerful? Is there not to be some rational basis to deciding what goes towards growth and what to the social sector – health, education, poverty alleviation and so on? Does Modi really expect the coterie that dominates the stock market to determine the share of the national budget that the poor might claim as their right?

Let us once again invoke Nehru from 1951: "Whatever plan we might make, the test of its success is how far it brings relief to the millions of our people who live on a bare subsistence level, that is the good and advancement of the masses of our people. Every other interest must be subordinated to this primary consideration."

Fourth, said the original resolution, the PC should "determine priorities". Does the Modi government not have priorities? And if it does, how will it determine them if they have no database to go on and no expert advice on the benefits and pitfalls of alternative models of resource distribution?

Fifth, the PC was to "define the stages in which the plan would be implemented". Of course, if there is no plan, there can be no defining its stages of implementation, but if we have no plan, and if the market alone is to determine the stages of implementation, then what becomes of the social responsibilities of the government? And what becomes of the parliamentary voice, that is, the voice of democracy? Obviously, parliament can say nothing about a plan that does not exist. But if parliament, the press and the public are to have a role in the formulation of economic policy, they will have to be told what is the government's policy. Else, the government will be left saying it has no policy and so it can change no policy!

Sixth, the PC was to "propose the allocation of resources". Note the expression "propose". Based on technical expertise, the PC would propose, but it would be the democratic, federal, political process that would dispose. If the PC has been insufficiently accommodating of the states or the private sector for resource allocation, the answer must lie in correcting the PC's excesses, not throwing the baby out with the bathwater.

Next, the 1950 resolution provided that the PC should "indicate which factors tend to retard economic development". *Kya ab itne achhe din aa gaye hain ki* there are no factors retarding economic progress? Is Sadhvi Jyoti going to determine what those factors are or are we going to get economists of repute to point out those factors to government for resolution? The same clause of the resolution also provided for the PC to "determine the conditions needed for the execution of the Plan." But, of course, if there is no Plan, no conditions can be created for its execution. But if we have no plan, then how is the ship of state to be steered? Or is that going to be left to the CII and FICCI to determine?

Finally, the PC was to "appraise the progress achieved in execution and recommend appropriate adjustments." Does the Modi dispensation believe that progress and failure require no appraisal? And if the PC is not to undertake the appraisal, who will do so and what will that authority appraise?

The fact is that apart from dismantling the Nehru heritage, the ruling party has no positive agenda. It somehow thinks that if the PC were abolished, the growth rate would automatically pick up, imbalances in the economy between agriculture and manufacturing, rich and poor, educated and ill-educated, healthy and unhealthy, and environmental issues would be resolved swayambhu. Nothing would lead us more quickly to anarchy and ruin than not having an institution to carry out the tasks allotted in 1950 to the PC.

Modi may dissolve the PC if he so wishes, for he has the brute majority in the Lok Sabha to get away with it. But in place of the dissolved PC, he has to put up another PC, by whatever name called, for the tasks entrusted to the PC by the Nehru government are vital national tasks that only a body constituted of the experts with which the PC once sparkled can do.

If in recent times, the PC has lost much of its shine, it is because the Planning Commission has been run by people who do not believe in planning. Therefore, it has become an instrument for the unelected (and unelectable) to strut the corridors of power, throw their weight around, be obstructive, and usurp functions that are legitimately the domain of the political authority. If the political authority has surrendered so much of its space to the PC, that is the fault of central and state ministers, not the PC. And if the National Development Council (NDC) has contributed next to nothing to the planning process ever since we took to liberalization and globalization, that is primarily the fault of the NDC and its member-chief ministers, not that of the usurper.

Yes, there is much to reform and rejig after more than half a century of planning. But to destroy the Planning Commission and abandon the road to planned development is to betray the people who expect government decision-making to be something more than the aggregate of corporate decisions. Hence, we need planning; and without a Planning Commission, by whatever name called, we cannot have a plan.

Modi's current exertions, like all his drama-*baazi*, is just showmanship without a show.

NDTV.com

NUKE DEAL WITH RUSSIA
NO REASON TO CHEER

15 December 2014

On the same day that visiting Russian President Vladimir Putin committed himself to supplying 12 nuclear reactors to India, oil prices slipped below $60 and looked set to drop to a band between $35 and $40. This makes the nuclear deal less enticing than it might otherwise have been. For it underlines the impossibility of substituting nuclear power for petroleum in our energy basket. Under the present circumstances, Modi would have been better advised to ask Putin how he thought Russia might network India into an Asian gas and oil community to meet her energy requirements than focus on nuclear cooperation.

This is not the popular or even the media perception and, therefore, needs to be explained. Even under the most optimistic assumptions, nuclear energy, which now constitutes between 1-2 per cent of India's energy consumption, could not rise above 6 till well into the middle of the century. Therefore, our prime requirement is not nuclear power but fossil energy.

Second, as Kudankulam has demonstrated, finding locations for nuclear plants is always going to be problematic and will increasingly be so. For while no one objects to nuclear energy, almost everyone objects to locating nuclear plants in their vicinity. We have seen this at Jaitapur in Maharashtra as well as in Haripur, West Bengal. Fukushima has shown that even in a highly developed country like Japan with a deeply embedded industrial culture and a highly disciplined workforce, nuclear accidents can happen and leave a trail of destruction over decades, indeed over generations, that make the Bhopal tragedy look like a small accident.

That is why the Three Mile Island nuclear accident in the US in 1979 led to a complete stoppage of all new nuclear plants in that country for nearly four decades. The most intensively industrialized country in the world, Germany, which has no fossil fuel of its own, decided in the wake of Fukushima that it would phase out all its existing nuclear power plants, build no new plants and move towards one hundred per cent dependence on fossil fuels and renewable energy. France alone continues to rely on nuclear power but has the safety backup of ample supplies of gas from Algeria by pipeline. For India to be celebrating 12 new Russian nuclear plants is like dancing the Dance of Death twelve times over.

Third, while Obama could tick off BP that the US would not accept "nickels and dimes" for the damage done to the country's environment by the deep sea oil rig disaster in the Gulf of Mexico (which killed no humans but did polish off a few seals) and thus get compensation of 68 billion dollars, India screwed no more than $480 million out of Union Carbide despite the loss of hundreds of lives and severe injuries to thousands of others – and still counting. Yet, our law on liability for nuclear accidents is considered too drastic for a single American nuclear plant manufacturer to come forward with supplies to India.

Fourth, the Russian nuclear deal comes at just the time that oil prices are plummeting, taking the sheen off much costlier nuclear power and pointing to the restoration of stability in the global oil and gas market.

As Russia is a leading producer of oil and gas, what Modi should have talked to Putin about (but did not) is the possibility of India-Russian cooperation in securing the diversion towards India of Russia's rich resources of oil and gas. He should have done so bearing at least two other factors in mind. One, that incremental Russian production is much more likely to come from its Siberian fields to the east of the Urals than from the traditional fields in western Russia which are getting increasingly depleted. What the Russians call Siberia is what, we should point out to them, constitutes north Asia. Moreover, the island of Sakhalin, where ONGC is partnering BP, clearly lies in Asian and not European Russia.

Also, Russia continues to have tremendous influence, particularly in the complex petroleum sector, over its former Central Asian republics – Kazakhstan, Turkmenistan, Uzbekistan and Azerbaijan, who are flush with oil and gas. It is from these sources that China has sourced much of its huge incremental requirements of oil and gas. There is still plenty left over. And we should be much more actively pursuing oil diplomacy in Central and North Asia than has been in evidence recently to access these resources. The prospects for this have significantly increased since the Ukraine snafu has led to the West boycotting Russian fuel supplies. Also, the fall in international oil prices makes it incumbent on Russia to look to newer and more reliable partners – and there can be no more reliable a partner than "time-tested" India.

It would appear, however, that oil was not even whispered in Modi's conversations with Putin. By focusing almost exclusively on nuclear reactors, Modi gave Russia a market to flog their reactors that few others want but which will barely contribute to meeting our growing energy requirements while subjecting the country's future to the utmost danger of nuclear catastrophe.

What Modi's advisers need to recognize is the dramatically altering geopolitics of oil and gas. Asia is the world's biggest producer of oil and gas. It is also the largest growing market for oil and gas with a huge unsatisfied appetite for fuel to sustain its growth. That is why, within an overarching goal of progressively establishing an Asian Oil and Gas Community, attention should be centred on first putting in place the elements of an Asian gas grid.

From an Indian perspective, the first leg of such a grid should be to link Iran with India either overland through Pakistan or by the undersea technology that has only lately become feasible. Such a core gas pipeline can then be extended to Qatar and other Gulf countries, and beyond to Iraq, and include a major branch line to Azerbaijan. Supplementing this western gas network, we should be expediting the Turkmenistan-Afghanistan-Pakistan-India (TAPI) pipeline that is on the drawing boards but is still to takeoff for want of the necessary political will. Tapping all these sources might provide such huge surpluses over and above India's immediate needs as to make it possible to extend the pipeline right across India to south-west China through Myanmar. We would earn far higher transit fees from any such arrangements than we might have to pay out to get west Asian and central Asian gas into India.

To promote this as a pan-Asian project, we should extend TAPI to send out tentacles to Uzbekistan, Kazakhstan and Russia itself – for the Caspian petroleum-rich port town of Astrakhan lies in the Russian Federation. If Astrakhan were to be a key hub of the proposed Asian Gas Grid, the other Central Asian Republics might have the greater confidence to become part of this revolutionary new network.

As far as north Asia is concerned, while a pipeline all the way from Siberia or Sakhalin to India might not at present be technically feasible, swap arrangements might be possible between India and Korea, as well as India and Japan, to supply them gas from our contracted lots in north Asia (particularly Sakhalin) in exchange for our getting the LNG they have contracted from Indonesia and possibly Australia.

To do all this requires, however, a revival of the Nehruvian vision that led to India convening the Asian Relations Conference under Jawaharlal Nehru in March 1947 even before we were wholly independent. Asia is the continent that led the world in the progress of human civilization from the earliest recorded times till the onset of European colonialism some 300 years ago. But Asia remains the most divided continent despite the Nehruvian initiative of 1947. That is because, in spite of progressively shaking off the colonial yoke, Asia has been the playground of Great Power rivalry in the second half of the 20th century and into the 21st.

This must change. We should take note from the European experience of having first set up the European Coal and Steel Community before moving to the European Common Market, the European Community and now the European Union.

An Asian Union might be a century or more away but we can move towards that goal by establishing an Asian Gas Grid as the first step towards an Asian Oil and Gas Community that might over time then evolve into an Asian Union.

But how can an India narrowly wedded to Hindutva and a Hindu Rashtra, and controlled by the likes of Sakshi Maharaj and Sadhvi Jyoti, even begin to have the all-encompassing vision that guided the Father of our Foreign Policy? No wonder Modi prefers to limit himself to buying nuclear reactors that no one else wants.

NDTV.com

MODI'S PARLIAMENT: A KISS & KICK STORY

22 December 2014

Most bullies are cowards. What else could be the explanation for Modi refusing to come before the Rajya Sabha for five full days? He is after all a renowned orator. He also claims to be in full command of his ranks. Why then allow five days of legislative business in which his government has a vested interest to be indefinitely postponed only because he shies away from being held responsible by the House for the lapses of his legislators and ministers? He is, after all, not just the Prime Minister. He is also a Member of Parliament. And it is his first business to be available in the House when Parliamentary business demands his presence. Even the meanest and smallest of us have to heed a three-line whip. What could be more important for nurturing our democracy than a Prime Minister who believes it is his duty to sit in the House, listen to the debate and then defend himself as best as he can?

My mind flies back more than half a century to my first visit to the Lok Sabha. The year was 1960. The month, I seem to remember, was February. A friend far better connected than I, as a small-town hick could hope to be, had secured passes for himself and a few friends to attend a debate in Parliament. The debate was on the most exciting event of the time – the dismissal by the Union government under Jawaharlal Nehru of the first-ever elected Communist government in history, the government of Chief Minister EMS Namboodiripad in Kerala. His government had nationalized all schooling in the state. Since many of the educational institutions were run by Christians, including the 2000-year-old Syrian Christian community, there was outrage at this abrupt end to private education which had propelled Kerala to the first position in school and college education in the country. People had taken to the streets in large numbers, and Indira Gandhi, as President of the Congress, had seized the opportunity to lead the protestors. As public order broke down, Nehru's government resorted to President's rule. The motion before the House was to debate the merits of the action taken. The Nehru government was clearly on the back foot.

The bus we took from college deposited us at the Parliament House bus-stand, which was then sited at the very spot where Mahatma Gandhi's statue is now seated. We took our place in the Visitors' Gallery and then listened spellbound to Comrade SA Dange flailing Nehru and the Congress for the error of their ways. He was heard out in pindrop silence, Nehru in deep thought just in front of him and the Treasury benches in disciplined decorum, writhing in their seats but not interrupting or erupting into slogans. Dange ended his speech in words that reverberate in my memory 50 years and more later. Comparing Nehru to Yudhishthira, whose chariot always rode above the ground for he never told a lie, Dange recalled that when Yudhishthira was persuaded to tell the white lie that Ashwatthama was dead – misleading Dronacharya to believe his son had died when in fact it was the elephant, Ashwatthama, that had been killed – Yudhishthira's chariot fell to the ground. So, said Dange, had Nehru's chariot fallen to the ground with this one action of his.

Nehru then rose to reply. I remember nothing of his rebuttal. What remains in memory is of the doughty warrior fully observing parliamentary protocol and democratic proprieties by giving the others every chance to have their say, and taking their barbs on his chest, before rising to defend his actions.

That is what we have been expecting of Modi. But he has shown himself to be indifferent to democratic practice and contemptuous of Parliament – or merely just frightened of public reprimand – to come to the House and bear like a man "the slings and arrows of outrageous fortune". Instead, he has simpered – rushing off to Kashmir to campaign when he should have been facing the House. A sign, perhaps, of how nervous he is that the J&K elections will signal the end of the Modi wave.

I recall too finding, on the back page of the *Hindustan Times* of 26 October 1962, a small news item informing readers that the leader of the Jan Sangh in the Rajya Sabha, one Atal Bihari Vajpayee, then all of 36 years of age, had called on the Prime Minister, then 73, twice Vajpayee's age, to demand that although the Lok Sabha was in recess, the Rajya Sabha be called immediately to discuss the then ongoing war on the India-China border. Unlike Vajpayee in1999, who refused a similar request, Nehru agreed with alacrity. The Rajya Sabha was summoned on 8 November 1962 and young Vajpayee launched into a vitriolic attack on the Prime Minister that the Prime Minister of the day bore with his usual dignity and then responded to with parliamentary punctiliousness. If that 'Gentle Colossus', as Hiren Mukherjee described him, had not thus nurtured democratic institutions, India today, like all 150 countries that have come to liberation since our Independence, might also be floundering like neighbouring Pakistan.

Modi does not seem to realize how fragile the plant of Parliamentary democracy is. Perhaps he does not even want to tend the plant so that he can always and all times have his own way, just like all the authoritarians who disfigure the pages of history. However that may be, the fact is that the Prime Minister has refused to heed the majority call in the Upper House that he come to Parliament to listen to what his fellow-Parliamentarians have to say about the conduct of his partymen, his backbenchers and his Ministers. He considers his Home Minister as his inferior in everything but responding to Parliament!

Nehru, on the other hand, had never flinched from his democratic duty. Whether it was the jeep scandal in the early years of Parliament or the Mundhra scandal that rocked the House in 1957-58 at his own son-in-law's instance, there would be Nehru sitting at his appointed place in the House, ever willing to listen with quiet dignity to whatever was hurled at him and to respond in measured tones to whatever had been alleged. More – to take action. For he had suspended in 1952 the first Congress MP charged with manipulating the stock market and then had removed his much-favoured Finance Minster, TTK, for the sins of Mundhra. He even allowed Lal Bahadur Shastri to follow his conscience when, as Railway Minister, Shastri resigned over a rail accident at Ariyalur in distant Tamil Nadu.

Modi prefers to cling to his discredited colleagues. A man accused of rape continues to adorn his Council of Ministers. The intemperate Giriraj Singh, who wants all those who do not vote for Modi to be hounded out to Pakistan, is rewarded with a ministerial assignment. So is a lady who does not deserve the name of lady because of her preference for filthy language remains on her perch. A back-bencher, swathed in a sadhu's robes, who appears to have more of the Devil than God on his tongue, is allowed, indeed encouraged, to get on with nonsense directed against another religious community.

This is what the country has got from voting in a diehard RSS pracharak as Prime Minister. His extremist cohorts receive the Prime Minister's protection because they speak the Prime Minister's thoughts. We have never had a more dangerous threat to our national unity than this authoritarian who little respects the sanctum sanctorum of our democracy despite having hypocritically kissed its doorstep when first stepping into its sacred precincts.

NDTV.com

BEST FOR J&K: PDP, OMAR AND CONGRESS TOGETHER

29 December 2014

Adolescent maidens in Elizabethan England would pluck daisies from the fields and peel the petals one by one, alternately reciting, "He loves me; he loves me not"! The curious election results from the state of Jammu and Kashmir have left politicians indulging in much the same exercise as they try to work out which of several possible combinations is the most attractive and feasible.

The obvious combination in purely arithmetical terms is the BJP going with the PDP. Together, they would have some 53 seats in a House of 87, thus ensuring an apparently stable majority. I stress the word "apparently" for hidden behind the bare figures is the incompatibility of programmes and purposes and the cleavage along religious and regional lines.

All the 25 seats the BJP has won are in Jammu. In Kashmir, the BJP lost its deposit in 35 of the 36 seats it contested. The PDP did secure two seats in Jammu, but 26 of its 28 seats are from the Valley. The virulent rhetoric of the election campaign showed the wide distance between the two parties in their respective approaches to the governance of J&K.

The BJP then and earlier accused the PDP of being "soft" on militancy and inclined to be understanding of the protestors who are collectively labelled "stonethrowers". The BJP loves to project itself in Jammu and the rest of India as the most muscular of Indian parties, determined to firmly and unrelentingly stamp out militancy and infiltration at any price. If the BJP were to go "soft" while in the J&K government, it would be castigated by the RSS and the Sangh Parivar and lose much of its appeal in Jammu and the rest of the country; if the PDP were to take a hard and cold line, it would instantly lose much of its new-found support in the Valley.

Similarly, on the continued application in the Valley of the Armed Forces Special Powers Act (AFSPA), the PDP insists on the progressive reduction and eventual removal of the Act, while the BJP reacts with alarm to any suggestion of dilution or elimination. AFSPA cannot be strengthened and weakened at the same time. Yet, Jammu, as a whole, demands the implementation of the Act be strengthened, while Kashmir, without a shadow of doubt, has voted definitively against AFSPA.

On Article 370, which confers a special status on J&K in that no Central law can apply to the state unless and until the state Assembly votes in favour of it, as well as enables the state to have a Constitution of its own (with special powers to the Governor that no other Governor enjoys), the BJP has for years been insistent that it is Article 370, above all, that has stood in the way of the full integration of the state with the Union of India. The PDP, in line with all other political formations of the Valley, is adamant that Article 370 is the bulwark that enables the state to maintain its separate identity. It also allows the Kashmiri parties to campaign on their right to "self-rule" (PDP) or "full autonomy" (National Conference). The Congress, for its part, is pledged to "the sky is the limit" as far as autonomy is concerned and all parties in Parliament (other than the BJP and Shiv Sena) are in favour of the retention of Article 370. The government of Jammu & Kashmir cannot both have and not have Article 370. The BJP has, therefore, sought to appease its ranks and its opponents by saying that it wants a debate on Article 370 and will abide by the verdict. They little seem to realize that a debate that throws the issue seriously into question will itself inflame passions in the Valley.

In any case, the debate has been on ever since the founder of the Jan Sangh, Syama Prasad Mookerjee, broke away from the Nehru government, of which he was a Minister, to demand, among other things, the abrogation of J&K's special status. (In fact, he died in Srinagar while protesting Sheikh Abdullah's government). So, what is there new to debate? And where will the debate take place? In the J&K Assembly? God forbid – for the current political divide between the regions will then become a powder keg. And any Kashmiri political party that agreed to formally allow the state's special status to be questioned would be left with the mark of Cain on its forehead – doomed to suspicion of "fifth-columnism" forever.

Then there is the question of "development" – a point being underlined by the BJP in a vain attempt to keep attention away from more fundamental questions raised by "ghar wapsi" and other such divisive religion-based issues. The BJP economic agenda is founded on bringing not only foreign direct investment into the state but also on encouraging domestic investment from outside the state. This immediately raises the question of land, that, under state law dating back nearly a century, is reserved for state residents and cannot be bought or sold by outsiders. This poses no problem for the public-sector enterprises, but when the BJP's Central Government emphasizes big-business private enterprise as the road to economic Valhalla, and at the same time threatens to dilute the Land Acquisition Act that they themselves voted for but a year ago, any thinking Kashmiri is bound to wonder whether, in the name of "development", the real aim is not to expropriate Kashmiri land and render the aam Kashmiri deprived of the very rights that Sheikh Abdullah fought the Maharajah over in the 1920s and that led to his being hailed as the Sher-e-Kashmir.

These are not minor differences of policy that can be ironed out in a hypocritically-drafted Common Minimum Programme. These are fundamental differences that go to the root of J&K's existence as a special and separate entity. A BJP-PDP coalition will, therefore, be opposed tooth and nail by many, perhaps most, PDP legislators – whatever Muzaffar Hussain Baig (the PDP's leading advocate of such an alliance) might have to say. Even if such a coalition were to be opportunistically cobbled together, it just cannot last. Thus, what arithmetically constitutes a "stable" government would, politically, be a bundle of contradictions, bound to collapse sooner than later under the weight of its own internal incompatibilities.

That leaves open the option of a BJP-NC coalition. Along with Sajjad Lone's two-member People's Conference and a couple of independents, a bare majority can be forged. But the discredited National Conference would find itself further discredited within minutes of such a coalition being formed. The argument that both Farooq Abdullah and Omar Abdullah have been members of BJP-led coalition governments in the past will not wash because they were with the BJP when a moderate like Atal Bihari Vajpayee was at the helm. Now we have at the head of the BJP central government a fanatic RSS pracharak who has spent a lifetime preaching all the things that have so totally alienated the Valley from the saffron forces, reinforced by his refusal to rein in the Yogi Adityanaths and Giriraj Singhs and Sadhvi Jyotis that adorn his parliamentary ranks and the Togadias and Singhals who articulate what he clearly thinks.

Omar's NC will be seen as sliming its way back to power through the backdoor after losing the confidence of the people of the state – and that too in the company of the very elements whom the Kashmiris have demonstrated in these elections as anathema to them. Moreover, for the same reasons as those adumbrated above in respect of a PDP-BJP coalition, any NC-BJP coalition would be riddled with the same contradictions and denigrated as amounting to sleeping with the enemy.

A third alternative might be a PDP-Congress coalition with the outside or inside support of a few independents. While mathematically possible at a pinch, the coalition would be fragile and little able to withstand the stresses and strains of ruling for six long years. (In Jammu and Kashmir, elections are held once in six years; for the rest of the country, every five years: that distinction would go if Article 370 were abrogated.) The PDP would have the advantage in such a coalition of explaining to its followers that the Congress has secured representation in this election in all three regions of the state – Jammu, Kashmir and Ladakh – but that might prove frail compensation for a government that survives on a hair's breadth.

That leaves the fourth option of a coalition between the PDP and the NC, an impossibility at first sight but, on taking a second look, entirely feasible to keep Jammu and Kashmir together and safe from the malignant designs of the BJP, united in the aims that unite the people of the Valley, ready and able to pursue "autonomy" above all. If, moreover, the Congress were to render outside (or inside) support to such a coalition, the coalition would be stable, constructive, purposive and representative of all three regions of the state. Will the parties have the wisdom to follow this last course? We will know very shortly.

NDTV.com

ACTS OF CONVERSION

29 December 2014

Is there a right to convert? Can it be banned? The short answer is that there is no right to convert, but there is a right to be converted. Hence, there cannot be a legislation banning conversion. Yet, such anti-Constitutional legislation is precisely what Parliamentary Affairs Minister Venkaiah Naidu has proposed with enthusiastic backing from the RSS and BJP MPs.

It was none less than the Father of our Constitution, Dr BR Ambedkar, who at a Dalit rally in Bombay in 1936, urged: "Religion is for Man, not Man for Religion. For getting humane treatment, convert yourselves. Convert for getting organised. Convert for becoming strong. Convert for securing equality. Convert for getting liberty. Convert, so that your domestic life should be happy." He followed up by getting lakhs of his Dalit followers to convert to Buddhism. Can the Father of the Constitution be said to have trampled on the Constitution?

The fact is that Article 25 gives citizens of India the fundamental right to "freedom of conscience and free profession, practice and propagation of religion". However, the wording of the article begins by making this right "subject to public order..." Because religion is a highly sensitive subject, possibly the most sensitive subject in a country of diverse religions where religion is seriously practised. The Supreme Court has recognised the right of the state legislatures to make laws for the regulation of conversions, so as to enable the states to ensure that "public order" is maintained in matters pertaining to religion. This general endorsement is being used to push the idea of a ban on religious conversion. That is unacceptable because you cannot have a right to propagate when there is a ban on being influenced by such propagation. Hence, the word "conscience" right at the start of the article. Anyone is entitled to follow the dictates of his conscience and that includes the right to change the religion an individual happens to be born into or to change to no religion at all.

Of course, the second sub-clause of the article also grants states the authority to regulate "any activity which may be associated with religious practice". But regulation is one thing; banning is another. In the 1967 and 1968 acts of Orissa and Madhya Pradesh respectively, which are cited in this regard as having been upheld by the apex court, the principal thrust was on prevention of conversion by "force, fraud or allurements". Precisely because force, fraud and illegitimate allurements are already covered by the Indian Penal Code, when attempts were made in 1954 and 1960 to introduce a Central legislation to regulate conversions, Nehru explained that "the major evils of coercion and deception can be dealt with under the general law". He added that further legislation "will not help very much in suppressing the evil methods of gaining converts but might very well be the cause of great harassment to a large number of people". He also said that "to suggest that there should be a licensing system for propagating a faith is not proper. It would lead in its wake to the police having too large a power of interference".

Finding themselves cornered, advocates of *ghar wapsi*, who are curiously the most vocal of the advocates of a ban on religious conversions, fall back on quoting Gandhi. Of course, Gandhi was against conversion by missionaries. But that was at a period of history when missionary activity had the protection of the imperial flag. Evangelical societies in the UK and the Western world made the change of religion an essential element of their "mission civilisatrice" – their mission to "civilise" the uncivilised. It was this manifestation of colonialism that Gandhi pitted himself against. To miss the historical context of his remarks, particularly by those who reject Gandhi in everything else that has to do with religion, is a classic case of the devil quoting the scriptures.

The Week

WHERE IS THE FDI, MODI?

5 January 2015

The Government of India's official, routine Mid-Year Economic Analysis has just been published – and a more damning indictment of Modi's economic policies would be hard to find. Not only has there been little development, all his energies seem to be directed at clandestinely pushing the extremists in his ranks to redouble with vigour their not-so-well-hidden agenda of precipitately pushing the country down the abyss of Hindutva.

GDP growth is negligible – all of Modi's rhetoric has pushed up the rate by no more than an unimpressive 0.6 per cent. Even that is the consequence of the last gasp of the previous government whose efforts were just beginning to take effect when the government changed and Modi was able to ride the tail wind. Gross value added in agriculture and allied activities is actually down – by an entire percentage point; the index of industrial production has gone up by a mere 2.8 per cent; and exports have collapsed from a growth rate of 15.2 per cent to a dreadful 6.7 per cent. The exchange rate vis-a-vis the US dollar is today the lowest ever in the history of our benighted country.

The Sensex may have soared to heights never before attained but that is principally on account of two factors: one, the Modi government having given up its efforts to bring back black money (thus reneging on a core election commitment) and winking at the perennial round-tripping of fresh black money through the Mauritius route, thus making speculation on the stock market, the main engine of "growth" in our country. So, Foreign Institutional Investment (FII) floods in, mostly from Mauritius, but it is unreliable "hot money" that enters or exits the economy at the press of a computer button. The real McCoy, Foreign Direct Investment (FDI), which is a genuine growth engine, shies away from India because real investors know that Modi's claims are bogus and the economy will stagnate under him at 5-6 per cent, no more, perhaps less.

The Economic Analysis tells us that over the six-year period 2005-

2011, the average growth rate of GDP was nearly 9 per cent per annum. It fell thereafter to below 6 per cent, but Jaitley has his work cut out for him to restore the UPA I growth rate. Recovery had already begun in the latter phase of UPA II, but all Modi has been able to do is not fall below. There are no signs of the economy accelerating towards the growth rates with which Dr. Manmohan Singh had wowed the world.

What then is there to celebrate? Inflation, certainly. But that has nothing to do with the exertions of Arun Jaitley. International oil prices have plunged thanks to a combination of four factors: low to negative growth rates in the developed West; bear sentiment in the New York Mercantile Exchange; the steep rise in domestic shale oil and shale gas production in the US that has reduced their petroleum imports to virtually nil; and sanctions against the Russian Federation for the people of Crimea having had the temerity to vote in favour of leaving the Ukraine to rejoin Russia. Plus, of course, OPEC's decision to keep their oil output at pre-crash levels instead of attempting to keep oil prices higher by cutting back on production. And El Nino having at the last minute decided to bypass India. So, the silver lining has everything to do with the global sun peeking out from behind the black cloud and almost nothing to do with the black cloud backing off from the Indian economic horizon.

Indeed, the Mid-Year Economic Analysis confirms that UPA II was punished for its economic woes just as its Herculean efforts to arrest the downslide were coming to fruition. The general index of consumer prices had steeply fallen from its September 2013 high of 11 per cent to below 8 per cent three months later, while food inflation fell over the same period from 14 per cent to below 10 per cent. The trend has continued.

While Modi has received extended applause for his "Make in India" slogan, that has remained only a slogan. No one is making (it)in India, not domestic investors, not foreign investors. No one explains this better than the Mid-Year Economic Analysis that deserves quotation in full:

"Growth in real capital formation was around 15 per cent and private corporate investment surged, East Asia-style, over a very short period from 6.5 per cent in 2003-04 to 17.3 per cent in 2007-08, amounting to an increase of nearly 11 percentage points of GDP. Investment was based largely on the perception that growth rates of 8.5 per cent would continue indefinitely and banks, especially public sector banks, could lend to private sector investors in infrastructure." (para 1.43)

That is, indeed, a true picture of the economy under UPA I. Then came the delayed impact on India of the global downturn:

"As the growth boom faded, projects turned sour, leaving a legacy of distressed assets. This stock problem is weighing down assets and hence investment. The problem is compounded by weak institutions." (para 1.44)

So, what is Modi doing? Weakening our institutions even further! Ordinances galore are weakening parliamentary institutions that are the very foundation of our democracy. Hitler did the same thing – only by a different route. Immediately on coming to office through the democratic route, he got the German Reichstag (Parliament) to pass the Enabling Act that enabled him to rule by decree. Modi too is ruling by decree, not parliamentary consent. Fortunately, ours is a seven-decade old, established democracy and, therefore, unlike the short-lived Weimar constitution that Hitler overthrew, capable of surviving Modi's assault on its sanctity.

But as we turn the New Year, the country is beginning to realize that it has been taken for a long ride of which the foredoomed failure to bring back black money is but symptomatic. The government is clearly clueless about how to tackle the fundamental malaise that afflicts the economy – the inability of the private corporate sector to rise above governmental sops to display some entrepreneurial spirit. What our businessmen are good at is leveraging their influence with those whom they helped with monetary donations to elect to power. They use this influence to squeeze more and more concessions out of government so that, through rent-seeking rather than 'animal spirits', they are able to salt away their gains. Yet, it is on the backs of this private sector that Modi hopes to play out his take on Margaret Thatcher. His chances of success are exactly the same as those of a snowdrop in the furnace.

NDTV.com

STORM OVER MY REMARKS ON CHARLIE HEBDO ATTACK

12 January 2015

I was on my way to the airport to catch a flight to Bahrain, where I had been invited to speak on the one hundredth anniversary of Gandhiji's return to India from South Africa, when my family rang to say that the usual suspect had gone bonkers on his TV channel lambasting me for something I had said to a TV agency earlier in the day in connection with the terrorist attack in Paris. As I hold this hysterical humbug in the uttermost contempt, I have not bothered to find out what the anchor was screaming about, but I do believe that in justice to myself, I should clarify my position to readers who may have been misled by what he has distorted and misrepresented.

I was as horrified as you to hear of 12 lives being lost in the armed assault on a Paris satirical weekly for their repeatedly sneering at the Prophet of Islam (PBUH) and running cartoons denigrating him and the religion he has brought to hundreds of millions of families the world over. That such horror at terrorism was not just my reaction as a non-Muslim to the Paris outrage, but widely shared by Muslims too was brought home to me by a statement issued by a collegium of Imams and preachers of Bahrain who said: "Violence and extremism have always been – and still are – the biggest enemies of Islam, and contravene its teachings, tolerance and genuine precepts. All countries should take unified stances against terrorism. We call for the need to devise a unified international strategy to combat its forms and manifestation everywhere."

That precisely reflects the position taken by the Dar-ul-Uloom. It precisely reflects my own personal position. To go by the Congress President's reaction, it also reflects my party's position: "The Congress President, Smt Sonia Gandhi, has condemned the cowardly and dastardly terror attack on media in Paris. Shocked at the audacity of the gruesome act, Smt Gandhi said that extremism and intolerance will never be able to curb freedom of expression and will only result in perpetuation of violence."

What then is the controversy about? It is about my describing the incident as a "backlash" to the War on Terrorism. That is not a justification of terrorism. It is an explanation. The distinction is important. I condemn terrorism. I do not commend it. If, however, war is declared on terrorists, it is stupid to imagine that the terrorists will take it lying down; inevitably they will hit back – that is a consequence we have to be prepared for.

Charlie Hebdo, the satirical weekly, was so obviously on the hit list that it was virtually inviting a reaction week after week. The threat to the Editor was so palpable that he had been personally provided with just about the highest level of security that France could offer. Why the magazine's office was not protected with an adequate posse of armed security is being investigated. But it also reflects the mindset that thinks the West can mount a war and get away with little or no loss to themselves. The West is so militarily powerful and so technologically superior that it is able to unleash an unequal war in which their resources in money and machines cannot be matched even remotely by those whom they are combating.

Therefore, terrorists resort to an asymmetrical response. They target non-combatants by way of avenging themselves on those whose war machines kill – daily – scores, hundreds, even thousands of the non-combatants in whose midst the terrorists live and shield themselves.

A dead innocent is a dead innocent. Terrorists deliberately target the innocent. The War on Terror does not target innocents. It kills them indiscriminately by way of what is delicately called "collateral damage". But the loved ones and the community are equally affected – whether the killing is deliberate or incidental. The rage is the same. The urge to revenge is the same. For, as Gandhi said – and I quoted him to the TV agency – "Violence begets violence."

The West is near perfecting the art of killing their enemies (plus "collateral damage") without risking their own lives. When eight American body bags returned from Somalia after Islamic militiamen shot down two UH-60 Black Hawk helicopters in 1993, President Bill Clinton immediately called off Operation Gothic Serpent. When eight

Pathan bodies of helpless mothers, hapless children, and innocent by-standers lie in the midst of the carnage wrought by a Drone attack, the wailing families do not react differently. They seek justice, each in his or her own way. The Drone wins out because even if it is downed, as it is unmanned, no American family is left with a tear in its eye. When terrorists attack, they know they are going to be killed – or kill themselves. They take the vicious consequences of their vicious action. The Drone just flies away – to come back another day.

Till even the First World War, war was fought on the terrain of war – the battlefield. Those who died or got injured were soldiers.

Civilians only accidentally got in the way. That changed when the Germans started assassinating mayors of towns where snipers shot at German soldiers. It horrified the world and contributed more to Britain coming in against Germany than perhaps any other single action. Not even into the Thirties had men been desensitized to the atrocity of civilian beings killed in armed attack. Picasso earned eternal fame because his painting captured and symbolized the horror experienced by all civilized people at the aerial bombing of the Spanish village of Guernica.

But by the Second World War, these niceties were abandoned. The terror opened by the Nazis through their Blitzkrieg on England, followed by their merciless genocide of Jews in the East European countries they occupied, started the process of desensitizing the hitherto unknown horror of innocents being mown to death.

Stalingrad finally dulled sensitivities to the point where Churchill could order the bombing of Dresden and kill more innocents in a single night than all the terrorist attacks since 9/11 and after.

Truman's atom bombing of Hiroshima and Nagasaki removed the final constraints on sparing non-combatants the terrible fate of the battlefield. Since then, it has been open house for those with the military means to do so.

I was posted as a young diplomat to Hanoi in the middle of the US-Vietnam war. Day after day, twice a day, US Air Force planes would pound the city without regard to civilian habitation or military target, shooting to death and severely injuring any living being – man, woman or child – they could fit into their sights. Uncounted millions died. Many were non-combatant civilians. A young British colleague remarked that the American U-2s flying at such speed could cross the country in 10 minutes at a height of 60,000 feet. "They could take a photograph of the saucer I held in my hand and that would be more accurate than my naked eye could see!" He paused and asked, "How do you think these guys on bicycles will ever drive them out?" The bicyclists did; they won. But only after millions of civilians had been slaughtered.

I condemn what happened in Paris with all the strength in my voice. It was dreadful. But I regard all forms of terrorism, especially by armed forces that take the lives of non-combatants as equally – perhaps even more – terrible. That is why my heart bleeds when 1500 Palestinians are killed in their homes by bombs rained on them from the skies because they have the temerity to ask for the right to return to their homeland. The Modi government had little or nothing to say about that outrage. It is this lack of balance in the BJP's approach to terrorism that fills me with dread and despair.

Most of us Indians, except the fringe lunatics of the BJP-RSS-Sangh Parivar, have learned millennia ago to live with diversity, indeed to celebrate our diversity, for out of it is forged our unity as a nation.

For the West, however, diversity is a totally new experience. They have been compelled for economic reasons to import millions of Third World labourers, and since an arc of Arab countries lies immediately south of France on the other littoral of the Mediterranean, most of France's imported labour comprises Muslims from the Maghreb. France wants them to become Frenchmen as if the Arabs had fostered 1789 and never been subjected to colonial rule. The Arab Muslims wish to remain themselves, notwithstanding their having emigrated to France for the same economic reasons that have led to France and other Western countries importing them in such large numbers. Hence, stupid measures like insisting that no Muslim schoolchild in France may wear the hijab that her sisters wear in their home countries will result in a backlash.

NDTV.com

172

IF MODI IS DON QUIXOTE, JAITLEY SANCHO PANZA

19 January 2015

I write this from Colombo where I have arrived in the aftermath of an extraordinary election that has seen the largely unanticipated exit of the Strong Man of Sri Lanka, President Mahinda Rajapakse, a kind of Sinhala version of our own 56-inch wallah, Narendra Modi. The two men have much in common: a public image of decisive leadership; a great oratorical talent; mesmerizing charisma combined with a dismissive attitude to precedents and procedures; a penchant for centralization; an autocratic bent of mind; a passion for building a personality cult; megalomania joined to paranoia; an unwillingness to listen to contrary advice; a predilection to play on societal divides for political advancement (and a preference for throwing shawls around their shoulders as a fashion statement).

Where Modi talks of "development", Rajapakse talked of "infrastructure", both men believing that the invocation of the word would feed the general desire for palpable progress. In Rajapakse's case, there was the actual achievement of the agenda; with Modi, we yet have only words, slogans and one-liners. But the cautionary tale is that if Rajapakse's nationwide network of excellent roads and railways did not quite impress a non-gullible public, Modi too will discover in good time that a bullet train from Mumbai to Ahmedabad is not going to impress the electorate as "development". Modi will also discover, as Rajapakse has, that favouritism in channelling enormous investment, such as the Chinese-built port and a flashy new international airport to his hometown of Hambantota only stoked resentment elsewhere; even so will the privileging of "Vibrant Gujarat" over other states be perceived as discriminatory mollycoddling.

Sri Lanka has very impressive social indicators – health and literacy rates are the highest in South Asia and akin to those of fairly high-income countries. Sri Lankans, therefore, expected social progress to accompany economic growth. The emphasis on "infrastructure" meant, however, the relative neglect of the social sectors. This rebounded on Rajapakse at the polls. Modi too is going to find that "development" has little appeal unless it is development at the grassroots. The way his government is going around throwing environmental regulations to the winds and amending labour laws with the interests of capital alone and not the working class in mind, is bound to result in the alienation of those who are unemployed. Modi's belief in big business private enterprise is going to translate into jobless growth as private enterprise discovers that, through hi-tech labour-saving devices, productivity per unit of capital can be vastly increased with no increase – indeed, a diminution – in the overall wage bill.

What Don Quixote Modi and his Sancho Panza, Arun Jaitley, have done tilting at the windmills of the 2013 Land Acquisition Act, which they supported in the last Parliament, is a striking example of leveraging the real estate mafia at the expense of small landowners and the marginal or landless labour that works these small plots. Rajapakse was confident of his rural base. That has been substantially eroded because the benefits of "infrastructure" did not reach down to the rural garib. Similarly, the protection that the Land Acquisition Act gives this vast segment of the electorate is being snatched from them by the BJP government. The rural masses are already sharpening their claws in preparation for electoral revenge.

Rajapakse thought he could appease his rural Sinhala voters by keeping ethnic tension simmering while repeatedly calling attention to his military victory over the LTTE. Modi thinks that by keeping the communal pot (and differences with Pakistan) simmering, while repeatedly calling attention to his huge electoral victory, Hindus will see him as the saviour even if Muslims turn from him. Now he can see how the Sri Lankan minorities – Tamil and Muslim – turned from Rajapakse. Indeed, the Rajapakse regime anticipated the Modi regime by turning a blind eye towards a section of Buddhist monks provoking attacks on Muslim mosques. But the secular electorate sees through such games of narrow, divisive self-interest. Hence, Tamils and Muslims came out in huge numbers to join the large numbers of Sinhalas who wanted an end to ethnic tensions and the beginnings of a true dialogue on reconciliation. Modi will come to the same pass since he is instinctively disinclined to rein in his fringe – for the good reason that he himself has risen from that fringe and, at heart, belongs to it.

Modi, like Rajapakse, believes in himself – and only himself. Centralised administration, ruthless authoritarianism and massive self-promotion have the short-term advantage that all the credit goes to the One and Only, while dissent is stifled for fear of exclusion from the inner circle. Apparent success – infrastructure in the one case and MoUs in the other – reinforce and validate the Leader's sense of his indispensability. The future is hidden from vision because no one dare tell the Emperor that he is wearing no clothes. In Rajapakse's case it has been the hilarious story of his much-trusted astrologer who not only enthusiastically endorsed Rajapakse's confidence in his inevitable victory, calling elections two years in advance of the stipulated term, but also advised him on the specific minute – 1.04 PM on 20 November 2014 – as also the particular direction in which he should look as he signed the papers calling the election. Now that Rajapakse has suffered a crushing defeat, the astrologer (who has lost the keys to his official car and has been kicked out of his government bungalow) cries that even Nostradamus was not always correct, and he actually knew Rajapakse faced inevitable defeat but dared not tell him so for fear that he too would be thrown in jail for warning of defeat as his predecessor astrologer had been for wrongly forecasting that a previous election would be lost!

The Myth of the Strong Leader by Archie Brown, Emeritus Professor of Politics at Oxford, has been making waves in academic circles since its publication a few months after Modi came to power. Prof. Brown argues that true leaders are "inspirational leaders" who do not require public office to make for revolutionary change. "It would be hard to think," he says, "of a more politically significant example of an inspirational leader than Mahatma Gandhi, though he never held governmental office." Challenging "the widespread belief that strong leaders – meaning those who dominate their colleagues and the policy-making process – are the most successful and admirable," Brown shows that it is "the most cooperative leaders who have the greatest impact." It is a lesson that Rajapakse failed to learn. It is a lesson that Modi is constitutionally incapable of learning. It led to Rajapakse's downfall. It will lead to Modi's downfall.

NDTV.com

AN OPEN LETTER TO
BARACK OBAMA

24 January 2015

Dear President Obama,

Might I add my small voice to millions of other Indians in welcoming you as our guest for Republic Day? You are not, however, a wedding guest but the representative of a great superpower with whom we seek to have sound and strategic relations. The pursuit of those relations involves our availing of your presence to carry forward the Indo-US dialogue on matters big and small. I stress "big and small" because what might seem small from one perspective might be the biggest thing for those caught like tiny fish in the mesh of great matters. This is the case with the young Indian diplomat, Devyani Khobragade, our former deputy consul general in New York.

The facts of the case are well-known. Your very competent staff can readily provide you with a one-page summary. My principal plea is that you regard this not only as relating to an Indian diplomat but also as impinging directly on the life of her husband, who is an American citizen, as also her two children who are Americans by right of birth.

These American citizens are caught in the maw of a bureaucratic catch-22. The case involving their wife/mother is being handled by the US Department of Justice (DoJ). India cannot deal directly with the US DoJ. It is obliged by protocol to restrict itself to the US Department of State (DoS) which can, if it so wishes, allow another department to interact with another government, but not without such authorisation. In the instant case, DoS has thus far refrained from intervening with DoJ. No action by the Indian diplomat or her American husband and children is possible without your personal intervention to direct the departments to look into the wider ramifications of the issue.

In the normal course, I would leave this to our Prime Minister. But although his party, the BJP, then in opposition, had joined in the national outrage over the arrest, search and persecution of an officer of the Indian Foreign Service, now that it has come to high office, it has gone possum.

I am, therefore, hoping someone on your large staff will read this open letter and bring it to your attention. For all of us believe yes, you can – if you wish to. My plea with you is a humanitarian one. The lady concerned is one of whom I am sure you (and Michelle and your daughters), as believers in women's empowerment, would want to see advance in her career. There has been no mollycoddling of her, as used to happen in the distant past when women officers were believed to be in need of protection from difficult postings. This woman has served in difficult Pakistan and dangerous Afghanistan without protest and with such professional competence that she was subsequently selected for the demanding job of deputy consul general. Please ask yourself whether you would wish to be responsible for the abrupt termination of an otherwise outstanding career that carried much promise.

Then please ask yourself whether a family should be divided by the dilemma of choosing between the US and India when, by birthright, both countries should be equally welcoming to them. Her husband has already lost his professorship at a reputable US university because of the adverse publicity that has hounded the family over the past 15 months. Should the US husband return to his country, that is, your country, he will have to leave his wife behind. He will also have to leave behind his American children because they are too young to be deprived of their mother's love and care. Should he remain in India, the promising career he was making for himself as a respected citizen of your country will have to remain in abeyance. Should these three American citizens be put in this impossible position?

Please consider these "emotional" and "personal" issues alongside the technical issues and direct DoJ to engage with our government on finding a way out. I ask no more. I leave the rest to my government. That, surely, is not too much to ask, nor too much "audacity of hope" – even if my government is shying away from asking you for simple justice?

Yours sincerely,

A fellow human being

The Week

RELAX, OBAMA'S ONLY A LAME-DUCK PRESIDENT

25 January 2015

For all the pomp and hype accompanying Obama's Republic Day visit to India, the fact is we are welcoming a lame-duck President who has lost control over his Congress (Parliament) because he has lost the confidence of his people. He is eking out the last days of his Presidency without being in a position to do anything very much more than he already has to carve his niche in history.

What a contrast to the Obama we welcomed in 2010. Then was the spirit of "Yes, We Can". He had caught the imagination of the world by becoming the first person of colour to attain the most powerful position in the world. He had opened his innings with a bang by a speech in Prague that signalled a definitive move towards the end of nuclear weapons. For this mere declaration of intent, he was rewarded with a Nobel Prize for Peace. It was within months of the grand reception in Oslo to receive the award that he landed in India. The longest paragraph in the joint statement he signed with Prime Minister Manmohan Singh related to the dismantling of nuclear weapons. He has since done nothing of substance to fulfil the high hopes he had raised of being a 21st century Mahatma. It underlies the importance of giving the Nobel Prize for solid achievement, not high rhetoric. It also shows that Joint Statements, even at the highest levels, are worth little more than the paper they are written on, if not followed up by either or both sides, as has been the case with the disarmament provisions of the November 2009 statement.

The Indo-US dialogue then was dominated by the Indo-US nuclear agreement (and the Defence Cooperation Framework that paved the way to the nuclear agreement). The nuclear agreement was the first and most dramatic confirmation of the "strategic partnership" between the two countries that India and the US had been working for ever since

Vajpayee declared that the two were "natural allies".

How a nonaligned country can be the *natural ally* of anyone was not explained, either by Vajpayee or his successors, for they were in fact riding two horses at the same time: the Non-Aligned horse, which was India's great gift to the post-colonial world, and the avid desire to be recognized as a special friend and partner by the world's solitary Superpower. It was always an alliance of unequals, but it ended nuclear apartheid and fostered dreams of India becoming a Nuclear Energy Superpower when (and if) the thorium route to nuclear energy would become technically and economically feasible.

For the Americans, it was the opening up of one of the world's biggest markets for nuclear power plants for their moribund nuclear energy industry that had been starved of orders ever since the 1979 Three Mile Island nuclear disaster in the US. So pleased was Dr. Manmohan Singh with this win-win achievement that he proclaimed on TV to President Bush (then on the verge of being kicked into the dustbin of history) that, "The people of India love you." I – as one of the people of India – demurred, but the euphoria was catching.

Two developments pricked the euphoria. One, Fukushima. That put real energy into the public demonstrations at Kudankulam, Jaitpur, Haripur and elsewhere against the siting of nuclear power plants in or near people's habitations. Everyone loves nuclear power – but no one wants to live in the vicinity of a nuclear power plant. Indeed, the only way to persuade the aam aadmi to accept that nuclear power plants are harmless neighbourhood creatures would be to site the next plant on Race Course Road, adjacent to the Prime Minister's residence.

But it is the second hurdle that really brought Indo-US nuclear power-sharing to an embarrassing standstill. Reminded of the Union Carbide disaster in Bhopal on the night of 23 December 1984 – for which the American multinational got away virtually scot-free, the Indian Parliament insisted on a Nuclear Liability Act that made the supplier substantially responsible for any disaster that might overtake their nuclear plants. The Americans baulked at having to rise to their responsibilities for causing untold harm to others. They wanted the billions upon billions of dollars they would get from flogging to us the nuclear power plants they found too dangerous to put up in their own country, but insisted on limiting to peanuts their liability as suppliers.

The result is that while Russia and France have agreed, within the existing legislative framework, to supply additional nuclear power plants, the US stands cut out of the deal. They did not sign the nuclear deal to enrich France or Putin's Russia – but that's the way it is going. So, once the kissing stops, Obama is going to apply all the pressure he can on getting Modi to dilute the Indian position.

If he succeeds (as he might) and US suppliers get themselves lucrative contracts, they will discover that villages selected as sites rising in revolt as has happened at every such site since the dangers of nuclear accidents became widespread public knowledge. Thus, either way, whether Modi relents or not, the Indo-US nuclear agreement is going to remain a dead letter. Moreover, Parliament's objections to giving Americans Warren Anderson-like concessions to wreak more Bhopals are going to be virtually impossible to overrule, even by a didactic autocrat like Modi.

When a freshly-minted President Obama visited India in November 2010, there was an 'Audacity of Hope' in the air. He now comes tired and dispirited. He has disappointed hordes of those who hailed him when he won his first Presidential bid in 2008. He personified then the dream of a final end to both racism and the Quest for Dominance. His track record as a senator for having voted against Bush's disastrous intervention in Iraq was hailed as the foresight of a truly enlightened leader who knew how to give the lead. Today, with Iraq still an albatross around the American neck, the IS running riot in the Levant, relations with Russia at their lowest ebb, the impasse over Iran unresolved, and the scuttle underway in Afghanistan, Obama has become, alas, a discredited President.

No wonder he has grabbed an opportunity such as the one offered to him by Modi to recover some of his erstwhile standing in the world. At least someone wants him to review a ceremonial parade.

What he now hopes to achieve is to carve a deeper niche for himself in history by snaring India into a security ring around China in the current build up to Cold War II. He might yet succeed, for Modi has little time for the rationale of Non-Alignment and is paranoid about security. He does not realize that it was Non-Alignment that kept us out of the conflict zone in Cold War I. If he allows himself to be seduced by Obama's siren song, as he seems inclined to do, we might find ourselves being dragged along, as a very junior partner, into precisely the web of military alliances among the Big and the Small that insidiously brought on World War I with no one desiring it.

I cross my fingers with the prayer that the worst may not happen between a loser US President and a naive (but authoritarian) Indian PM.

NDTV.com

MODI TURNING US INTO AMERICA'S NEW PAKISTAN

3 February 2015

During Cold War I between the US and the USSR in the 20th century, the US co-opted Pakistan as its "most reliable ally". With the onset of Cold War II in the 21st century, now between the US and China, Barack Obama made his Republic Day visit to India to woo Narendra Modi to become the US's most reliable ally. Modi doubled over backwards to oblige.

We are being rapidly dragged into the abyss of confrontation, abandoning the signature tune of Gandhiji and Nehru – peaceful coexistence. We are on the edge of becoming America's Pakistan at the brink of Cold War II. History must serve as our guide as Modi takes the plunge.

India under Nehru reacted to US overtures in the mid-20th century by setting our face against all forms of military involvement with one side or the other. It was called Non-alignment. We were the first and, at the time, only Non-aligned country in 1947. 36 years later, when the seventh Non-aligned Summit was held in New Delhi in 1983, two-thirds of the Member-States of the UN turned up in our capital at the Head of State/Head of Government level. No foreign policy of any country in the 20th century turned out to be as widespread in its global influence as Nehru's. Nehru showed the way. Virtually every newly independent nation followed. Until we got embroiled in the 1962 war with China, Non-aligned India was the country of choice for settling almost every international crisis-Palestine in 1947; Korea in 1953; Indo-China the following year; Suez in 1956; the Congo in 1960. Even when the world initially disagreed, as with India's recognition of China after Mao's revolution, everyone eventually came around to accepting the reality.

On decolonization, India's was the first and last word. We were the first to boycott racist South Africa and the first to rejoice when half a century later Nelson Mandela joined with Willem de Klerk in Africa's

Gandhi moment. From Algeria to Namibia, over three long decades, India was the acknowledged champion of the End of Empire. On disarmament, India gave the lead. On mobilizing the world to regard development as a global responsibility, India again led the rest in securing global trade concessions for developing countries in GATT and establishing the Group of 77 in the United Nations Conference on Trade and Development (UNCTAD).

Meanwhile, independent India's development was so impressive compared to its colonial past that when Walt Rostow published in 1960 his breakthrough work, *The Stages of Growth,* and was asked which underdeveloped country he thought would first reach the "take-off" stage, he unhesitatingly pointed to India. Besides, of course, among about 150 countries which have attained independence along with us, we alone have translated liberation into many expressions of freedom for our people, combining full-scope democracy with a socialistic pattern of society and sincerity in secularism, backed by a voice of our own in international affairs that was respected by all even when disagreement was strong. We established that foreign policy is the external expression of internal sovereignty – and although the West balked at that, it did not prevent us from essentially "viewing the world with clear and friendly eyes", as Nehru remarked on the day we became independent. We were friends, but not allies, of both the East and the West.

Pakistan, by the turn of the century, was left a client State of an increasingly disenchanted patron. Since Clinton, it has been downgraded as the preferred partner for the 21st century, cast aside like a used glove. Today, its most sturdy patron is China.

Readers as old as I am will remember Vice-President Lyndon Johnson visiting Pakistan during Kennedy's Presidency and taking Pakistan swirling into euphoria when he invited a Pakistani camel-driver to the US as a State guest. A decade later, the US-Pakistan partnership reached its highest (or lowest) point when the US stood rock solid behind Pakistan as the Pakistani army butchered ordinary East Pakistanis and drove ten million of them as refugees into India, thus sparking the war that led on 16 December 1971 to the dismemberment of Pakistan and the emergence of Bangladesh. Small reward for Peshawar having served as the base for U2 spy flights over the Soviet Union and as Kissinger's launch pad for his rapprochement (now breaking down) with China.

In the years that followed, the US led Pakistan by the nose into the mess of Afghanistan. The Mujahideen, transported from the Arab world and Central Asia to the Af-Pak border, and trained and supplied by the US on the soil of its most reliable partner, has now become the Frankenstein that has rendered Pakistan both the hub of global terrorism and its biggest victim. Meanwhile, the people of Pakistan have been denied the democracy that had come so readily to India because India eschewed military engagement with the US while the Pakistani armed forces became the US's principal client and, therefore, the rulers of Pakistan or in between the puppeteers of civil governments. Seventy years of servitude to America has ended in America becoming the most hated, if most desired, country in Pakistan.

At the end of a half-century and more of becoming a military ally of the United States, Pakistan's society, polity and economy lie in tatters while non-aligned India rides high. Modi does not seem to have learned the lesson. Quite taken at his transformation from a communalist denied a visa to the US to being feted by the US President, India under Modi is being enticed into a military partnership with the US as it attempts to encircle China in the way the US in the twentieth century had sought to encircle the Soviet Union. From being a disengaged peace-maker, and therefore, a highly influential independent operator in foreign policy, as India was from Nehru to Indira to Rajiv Gandhi, we now have Modi cozying up to the United States in the military sphere as if he were a Liaquat Ali Khan, a Feroze Khan Noon or a civilian Ayub Khan/ Yahya/ Zia-ul-Haq. That is the real story behind the recent Obama visit that has dragooned India into the disputes of others in the South China Sea.

One final warning and I am done. Cold War I was a far-away war, the potential battlefield being Europe. Cold War II is much nearer. It is burgeoning on our doorstep. If it comes to hot war, the most likely battlefield will be India. Is that how we wish to transmogrify the India of Mahatma Gandhi by the time we reach the centenary of our Independence?

NDTV.com

HOW MODI AND AMIT SHAH LOST DELHI FOR BJP

11 February 2015

Is this the End of the Beginning for Modi – or the Beginning of the End?

Kiran Bedi, whose aesthetic judgement has Modi's "beautiful face" as its benchmark, might step forward to claim the credit for the BJP's spectacular defeat in the Delhi elections, but the palm leaf should surely be shared by Modi and his beautiful companion-at-arms, Amit Shah. Between the two of them, they have delivered the BJP such a sound thrashing that for exactly the same reason that till yesterday, their dual performance at the polls used to be hailed as "masterly". For that same reason, they now need to be held up to ridicule. But for the two having so needlessly taken over what, after all, was an election to India's smallest state, the BJP would certainly not have suffered the rout it has.

It was the two who decided that Kiran Bedi should be rewarded for her tasteless sycophancy by being selected to grace the Throne of Delhi. In a single stroke, they antagonized dozens of Delhi's homegrown BJP leaders and thousands of its workers. Here is a party that in the two decades since Delhi was granted statehood has produced a sheaf of Chief Ministers ranging from Madan Lal Khurana to Sahib Singh and Sushma Swaraj. Their leaders have included men of political standing like Vijay Kumar Malhotra, Harshvardhan and Jagdish Mukhi. All of them, and scores of other aspirants, were pushed to one side by a single decree emanating from the very top of the party: the crown, they ordered, is being awarded to Kiran Bedi. The precipitate decline in the BJP's fortunes coincided exactly with that decision. Till then, pollsters had thought the BJP would carry the people of Delhi with it. In fact, Modi and Shah between them ensured that Kejriwal's *jhadu* would sweep the elections. A foul-mouthed Sakshi Maharaj pushed women into the AAP marquee by dictating that each one of them must produce four children.

The next mistake of the Modi-Shah duo was converting a small state election into a referendum on the Centre's performance by inducting into the campaign every single central minister and no less than 120 MPs, besides its Chief Ministers and other senior leaders from the Hindi belt. Never – and this is worth emphasizing – never have so many been deployed to achieve so little. The twosome wanted to claim victory in Delhi as vindication of nine months of BJP rule at the Centre. In the event, the elections have only exposed the growing disillusionment and disenchantment of the people of India with the empty bombast that has characterized those nine months of insubstantial image boosting.

A third major boo-boo was the Modi-Shah decision to delay the elections in Delhi from the summer last year to the present. Had they recognized the temporary nature of the wave that took Modi to power, they would have understood that the wave had crested and the ebb had started. But so puffed up were they with their arrogance and certitude that they failed to see that every wave must ebb. Hubris has arrived. As the ancient Greeks used to say, "Those whom the gods wish to destroy, they first make mad!"

That there is such a syndrome operating is best illustrated by Modi-Shah's refusal to take a stand on communal disturbances. Both Trilokpuri and Bawana have been buffeted by communal riots in the aftermath of the May 2014 elections. That disturbs the aam aadmi and the khaas aadmi. But neither Modi nor Shah has had a word to say in sympathy for the victims. Notwithstanding the ten-year moratorium on communalism that Modi sought fit to declare from the ramparts of the Red Fort, again and again he has failed to rein in the lunatic fringe of the Sangh Parivar – for the good reason that it is this fringe which brought him to power and it is this fringe that is his natural home. The so-called "development agenda" has long been put on the back-burner while the real agenda is brought to the fore through "love jihad", "ghar wapsi" and forced conversion/reconversion, aside from pre-election riots of the kind the nation witnessed at Saharanpur. Five churches have been attacked or burned down in Delhi itself. Not a word about this outrage figured in the Modi-Shah campaign. It alienated every segment of the voting public.

There is also the notorious praise of the "patriotism" of the murderer of the Mahatma, Nathuram Godse, and the building of temples to him and statues of him. Modi's response was to refuse to fulfil his parliamentary duty of coming to the Rajya Sabha to explain himself, thus sabotaging his government's entire legislative agenda. He did it because he and Jaitley had already hatched their dirty plan of bringing through ordinances legislation that would not have stood the scrutiny of Parliament.

One of these ordinances relates to the Land Acquisition Act that the BJP had voted for only a few months ago. By taking away from the aam aadmi the right to not lose land without his consent and due compensation, the BJP has alarmed small and marginal landholders the country over. The first test was on the rural and quasi-rural outskirts of Delhi that have been the worst victims of the real estate mafia. It was in this rural periphery that the BJP had won most of its seats in the December 2013 elections. It is here that the BJP has now been roundly defeated. The implications are nationwide: that Nariman Point and Malabar Hill may thrill at the thought of land being acquired at a pittance by the State for exploitation by Big Business, but the farmers and the labour that work these lands are going to reject the BJP all over the countryside if it persists, as it seems likely to do, with the amendments it has made by ordinance to the Land Acquisition Act.

The ordinances reflect, of course, the authoritarian bent of mind that is so characteristically Modi's (and Shah's). They got away with it in Gujarat. So, they thought they could get away with it at the Centre. Delhi has taught them a lesson – namely, that democracy does not care for dictators. The deft playing of the communal card in Gujarat gave them ten years of arbitrary abuse of power in the name of "development" in that state; Delhi, in keeping with India's civilizational ethos, has not only said a big NO to creeping communalism, it has also said No to the undermining of democracy and democratic practice.

But perhaps Modi's biggest contribution to his own resounding defeat has been the dus-lakh suit, embroidered repeatedly with his name, that he donned to show off to Obama. That is manic vanity. People were revolted at the idea of their Prime Minister dressing up like a mediaeval monarch. Remember the story of the child who cried out that the Emperor had no clothes? Delhi has asked the same question.

NDTV.com

WHY AAP WIN IS ACHHI BAAT

14 February 2015

I do not usually read the comments on my weekly blog because they are mostly so illiterate, misspelled and ungrammatical as to make any perusal of them a waste of time. But I did go through every comment on my last blog explaining the BJP's resounding defeat in the Delhi elections. One theme running through the comments did, I thought, deserve consideration – namely, what I had to say about the Congress failing to open its account and 63 of its 70 candidates losing their deposits? I intend to do this today, but only after clarifying that I write this column not on behalf of the Congress, but as a way of airing my own opinions on issues of the day. Some of the time, I dare say, this coincides with the official Congress position, but it is precisely because much of the time I am out on my own limb that the Party takes such great care to ensure that I am not its official spokesman. I have too much of a mind of my own to toe anyone else's line.

I think it was evident to every Congress supporter after the December 2013 Delhi elections that the capital's voter felt that after giving the party three straight wins, it was time for a change. That is par for the course in a democracy. Can you immediately think of any party having won four elections or more in a row? Apart from the Congress' own record of five straight wins in the first five general elections, when our democracy was still very young, I can only think of one: the Sikkim Sangram Parishad. Perhaps the CPI-M will equal that record next time in Tripura and the BJD in Odisha. The point is that defeating the ruling party after giving it three straight wins is the norm in a vigorous democracy.

What was telling, however, about the December 2013 defeat was the scale of the Congress defeat – down to 8 from a huge, consistent majority. That had everything to do with the reverberations of the India Against Corruption campaign that had caught the imagination of the people of the capital – although, curiously, it had failed to click anywhere else, perhaps because the political elite is nowhere more visible than in Delhi. At a time when IAC was abusing every politician in sight, I had advised Arvind Kejriwal on a TV programme that if he wanted to make a difference, he should stop trying to do it from within civil society and instead enter the political arena. At the time, he appeared to demur, but subsequently formed a political party and threw himself, with energy and innovation, into the only proper sphere for politics in a democracy – which is politics. We knew during the 2013 campaign that his appeal had traction in the city, but I am sure it came as a surprise – albeit a welcome surprise – to Kejriwal himself when he won as many seats as he did. The lesson the Congress had to learn then was that while Delhi's voters were shying away from the Congress they had voted to office for 15 long years, they would not vote for the BJP if they had a credible alternative. That alternative was Kejriwal, then in the wings.

Although the defeat of the Congress was crushing in 2013, at least it was not a double whammy: the BJP did not get Congress votes and that was a huge relief. For our enemy could never be the up and rising AAP; it was at best a regional rival. The real enemy of the Congress (I deliberately do not use the word "opponent" but "enemy") is the BJP. The BJP and its army of Sangh Parivarists and assorted communal fanatics stand for an India that is the polar opposite of everything that secularist socialist Nehruvians like myself stand for. They represent those who encouraged and caused the murder of Mahatma Gandhi. They venerate the likes of VD Savarkar, author and philosopher of the word "Hindutva". They are those who emulated the massacres of Hindu minorities in Pakistan by carrying out at Partition a similar pogrom against Muslim minorities in India. It is their politics that is based on a denial of Indian pluralism, particularly in the religious sphere, of the synthesis and the sharing of spiritual ideas that has characterized the evolution of India's civilization for five millennia. It is they who have nutty notions of the history of India, in particular of the 666 years, from 1192 to 1858, that there was always a Muslim sultan on the throne of Delhi – a period that witnessed the rise of the Bhakti movement, climaxing in the Ten Gurus of Sikhism, under the influence of the egalitarian ideas that had invaded the Indian psyche with the advent of the Message of the Prophet (PBUH), leaving the Hindus in a majority of 76 per cent after close to seven centuries of Muslim political rule. It was under the stewardship of the great Mughals that India as a civilization gained its highest expression, becoming an economic superpower in the 16th century.

It is also they who ignore the entire history of Buddhism being driven out of the country of its birth and Buddhist shrines desecrated that characterized the end of a millennium of India having been less a Hindu than a Buddhist and Jain country. It is they who know not that India was the first country in history to have an organized Christian church – the Syrian Christian church that flourishes to this day in Kerala. It is they who have bizarre notions of technological development in ancient India which obscure real achievement with fantasies. The BJP and its cohort constitute an omnipresent threat to the India that all Indians (other than the Sanghis) want. Hence, my choice of the word "enemy" to describe them. To all other opponents of the Congress – and they are legion – I restrict myself to the term "opponent".

In some measure, most Congress supporters recognize that while our fundamental idea of India is shared by the entire non-Congress spectrum from the extreme left to right, the Sangh Parivar represents all that we most fear about the future of the India of our dreams. That is why any Congress voter disillusioned – for whatever reason – with the Congress, looks first for anyone other than the BJP to shift his allegiance. We saw that dramatically happening in 1977, when the Congress vote shifted bodily out of the Congress but went to the Jana Sangh only to the extent that the then Jana Sangh dissolved itself in the alternative secular identity of the Janata Party. We also saw it in the decisive rejection of the Jana Sangh, reincarnated as the BJP, at the elections of 1984 – an election which returned fewer BJP MPs to Parliament from the whole country than the BJP won from Delhi alone in the recent Delhi elections. In the states too, over long years, we have seen the Congress vote repeatedly drift to the regional parties and Left Fronts but not towards the BJP until the mid-1990s where credible secular alternatives to the Congress did not emerge (Madhya Pradesh, Chhatisgarh etc.). When a credible non-Congress, non-BJP alternative emerges, the Congress vote largely shifts to the secular alternative, not the BJP. We saw this with the long rule of the Samajwadi Party in UP, of Lalu and Nitish in Bihar, of the Left Front in Kerala, West Bengal and now most spectacularly in Tripura. We have seen this also with the two Dravidian principals in Tamil Nadu and regional parties like the BJD, the Trinamool, the Sikkim Sangram Parishad and the NC/PDP in J&K (generally, if not today, in tandem with the Congress).

It was, therefore, only to be expected that when a credible alternative to the Congress and BJP emerged in Delhi in the shape of the AAP, some of the disillusioned Congress vote should drift to the secular AAP, whose fundamental philosophy reminds one so much of the pristine Nehruvian Congress. The trouncing of the AAP (and of the Congress) in the country and in Delhi in the 2014 general election happened with Modi projecting himself as the Sikandar of Development rather than the Forerunner of Hindu Raj. Since the last eight months have seen no development, only slogans, and a great deal of Hindutva, the Delhi Congress voter, who was temporarily deceived into voting for Modi in the general election, found that with the restoration of credibility to the AAP, he did have a secular alternative to the Congress – and so voted for the AAP. Disillusioned BJP voters also voted for AAP since the committed BJP voter would never vote for the Congress for the same reason as the Congress voter, except exceptionally, does not vote saffron.

Which still leaves unanswered the question as to why I am gloating over the AAP victory instead of shedding copious tears over the resounding Congress defeat? Very simple, really. When the Delhi voter gets disillusioned with the AAP – after all nothing more than a Saturday evening club of mohalla *buddhijibi*s – he will come back to the Congress, not to the BJP. So, assuming the AAP stumbles, as I am inclined to believe it will, we only have to sit it out for five years. That may seem a long time to the BJP. But for the Congress, which has seen many ups and downs in its life of 129 years, five years is but a wink of time. To the distress of those who week after week abuse me, I am sorry to tell them that we will be back, sooner than later. Our preference is always for the last laugh. Haha

MODI, EVER THE RSS PRACHARAK

23 February 2015

The 56-inch mountain has at long last heaved – and produced the proverbial mouse.

After eight months of *maun vrata* over issues of religious tension, Narendra Modi has now disclosed that his "government will ensure there is complete freedom of faith" and "will not allow any religious group, belonging to the majority or the minority, to incite hatred against others, overtly or covertly".

Excellent – except that this is what he should have said – and done – at the Shah Alam refugee camp in Ahmedabad in 2002 when an anti-Muslim pogrom was taking place under his watch. There was neither a word of sympathy then, nor any action to establish that his government was with the victims, not the perpetrators. Indeed, it was not until he was compelled to accompany Prime Minister Vajpayee to the Shah Alam camp a full month later that he even made his first visit to the camp. And when, finally, a word of sympathy came from him a decade or so later, it was to compare the murdered, injured and looted Muslims to a puppy dog accidentally coming under the wheels of a car.

Nor is this the first time Modi has declared that he "strongly condemn[s] State violence". He had said it before to the BJP's Parliamentary Party. But with what result? Only the filthy statements from those he selected to represent his Party in the Lok Sabha and adorn his Council of Ministers. Perhaps he cannot deprive Sakshi Maharaj of his seat but by what standards does he continue to include Sadhvi Jyoti among his Ministers? In the behaviour of a whole cohort of his most ardent supporters, there is no indication that "equal respect for all religions" is in their "DNA". If they do not have that in their DNA – as manifestly they do not – what are they doing sitting beside and behind him in Parliament?

And talking of Parliament, why did Modi so adamantly refuse

to come to the Rajya Sabha and say exactly what he did to the Syrian Christians? The Opposition was demanding no more. They wanted him to unequivocally declare on the floor of the sacred precincts of Parliament that he "consider[ed] the freedom to have, to retain and to adopt, a religion or belief [as] a personal choice of a citizen". He did not because he was afraid of being questioned about the gap between such an oral declaration and the ugly effects of *ghar wapsi*, love jihad and election-oriented riots strewn around him.

The RSS *pracharak* in Modi is manifested in virtually every sentence of his speech. Note that all his quotes come from the Hindu religious texts. He finds nothing in the *Dhammapada* or the Holy Quran, in the *Zend Avesta* or the Torah or even the Guru Granth Sahib to share with his audience. He talks of "spiritual exchanges thousands of years back" between "the Indian saints and Greek sages", but rears away from even hinting at the spiritual exchanges between Muslim saints and Hindu sages for more than a thousand years that have given rise to the synthesis of spiritualism that defines the whole of India today. Nor does Modi's constricted conflation of "India" with "Hindu" allow him to talk expansively of the profound influence of Buddhism and Jainism on Hindu spiritual thought and traditions and over most of the period from Asoka (3rd century BC) to Harshvardhan (7th century AD) – that is close to a millennium – which eventually gave rise to Sankara's Advaita which resolved the age-long disputation within the Hindu fold of whether Mind or Matter are one or separate. No, his quotes are all from the Rig Veda and "ancient Indian sayings". Nothing from Guru Nanak or Guru Gobind Singh, nothing from the saints of the Bhakti Movement. Indeed, given that Modi was in a Christian church, neither he nor his speechwriters could find anything to cite from the Bible or more recent Christian philosophers. Surely, Gandhiji's devotion to "Lead Kindly Light" or the Sermon on the Mount could have found more reflection in his remarks.

"Spiritualism," said Modi, "is rooted in India's heritage." Of course it is. But it is a spiritualism that derives from India being a confluence of virtually every religion the world has or has known. Compare any page of Jawaharlal Nehru's *Discovery of India* and Modi's speech, and the gap becomes glaring between a truly profound understanding of India's numerous spiritual traditions and Modi's one-way street. For Modi to affirm, however, that important religions have gone into the making of India's contemporary spiritual heritage would be to deny Savarkar's fundamental proposition that only those Indians are genuine Indians who regard India as not only their "pitrubhoomi" but also their "punyabhoomi". That is precisely why he spoke of "Mother India" having given "birth to many religious and spiritual streams" but completely ignored the many religions and spiritual streams that have come into India, that have been assimilated into our cultures and civilization over and over again. Consider the contrast between Modi's boast that "some of them [religions born in India] have even travelled beyond Indian borders" with sidelining the religions born outside India but which have travelled into India, crossing Indian borders and becoming part and parcel of our composite Hindu and non-Hindu heritage. Modi's speech privileges those religions born within India over those whose origins lie elsewhere. That is not the Hindu tradition. It is Hindutva at its naked.

Let us not forget that when Modi presented a copy of the Gita to the Emperor of Japan, he sneered that "secularists" back home would object. That is to totally misunderstand "secularism". Secularism is not about being anti-Hindu or anti-Gita. We secularists regard the Gita as integral to not just the Hindu Way of Life, but the Indian Way of Life. We would also applaud Modi presenting a copy of the Holy Quran, printed at the Darul Uloom, to Prime Minister Koirala when he next visits Kathmandu; or of Dara Shikoh's Persian translation of the Upanishads to Nawaz Sharif were Modi to ever meet Sharif again; or even a copy of the Torah printed in Jew Town, Kochi to the Israeli President: that would be to give full expression to India's pluralism. It is in the active celebration of all of its faiths and beliefs, in rejoicing that all things Indian are not only Hindu, in bringing together all Indians instead of sequestering some of them in khaki half-pants in Nagpur, that the true spirit of India lies.

The time now is for Modi to fulfil – particularly with respect to his own Sangh Parivar and associated outfits – that he really will "act strongly in this regard".

NDTV.com

BAKE IN NUCLEAR INDIA

27 February 2015

Will someone teach Modi the difference between M and B? For, his "breakthrough understanding" with Obama turns out to be India providing an additional $200 million in the event of nuclear disaster, whereas the Fukushima cleanup is projected to cost up to $200 billion. The Indian liability law recognises the virtually uncountable costs of a nuclear accident by allowing affected parties to sue both the operator and the supplier for adequate compensation. The Obama-Modi "understanding" does not cover even a fraction of the cost and leaves the supplier as vulnerable as before to the Indian law. To give Modi yet another Pyrrhic victory in foreign policy, Obama allowed him to get away with announcing a mysterious "breakthrough" but took the utmost care to ensure that none of this found its way into an actual formulation of words. We remain where we were: US suppliers can sell in India only on our terms. And if they don't like it, well that's their problem.

How likely is an accident to a nuclear power plant involving core damage? In the early days after World War II when the nuclear power industry was still in its infancy, there was a general untested belief that the risk was negligible, perhaps one in every 50,000 operating years – an operating year being the year for which a reactor is run multiplied by the number of reactors in the world. But as the number of reactors worldwide rose exponentially, the US government in 1974 appointed a committee under Prof Norman C. Rasmussen of MIT to take a closer look. The report estimated the risk at 1 in 20,000 reactor years. This was on the eve of the 1979 Three Mile Island partial core damage in the US that resulted in no additional reactors being installed in that country for the next four decades. The accident persuaded the US Nuclear Regulatory Commission to revise its problematic risk assessment to one accident in every 1000 reactor years. Three Mile Island was followed by the accidents at Chernobyl and Fukushima. The current assessment is:

one accident every 45 calendar years. But there have been five accidents in the last 40 years. Hence, the problem of risk assessment is a real one, not some anarchist fantasy of a Jurassic Park NGO, as the protestors at Koodankulam are being portrayed. To quote Mitsuhei Murata, the Japanese anti-nuclear activist, "Nuclear reactors are no less dangerous than nuclear weapons."

Fukushima has also given rise to the real fear that contaminated water might contain the deadly compound, tritium. Japanese Nobel laureate Masatoshi Koshiba and his fellow-researcher Akira Hasegawa have estimated that in Fukushima's contaminated water of 5,90,000 tonnes, there may be traces of tritium, 2 kg of which could kill 2 million people!

It is precisely because US suppliers like GE and Toshiba-Westinghouse know much better than our government does that nuclear plants are far from fail-safe that they baulk at being made to bear the costs of an all-too-likely civil nuclear accident. Hence, the fuss over limiting supplier liability to a few hundred million dollars when even the cleanup of the BP oil spill in the Gulf of Mexico, which did not kill a single human being but wiped out many seals, has risen from $18 billion to about $42 billion now and is likely to go up to $58 billion. How can a country that has experienced the awful injustice of Union Carbide contemplate letting foreign suppliers off the hook for a tithe of what is being paid out for dead seals?

I recall Rajiv Gandhi mentioning to me that a kamikaze pilot could fly his plane into the Bhabha atomic reactor on the outskirts of Mumbai and cause as much damage as Hiroshima or worse. He added that we could do the same to the Candu reactor on the outskirts of Karachi. The Modi plan, following on the UPA plan, envisages dotting the country with such potential nuclear targets. How then can we spread nuclear power plants through the length and breadth of the nation while baring our teeth at both nuclear Pakistan and nuclear China?

The Week

JAITLEY'S BUDGET IS FOR
SAHIB LOG

2 March 2015

Every year around the end of February, the *sahib log* and the pink papers (and now, increasingly the TV news channels) whip themselves into a frenzy over what the Union Budget holds for them.

There is no equivalent frisson of excitement among the broad masses of the Indian public. One reason, of course, is that the broad masses pay no direct taxes. Therefore, there is no incentive to discover how much less or more the taxman is going to snatch from them. But more important, I think, is that at least since we entered the era of neo-liberalism, the Finance Minister concentrates his attention on the corporates (who make or break his reputation) – and the corporates on him to see what's in it for them.

The vast majority of Indians working in agriculture and allied activities (dairying, fisheries), as unskilled labour on the farms, in construction and domestic services, in petty retail and nano-to-micro-industries, are neither looking to the FM nor is the FM looking towards them.

Of course, there is a ritual invocation of the poor and the *kisan* by every FM at the start of every budget speech, but once he has got over that hump, he quickly moves on to more congenial matters such as augmenting the annual ₹6 lakh crore subsidy given to fat cats and written off under the heading "revenues foregone".

(However, not one FM mentions the figure in his budget speech for fear that if the figure is boldly stated, sharp questions will be asked why if this subsidy to the rich can go up year after year, it is only the subsidies to the poor that come under annual attack from sources who wish to portray the rich as prudent and the poor as profligate).

Unsurprisingly, this has happened again this year. Arun Jaitley shed a few crocodile tears for the *kisan* and *khet-mazdoor* before devoting five-sixth of his speech to his real clients. And this despite the fact that in this year where the (statistically fudged) claim is that India is growing at plus seven per cent, will cross eight per cent next year and soar to double digits thereafter, the Government's Economic Survey 2014-15, Vol II, chapter 5, divulges the tragic truth that Indian agriculture has grown by only 1.1 per cent in this miracle year.

With nearly half our workforce engaged in agriculture and nearly 60 per cent of rural households essentially dependent on agriculture for their household income, this horrifying story of stagnation in a period of stratospheric growth has merited neither the attention nor the concern of the Finance Minister nor any of the sahib log. It took a heroic effort on my part to get in even a word edgewise on this in the televised budget discussion in which I was entrapped for some six hours on Budget Day. We, the sahib log, just don't seem to care.

Every single agricultural crop of significance is down. Our output of rice, wheat and coarse cereals (jowar, bajra etc) is down; our output of oilseeds and pulses is also down. Only monkey nuts are up! What has saved the rural economy is dairying and poultry. All this is spelled out in the Economic Survey but merits no attention in the Budget speech. Moreover, the Economic Survey details what needs to be done to pull this most vital sector of the Indian economy out of the mire in which it is stuck. But the Finance Minister (and his PM) appear to have skipped Chapter 5 which succinctly sets out the steps to be taken.

Chapter 5 emphasizes that the biggest lacuna in Indian agriculture is agricultural research and extension to address the twin problems of yield and productivity. It says "the paradigm shift in yield/productivity required for the second green revolution" renders it "imperative to make Indian agricultural growth science-led" and a nation-wide network of extension services provided to carry the message to the farmer. Studies show that two-thirds of Indian kisans do not even know that extension workers are supposed to inform them about all this free of cost. Yet, apart from ₹100 crore set aside in Jaitley's last budget for two additional institutes of excellence, the subject is not even mentioned in this year's speech.

Moreover, no recognition is accorded to the heartbreaking story of agricultural credit despite numerous studies, most recently the 2013 NSSO 70th round, establishing conclusively that "the crop loans are not reaching intended beneficiaries and there are no systems and procedures in place at several bank branches to monitor the end-use of funds". These alarming facts are underlined at a time when 40 per cent of farmers' credit requirements are still being secured from "informal sources" (which translates as the village middleman) and "usurious moneylenders account for a 26 per cent share of total agricultural credit", both "issues that need to be addressed on a priority basis". The share of long-term credit in total agricultural credit has collapsed from 55 per cent to 39 per cent. Worse still, the bulk of so-called rural credit is availed of by corporate farmers from urban branches, while a disturbingly large number of kisans are not even aware of the credit facilities being made available by the government.

Unless and until the Panchayat Raj institutions are integrated into the agriculture credit and extension services system, there is no way "last-mile connectivity", underlined by the Survey, can be ensured. Yet, the Finance Minister did not even whisper the word "panchayats" and drastically cut the allotment for the Union Ministry of Panchayati Raj from over ₹6500 crore to just ₹95 crore.

This is clearly a government that either knows nothing of India's real needs or is so obsessed with its corporate sponsors that it cannot look beyond the factory to the farm. The tragedy, therefore, continues of 60 per cent of India's population that lives in her villages having to make do with just 13 per cent of the nation's GDP.

Astoundingly, this neglect of the rural economy is received with applause by those who wish to see investment in private sector industry and PPP infrastructure rise exponentially. Agriculture's disaster in recent decades has been spelled by the drying up of public investment in the sector. For a whole decade, public investment has stagnated; it is now running at about one-eighth of total capital formation in agriculture. The Survey says, "Given the vast investment needs of this sector, greater public investment would only help increase private investment." Yet, the Finance Minister has seen fit to glide away altogether from this desperate need of the real aam aadmi – the kisan and the khet-mazdoor.

This is deeply depressing as growth is ultimately for the people and needs to find reflection in employment. Agriculture is the most employment-intensive segment of the economy. Investment, public or private, in private big business and PPP projects leads to capital-intensive and technology-intensive growth, that is, jobless growth of the kind we have suffered for the last two decades and more.

Where then should the priority lie? Please don't ask Mr. Jaitley because the poor man does not know. All he sees are the bulging bags of private domestic and foreign industrialists. Hence, a Jaitley budget that is principally addressed to these corporate bigwigs and their fellow-sahib log.

NDTV.com

BJP PUSHING ECONOMY TOWARDS DISASTER

10 March 2015

As the Budget figures sink in, the realization grows that by kidding itself, the BJP is presiding over an economy drifting slowly but surely to disaster.

The flaw essentially lies in the new technique its statistical advisers have provided of calculating GDP. Where all these decades, GDP has been measured at factor cost – that is the cost at which inputs have been obtained – the new GDP series has shifted the basis to the price at which output is marketed. This is in line with standard global practice and, therefore, not to be faulted. The catch, however, is that owing to some yet-to-be-discovered glitch, the growth rate thrown up by the new process is wildly out of sync with the growth figures for the three key sectors of the economy – agriculture, industry and services.

We saw last week that the growth rate of agriculture has been estimated at a mere 1.1 per cent last year. The same Economic Survey estimates the industrial growth rate to have been 5.9 per cent, a mere 1.4 per cent higher than the previous year and services alone topping double digits with 10.6 per cent, but a mere 1.3 per cent above the previous year.

How can such modest sectoral growth rates add up to a whopping GDP growth rate of 7.4 per cent, blasting us into being the "fastest-growing economy in the world"? Somewhere, someone has gone wrong.

But instead of prudently waiting to see how the glitch might be discovered and corrected, the BJP government is rushing headlong into assuming the figure must be correct and basing its Budget on that GDP growth figure. Principally, its revenue estimates are based on the economy growing at around eight per cent a year when, on the old basis, the figure would be closer to six. Such a huge margin of over-estimation will soon reveal itself in much smaller tax revenues and other government receipts than imagined, with the result that six months down the line, when the mid-term survey is prepared and the Revised Estimates have to be projected, the government will be shown up to have been living in cloud-cuckoo land.

Meanwhile, huge damage would have been inflicted on the poor, damage that will persist even if the avaricious classes have to revise their hopes for a bonanza. This is principally on account of the substantial increase in the transfer of Central tax revenues to the states having been raised from 32 to 42 per cent as per the recommendations of the 14th Financial Commission (the consequence of the UPA II having so drafted the Terms of Reference of the 14th Financial Commission – and so no credit to Arun Jaitley).

In itself, the increase in the share of the states is to be welcomed. We do indeed need "cooperative federalism". But such a major change needs preparation, which is why the 14th Financial Commission made the increase conditional on appropriate "institutional arrangements" being worked out between the Centre and the States to ensure a smooth transition. No such institutional arrangements having been made; there is going to be major disruption, particularly in measures to cater to the human development needs of the poor. Let us explain this point in detail.

First, the share of the states in Central tax revenues might have gone up, but their share in the overall resources of the Centre, tax and non-tax, is in fact projected to marginally decrease from 63 to 62 per cent. With no more money from the Centre at the disposal of the states than they had earlier, states are being conned into believing *ki achhe din aa gaye hain* when the reality is *ki wahi burre din badle nahin*. Not only will the states have to meet their Plan and non-Plan requirements from the same overall pool of resources, in addition they will have to take over many of the financial responsibilities which were till now being met by the Centre, particularly in the domains of agriculture, gap funding of backward regions, rural (including Panchayat) infrastructure, irrigation (major and minor), sanitation, drinking water, health and education, besides a myriad other schemes hitherto partially or totally funded by the Centre. True, their larger share of Central tax revenues will place at their disposal a large source of untied funds which they can deploy as they wish. This would have been all to the good if it had been matched by a similar or equivalent augmentation of total funds at their disposal. But as Jaitley has robbed the states with one hand of what he has so generously given with the other, the states are now saddled with huge additional developmental responsibilities without the financial wherewithal to rise to these new challenges.

Given that India may, with a slight statistical sleight of hand, have become the "fastest-growing economy in the world", on the UN's Human Development Index we still stagnate around 135th position, virtually the same as it has been through all the long quarter century since 1991 of neo-liberalism. The development model has made the rich unprecedentedly richer and the richest rich beyond their wildest imaginings, but the poor have had to make do with little more than crumbs from the table. We remain, in terms of what really matters – namely, literacy and education; malnutrition and hunger; maternal and infant mortality; unemployment and under-employment; destitution and minimum basic needs – poorer than much of our neighbourhood, far behind most fellow-developing nations, and, on some crucial parameters, equal to or below sub-Saharan Africa.

The Budget should be, but is not, measured against these parameters. What this Budget has done is to prospectively set us back even further.

This is not a matter only of sharply-reduced Central allocations for social sector and poverty alleviation programmes, although that is where the rots start. It lies in the assumption that what the Centre has reduced, the states will make up for. And of their own volition, at that. Is that at all feasible? One, many states have already prepared and passed their budgets. The money now being flung at them without prior preparation will take time to translate into government accounts and turn into spending for the purposes from which the Centre has partially or wholly withdrawn. Second, the temptation will be for many states to use the bonanza for what they see as their priorities within their old figure for total resources, not in any way as a significant additionality. Third, the Centre has lost all or much of its hold on ensuring at least some spending on what must be regarded as "national priorities" – such as education and health. However high-minded a state may be, if its overall budgetary resources have shrunk, why should it suddenly change its priorities and start doing all the (good) things the Centre has hitherto been doing? These, in any case, were being done through the states earlier, but without burdening their exchequer by as much as they are now required to bear.

Jaitley should have done two things before rushing in where angels fear to tread. First, he should have worked out in consultation with the states at least a modicum of understanding that the additional ten per cent they were getting would be spent in the sectors from which the Centre was wholly or partially withdrawing. Second, a cooperative consultative mechanism should have been set up to oversee, at least broadly, that the terms of the Centre-state understanding were being adhered to. Third – and most important – this was the key moment to ensure that "federalism" covers all three Constitutionally-mandated tiers – Centre, states and panchayats/nagarpalikas.

Sonia Gandhi has memorably said that our federalism requires "a strong Centre, strong states, and strong local governments". Arun Jaitley's budget has massacred the Ministry of Panchayati Raj by slashing its allocation from ₹7000 crore to a mere ₹94 crore – the most drastic cut of any Ministry, thereby confirming his and Narendra Modi's bias against the people's participation in governance and towards bureaucratic authoritarianism. Under these circumstances, it is ludicrous to talk of "good governance" – for the best governance is self-governance, and this is being extinguished.

It is precisely because the states failed to live up to their duty of funding the social sectors and poverty alleviation programmes that the Centre resorted to Centrally-Sponsored Schemes (CSS) to finance essential schemes for human resource development. And it was precisely because he perceived how inefficient CSS were if they were implemented by state bureaucracies alone that Rajiv Gandhi ensured Constitutional sanction, sanctity and safeguards for local self-government in every village of this country. That humongous endeavour at making the people of India masters of their own destiny has been disowned by

Modi and Jaitley.

The only good that will come out of it is that they are hastening their own end. The Delhi elections have revealed the BJP's Achilles' heel. It is their refusal to give the people their due share in the governance of the country. Jaitley's budget begins the countdown.

NDTV.com

HOW AFZAL GURU
WAS TURNED INTO A MARTYR

17 March 2015

In the week that has seen Mahatma Gandhi's statue being unveiled beside Winston Churchill's in London's Westminster Square, the question surely arises: what do governments gain by jailing political dissidents? Certainly, in the end, Gandhi, the convict, won and Churchill, the jailer, lost. Ditto Nelson Mandela, whose statue also stands in the same square. Home Ministers who arrest those they do not like might win temporary kudos, but inevitably, a term in prison enhances rather than diminishes an activist's reputation among his present and potential followers. It does not snuff out the cause for which he seeks incarceration.

With judicial hanging, the impact is even more decisive. Bhagat Singh remains an icon. Afzal Guru, who in his lifetime was a marginal player, has now acquired cult status as a martyr among his growing band of followers. His remains remain buried in an obscure, unmarked grave in Delhi's prison grounds, but memorials to him are being erected in the hearts of many, many Kashmiris. We have offered a hostage to fortune by hanging him – and hanging on to what is left of him.

There are only two ways of resolving disputes: the authoritarian way of putting away the other side on the principle of 'out of sight, out of mind'; or the democratic way of discussion, dialogue, negotiations. The problem with the former is that 'out of sight' does not take away from the mind's eye. Indeed, the silenced one put away from his followers gains immensely by being portrayed (and portraying himself) as one prepared to be punished for his beliefs – especially when he cheerfully accepts his punishment and even urges the unjust judge to be as severe in unjust judgement as the unjust law provides. The world discovered this in 1922 when Gandhiji was arraigned in front of the Ahmedabad district sessions court judge. At Gandhiji's instance, the poor man pronounced the harshest sentence possible, but then, in open court, expressed the hope that the executive would see it fit to reduce or remove the sentence. Gandhi at that moment emerged as the Mahatma, not only in the eyes of his followers (who had long regarded him a Mahatma) but to an ever-widening worldwide circle of admirers that has now resulted in the irony of Gandhi standing shoulder-to-shoulder with the same Churchill who had once denounced him as a "seditious fakir", under the benign gaze of the same Parliament where Churchill had so traduced him!

Afzal Guru would not have attained martyrdom status if he had been found guilty of a palpable crime, as Ajmal Kasab was. There was simply no doubt in anyone's mind – not even Kasab's – that he was guilty as charged. In Afzal's case, the case against him was fuzzy, so fuzzy that first the High Court discarded much of the evidence against him as being unproved or improperly obtained, followed by the Supreme Court relying exclusively on "circumstantial evidence" to sentence him to death avowedly to satisfy the "collective conscience" of the country. It led to a collective howl of disapproval in the Valley that propelled the PDP to a massive win in Kashmir in the December 2014 election. Since death cannot be reversed, even the PDP's arch opponent, the National Conference, demands the return to the family of the remains for a proper burial, a demand repeatedly endorsed by Omar Abdullah personally. While the issue festers, Afzal is perhaps as widely regarded as a martyr in Kashmir as he is regarded as a murderer in the rest of India. Keeping his remains in Delhi only causes the wounds in the Valley to fester further.

Temporary peace might be bought by keeping Masarat Alam incarcerated or Afzal's remains buried under an unidentified mound in Tihar. But a lasting solution to the challenge of Kashmir's emotional integration with India can come only through engagement. Of course, we will never succeed in changing the minds of hardliners like Alam and Afzal, nor will they in bringing us round to their view. That is not the point of negotiation. The more germane goal would be to expose them as "unreasonable" to a larger public – if our cause is just. Delhi must reveal itself as "reasonable" to the people of Kashmir. That is the litmus test, failing which stones will be thrown in Srinagar while detention "advisories" are drafted in Delhi.

The group of three interlocutors, led by Dileep Padgaonkar and comprising Radha Kumar and MM Ansari, opened the gates to dialogue. Delhi has since refused to walk through the gate, giving the excuse to the separatists to do likewise. It is out of the question that the Hurriyat will simple go away, or that Alam will lose his young stone-pelters, or that the dead Afzal will lose his sheen. They have to be shackled with words, not fetters.

However, progress will not happen in a political vacuum. Unfortunately, what we have today in the state is a political vacuum with two incompatibles embracing each other opportunistically to come to power together – only to exercise power against each other. Optimists see in this unprincipled coalition the hope that the gulf between Jammu and Kashmir will be bridged. Realists would argue that a bridge cannot be jointly built if one party is joining the cantilevers even as the other is bringing it down. There has to be engagement across the spectrum from RS Pura to Kargil, but we do not have engagement even between the two halves of the state government. That is why the first few weeks of the government have been so fragile. Differences are papered over only to burst wide open at the first move by either half.

The longer such a government lasts the more harm it will do before it finally bows out – which, as in the case of the similarly constituted Janata Government of 1977-79, will happen sooner than later. Another election has to be held – perhaps before the year ends. One can only hope that would throw up a House united, not divided, as this one is, against itself.

Obviously the same cannot be said of a militant as wedded to violence as Masarat Alam, but there is no gainsaying that far from reducing his following, every jailing weds his circle of followers. The paradox is that every attempt to cut him to size merely makes him grow higher. He is a more formidable opponent in jail than is outside.

NDTV.com

UNCOOPERATIVE FEDERALISM

21 March 2015

Ever since the 2014 election campaign, Narendra Modi has been hammering away at "cooperative federalism" as the distinguishing feature of his style of governance. Apart from the little-remembered Deve Gowda, Modi is the first Prime Minister to have served 13 years as a chief minister, making him something of an expert on how states' rights under the Constitution have been whittled away, leaving them subservient to the whims and finances of the Centre. His promise has been to rectify the balance and bring the states back into their own.

The man, however, is what he is – authoritarian, centralising and single-minded in building around himself a personality cult. That includes, of course, showing off a ₹10 lakh suit embroidered all over with his name, then having it flogged at an auction for a meretricious ₹4 crore. More subtly, however, are his preferred methods of governance that are revealing themselves for concentrating real power in his hands.

This is best illustrated by what the Modi government has done with the 14th Finance Commission's recommendations on financial devolution to the states. The commission recommended that the share of the states in the net divisible Central tax pool be enhanced from 32 per cent to a whopping 42 per cent. Modi and Jaitley have accepted the recommendation and are now tom-tomming their commitment to an exponential augmentation of the untied funds placed in state coffers. What is hidden from the public's eye is that the Centre's resources are not limited to Central taxes; they comprise also revenue from several other lucrative sources such as dividends declared by public sector companies and various types of cesses and levies. The totality of these, along with the proceeds of Central taxes, comprises the total net divisible pool of the nation's resources. The budget has actually reduced the total transfer of Central resources to the states, albeit by 1 per cent, from 63 per cent to 62 per cent. Hence, while the states' untied share of the national pool has risen, the total availability of their resources remains virtually stagnant. Notwithstanding the freezing of total available resources to the states, the Centre, in the name of "cooperative federalism", has passed on to the states the responsibility for more than 100 Centrally-sponsored schemes for social and human development and the direct assault on extreme poverty without adding a *khota paisa* to the states' kitty.

The same kind of game is at play in most of the ordinances issued in January to claim that Modi's is a government that works. While largesse is bestowed on the states by, for example, giving them the entire proceeds of the auction of natural resources, firm control is being asserted over sectors that the Constitution has reserved to states' jurisdiction, such as coal and other minerals. Clause after clause of the coal mining bill and the mines and minerals bill place the states under the disciplinary control of the Centre. This is not "cooperative federalism". It is uncooperative federalism!

Worst of all, notwithstanding the historic amendments brought into the Constitution at Rajiv Gandhi's instance for meaningful local self-government, the Modi schema simply puts Panchayat Raj out of sight. Where what true federalism needs is "a strong Centre, strong states and strong local governments", as Sonia Gandhi pithily put it over a decade and a half ago, Modi undermines the Constitutional responsibilities of the Centre by sidelining local self-government. Two lakh fifty thousand panchayats and municipalities, and the 32 lakh representatives elected to them, were altogether left out of the President's Address, consigned to oblivion in the 2015-16 Budget, and never mentioned in Modi's all-too-frequent speeches, as if the Union has no duty to protect and promote Panchayat Raj in Modi's modified version of "cooperative federalism". This is a travesty of constitutional propriety that needs to be exposed and condemned as a betrayal of his constitutional duty. Gandhiji would not have approved of Modi.

The Week

WHY I ATTENDED
PAK DAY RECEPTION

24 March 2015

I was at Pakistan's National Day reception last night, as I usually am. Unfortunately, I missed out on the kebabs and other goodies as I was able to spend only about 15 minutes there; the Hon'ble Vice President had invited me about the same time to an official banquet in honour of his Cuban counterpart. But I went nevertheless to Pakistan House because I believe Pakistan is the most important country on our foreign policy agenda.

I am a regular at Pakistan National Day receptions (so much so that I was once asked to be the Government of India's official representative, predecessor to General VK Singh). This is partly nostalgia. I spent three of the most fruitful and enjoyable years of my life as India's first-ever Consul General in Karachi (Dec 1978-Jan '82), and made so many friends there that 25 years after I returned, no less than 46 of them turned up for my daughter's wedding. They are a warm, friendly, hospitable people and I never cease to be amazed at our inability to turn that affection to political advantage. I also believe that there are at least three major factors that make it imperative for us to seize the opportunity by the forelock.

First, the Partition generation in Pakistan, those who were Indians for much of their lives before they became Pakistanis, has virtually phased out. That was the generation that could not but define their own identity in terms of NOT being Indian: "I am a Pakistani because I am not an Indian." The present generation of Pakistanis are Pakistanis – because they are Pakistanis! They were born there, grew up there, have always been Pakistanis and are quite comfortable with their Pakistani passports.

Second, their domestic problems, particularly homegrown sectarianism and terrorism, are so overwhelming that instead of hostility to India being the centrepiece of their national existence, as it was in the immediate aftermath of Partition, India has been so far pushed out of their national consciousness, that in the last two elections, neither India nor even Kashmir figured in any of the principal parties' campaigns.

Third, while hostility against India and Hindus is a running theme in the propaganda of the Islamist extremists, these extremists have so lost sympathy in Pakistan at large that in election after election, their position on the margins is confirmed. Our hostility only helps those in Pakistan who wish to play up that hostility. The mainstream response is to work, if at all possible, towards a viable relationship with India. Working out that viability requires, of course, dialogue – dialogue that, to be eventually fruitful, has to be "uninterrupted and uninterruptible". Yet, we have been shooting ourselves in the foot by repeatedly breaking off the dialogue, converting the relationship into a game of snakes and ladders where we progress significantly up the ladders of mutual cooperation only to let the snakes swallow us up and take us back to the beginning.

The reply I have received to a Question I posed in the just-concluded first half of Parliament's Budget session makes the point succinctly: that when we engage diplomatically, ceasefire violations virtually cease, and when we disengage, ceasefire violations increase exponentially. The figures I have been officially supplied show that in the years 2004, 2005 and 2006, when Dr. Manmohan Singh's special envoy, Ambassador Satinder Lambah, was consistently on the back-channel with his Pakistani interlocutor, Ambassador Tariq Aziz, ceasefire violations were just 1, 6 and 3 respectively. As, however, in 2007, when the dialogue seized up and eventually broke down, ceasefire violations rose to 21, shot up to 80, then 93 in 2012, and peaked in 2013 at 199. 2014 recorded a small decline to 153. There are approximately 150-200 times more violations when war clouds are gathering than when peace is on the horizon.

Does that not show that we have got cause and effect wrong when we insist that ceasefire violations must end for talks to begin? Past experience shows that the best way to end ceasefire violations is for us to talk to each other, rather than at each other.

Among my fellow-guests at the Pakistan reception were, I understand, Mirwaiz Farooq and a team of Hurriyat leaders. I would have liked to meet them, as I usually do at Pakistan National Day receptions. This time I was denied the pleasure for I was at the reception for far too short a time to really walk around. But on previous occasions, the Hurriyat have always greeted me fondly and invited me to Kashmir (an invitation that has, alas, never been followed up!) I greet them not because I agree with them, but because they are fellow human beings, fellow Indians (even if they do not always so regard themselves), and people we have to persuade to at least edge themselves towards us if we want not only Kashmir but also Kashmiris.

That is why Dr. Manmohan Singh's interlocutors – Dileep Padgaonkar, Radha Kumar and MM Ansari – made a point of meeting them and soliciting their views. That there was so little follow-up on the interlocutors' report is a tragedy, but one that will only be compounded if the government in Delhi tries to shut them out. Fortunately, J&K Chief Minister Mufti Mohammad Sayeed has a better grasp of ground realities in the Valley than his partners in government.

Of course, as a fellow Indian, it is my right (and duty) to meet the Hurriyat if I can. But do the Pakistanis have a locus standi? It was Atal Bihari Vajpayee, none other, who answered that one when he allowed (encouraged?) Pervez Musharraf to meet with the Hurriyat at the time of the Agra summit. Until August last year, it had become standard practice for the Hurriyat to not only be invited to the Pakistan National Day reception, but also to interact with Pakistani dignitaries visiting India. Indeed, the government itself facilitated a visit to Pakistan by the Hurriyat leadership. It has done us no harm – and done the Pakistanis precious little good.

Stupidly, Modi made a proposed routine encounter between the Hurriyat and the Pakistan High Commissioner, on the eve of the Indian Foreign Secretary's visit to Pakistan, the casus belli to kill that initiative at resuming the Indo-Pak dialogue. He has since been impaled on the horns of the dilemma that he has needlessly created for himself – To

Achhe Din? Ha! Ha!!

Talk or NOT to Talk? That is the question!

The process of climbing off the high horse has begun. Not only has the new Foreign Secretary been to Islamabad, Delhi is now beginning to walk the talk on dialogue. Instead of sending so graceless a representative, Modi should have ensured that we were more decently represented.

NDTV.com

MODI'S OVERTURES TO ISRAEL DEEPLY DANGEROUS

24 March 2015

An election in distant Israel would not normally warrant a column on NDTV.com. But last week's surprise victory of Benjamin Netanyahu for a fourth term as Prime Minister has such sinister implications for our domestic national identity, and our foreign and defence policy, that we must evaluate the outcome for its implications for us.

Compared to India, Israel is a tiny country of some 6 million people (of whom 1.7 million are Israeli Arabs), as is its neighbour, Palestine, with about 4 million in the West Bank and nearly 2 million in Gaza. But because we were deeply involved, as a member of two key UN committees, with the end of the British mandate in Palestine (which happened in the same year that we secured our Independence), the Israel story came to be closely linked to the India story. In India, the price we had to pay for Independence was Partition. We were, therefore, wary of endorsing the idea of partitioning Palestine to bring the Israeli state into existence. Nehru suggested a "One-State" solution – that the British should leave behind a composite, secular nation comprising both Arabs and Jews who would frame a federal constitution under which one part would have a Jewish majority and the other an Arab majority, but bound together in a federal state that would be jointly and democratically governed by Jews and Arabs together.

The Jews said no to this because they wanted their own separate homeland; the Arabs said no because they saw no reason to pay the price of losing their homeland for a genocide committed not by them but by European Christians during the Second World War. Initially, there was a majority in the relevant UN committees which argued that partition would only lead to even more and longer-lasting problems. Eventually, however, the US and the Soviet Union persuaded or pressurized an overwhelming majority of the international community to vote in favour of partition. India was the only non-Arab, non-Muslim member to stand out against partition.

The November 1947 partition of Palestine led to a brief war in April-May 1948 during which the Arab armies were roundly defeated by the US-armed and Western-backed Zionists seeking a separate State of Israel, and the Palestinian Arab population was largely driven like cattle from their villages to become a rootless diaspora. That disaster is known to all Palestinians and Arabs as Al-Nakba ('The Catastrophe').

There have been other wars since, but the present international position favours a "Two-State" solution which guarantees Israel's continued existence but adds that there must also be an independent, sovereign Palestine state in the territories occupied by Israel in the 1967 war on the West Bank of the Jordan river and the Gaza strip in the Sinai peninsula.

In the run-up to last week's election, which Benjamin Netanyahu seemed to be on the verge of losing, he suddenly turned around to assert that he would not allow the Palestinians to have a State of their own, and would continue to encourage Jewish settlements on Palestinian territory to preclude the emergence of an integrated Palestinian State. He also denounced the Arab citizens of Israel, who make up about 15 per cent of Israel's electorate, warning the Jews to come out to vote for him to defeat the Arab fifth column in their midst. That is how, by appealing to the basest fears of the Jewish voter, he suddenly came up from behind.

All this is relevant to us because Israel has emerged as Modi's favourite friend in West Asia in contradistinction to the Arabs, stretching from Oman to Morocco, whom Nehru had cultivated as the Arab bulwark of the Nonaligned Movement, thereby thwarting Pakistan's attempts to play the Islamic card against us. In more practical terms, it is the Arabs, not the Israelis who are hosting seven million Indian expatriate workers who constitute our largest single source of remittances in foreign exchange. India's consistent pro-Arab policy has been a principal cause of the warm welcome our workers have enjoyed. In trade too, Arab destinations like Dubai have emerged as principal outlets for Indian exports. Our stakes in the Arab world are high.

On the other hand, Israel is the largest supplier now of India's defence requirements. The security cordon has drawn us closer and closer over the years to an Israel whose domestic policies are repugnant to much of what we have stood for all these years, and been diametrically the opposite of our own approach to inclusivist nation-building in diversity. Much of the Israeli attitude to its Arab minorities and Arab neighbours has been anathema to generations of Indians, particularly since Gandhiji in 1938 proclaimed, "Palestine belongs to the Arabs as France belongs to the French and England to the English." This principled stand has now been distorted by being viewed through the prism of defence cooperation. More disturbingly, the Israeli attitude to Muslims and Islam reflects Hindu extremist views in India. Both the Israeli Jewish mainstream and the Indian fringe believe in religion-based nationhood, with Zionism sharing many of the characteristics and prejudices of the Hindutva brigade. That is what has led Modi to send his felicitations to Netanyahu in Hebrew, the Israeli language, as a special gushing gesture of delight at extreme views having catapulted Netanyahu to his last-minute win.

My mind goes back to the only visit I made to Palestine – in 1998 to join the commemoration of the 50th anniversary of Al-Nakba. I was taken to the home of a Hamas leader, then locked in a political battle with Yasser Arafat's party. After he told the amusing story of Arafat having asked him to bring out his cadres for the commemoration, to which the Hamas leader had replied that he could not because Arafat had locked them all up, I more seriously enquired how he could imagine that the Arabs would ever prevail. Pat came his answer, "We are making Palestine in our bedrooms!" He went on to explain that the Arab population of Israel was expanding so much faster than that of the Jews, principally because there was so much net Jewish emigration out of Israel to the glorious West that by the middle of the 21st century, Israel's Arabs would outnumber the Jews. I thought it another joke, but Netanyahu seems to have taken seriously the possibility of the Israeli Arab vote becoming the determining element in Israeli elections. That is a demographic trend that cannot be reversed so long as so many young Jewish citizens of Israel wish to seek their fortunes outside Israel, thus belying the Zionist argument that a Jewish homeland on Palestinian territory is a necessity that justifies any amount of discrimination against its own non-Jewish citizens, and any amount of aggression against its Palestinian neighbours.

Secular India should not be joining Modi in extending felicitations to the fourth-time Israeli Prime Minister, but in expressing our solidarity with Arabs everywhere in the tragedy of Netanyahu that has now overtaken them – a veritable second Al-Nakba.

NDTV.com

VAJPAYEE, THE BEST CONGRESSMAN WE NEVER HAD?

27 March 2015

Might Atal Bihari Vajpyaee be the best Congressman we never had? Given the company he has kept all his political life, he remains amazingly untainted by the vices of the family from which he has emerged – the Sangh Parivar. It was Govindacharya who chanced on this revelation when he called him a '*mukhota*'. Although it was Vajpayee who had coined the notorious equivalence between 'Hindutva' and 'Bharatiyata', it is hard to find in his words or action any extremism of the RSS kind. He seems to have instinctively learned that the exclusivism of his peers ill-suited an aspirant for the office of Prime Minister. He, therefore, kept away from Advani's Rath Yatra and the movement to demolish the Babri Masjid.

Indeed, he was the only BJP leader of eminence to stay well out of Ayodhya that Black Sunday of 6 December 1992 when the three gumbaz of the Masjid were brought down one after the other. It was perhaps the finest moment of his political life, to be a BJP leader and yet not part of the "*Ek dhakka aur do/ Babri Masjid tod do*" crowd. I do not recall his having lent his voice to the hypocrisy of the claim that Mir Baqi's structure was not a place of worship, but a "*vivadit dhancha*".

He was also much more a socialist than his peers. It was at his instance that the economic philosophy of the Bharatiya Janata Party at its foundation was described as "Gandhian Socialism", a phrase they have since abandoned. They switched to the free market only after Dr. Manmohan Singh's reforms began to get reflected in higher GDP growth figures.

Unlike his disruptionist followers, Vajpayee loved the cut and thrust of Parliamentary debate – and, indeed, was a master of the dialectics of democracy. I remember attending a function to celebrate the fiftieth anniversary of the inauguration of the Lok Sabha (2002) when he bemoaned that while, in the past, MPs would walk out when they wanted to show their opposition, now the Opposition was walking in the opposite direction – right into the Well of the House. The irony is that when a couple of years later, the BJP found itself in Opposition, it made the invasion of the Well its primary instrument of politics. Had Vajpayee continued to lead the BJP in Parliament, there might have been occasional disruptions but not the forcible closing of Parliament for days on end as we witnessed in the worst period when the BJP's Rajya Sabha chief whip, SS Ahluwalia, would repeatedly lead his 'shouting brigade' right up to the Chairman's elevated height.

Illness has now muted Vajpayee's extraordinarily powerful voice but evidence of his outstanding Parliamentary abilities is available to anyone who cares to look into the parliamentary records – preferably not in English translation but in the original Hindi. He spoke impeccable Hindi, almost never using an English word. His style of delivery was peculiarly his own – jocular but with rapier thrusts, never offensive but always telling. I spent hours in the Lok Sabha just listening to him speaking, fascinated by the long pauses, usually followed by a punch line. Not only did he command attention when he spoke, he was also an excellent listener, allowing the argument from the other side to flow over him without betraying anger or annoyance, without disruption. He also did me the great kindness of taking particular care to take his seat when I was on my feet.

On one occasion, when I was commenting on the Narasimha Rao government's decision to accord full diplomatic recognition to Israel, I thundered that we must not allow the Israelis to dictate to us the religion of the person we should be sending as our first Ambassador to Tel Aviv. I heard Vajpayee asking his neighbour in a loud sage whisper, "*Yeh kiski ki baat kar rahein hain?*" Pat came the reply, "*Unke dost, Hamid Ansari ki.*" Hamid, then our Ministry's most accomplished West Asia expert, is now the Vice President, and as such, the Chairman of the Rajya Sabha.

Entering Parliament in 1957 at the age of 31, Vajpayee quickly became the leader of his tiny Parliamentary party, but notwithstanding his party's minuscule numbers, had a voice that was listened to with much anticipation every time he rose to speak. His high moment came in October 1962 when, at the peak of the Chinese invasion, he led a four-member delegation to see Nehru to persuade him to convene the Rajya Sabha. Nehru agreed, and Vajpayee launched into a scathing attack on Nehru's foreign and defence policies. He was given his full head without interruption. It is a pity, therefore, that when the Opposition was calling for a debate on the Kargil invasion, Vajpayee ducked it, failing pathetically to rise to Nehru's stature.

His other notable passage of arms was with CN Annadurai over the role of Hindi in national affairs. Both were orators par excellence in their respective mother tongues. Vajpayee had the advantage of speaking in Parliament in his mother tongue, Hindi. 'Anna' responded in faultless, free-flowing English. They kept the nation riveted until Indira Gandhi's three-language formula quieted the dispute for a while.

When in 1979, the Janata government of Morarji Desai appointed Vajpayee as Foreign Minister, my first reaction was one of alarm. Why were they appointing a right-wing, anti-Islamist to this vital portfolio? Vajpayee fooled everyone. Taking to his assignment like a duck to water, Vajpayee became the first Foreign Minister since Swaran Singh to visit Islamabad. There, he delivered his banquet speech in flawless Urdu, much to the chagrin of his Madras-born counterpart, Aga Shahi, whose Urdu was non-existent. He then quickly rushed through a programme of normalization of relations, including the reciprocal opening of Consulates-General in Karachi and Mumbai. I heard the news over the radio in Baghdad where I had completed only two of my three-year posting and would, therefore, not even be considered for the assignment. To my immense delight, a few days later, a telegram arrived transferring me to Karachi. Vajpayee, who did not know me at the time, knew nothing of why I had been selected, but in later years in Parliament he did me the great honour of waiting in the chamber, or returning to it, to hear me out on Pakistan.

The single most severe challenge to his championship of higher values in politics came in the wake of the Gujarat pogrom. After Home Minister Advani had visited the state and given Modi a clean chit, Vajpayee went to Ahmedabad. At his press conference, he said, "I have just one message for the Chief Minister. He must adhere to 'rajdharma'. For the King or the ruler cannot discriminate between people, whether on the basis of birth, caste or religion." So stinging was the public rebuke that Modi butted in, "*Hum bhi wahi kar rahe hain, sahib.*" Vajpayee did not respond. It is now learnt that he intended to dismiss Modi. (I am indebted to Manoj Mitta's 'The Fiction of Fact-finding: Modi & Godhra' for these details.)

That was the moment Vajpayee could have been considered for the Bharat Ratna. But, after having privately complained, "*Is kalank ko mere muh par laga diya*," Vajpayee backtracked – and the same Modi who had never visited a Muslim refugee camp in the aftermath of Godhra except when, for protocol reasons, he accompanied the Prime Minister to the Shah Alam camp, found his road opened to becoming Vajpayee's BJP successor in Race Course Road. That lapse makes it clear that while Vajpayee might be deserving of a high Padma award, giving him the Bharat Ratna is really going too far over the top.

NDTV.com

MODI'S LEMMING MOMENT

6 April 2015

There is an enduring myth about the lemming, a rodent which inhabits the Arctic region, that they are prone to mass migration towards the steep cliffs of the Norwegian coast and, following their leader, topple over, one after the other, into the raging sea below. Much like the BJP over the Land Acquisition ordinance.

The ordinance has been re-promulgated and the BJP is now irretrievably committed to its bizarre lemming-like behaviour, hoping against hope that the nine amendments they have introduced after the debate in the Lok Sabha will exculpate them from the charge of being anti-farmer and pro-corporate.

It is a vain hope. The amendments are an eyewash, designed to buy the support of their own allies, within and without the Sangh Parivar, who have fierce reservations over the course of action that Modi has chosen to take. The amendments do nothing to alter the vicious undermining of the interests of the most discriminated against segment of the Indian population – the kisan and the khet mazdoor. This segment makes up close to 60 per cent of the electorate. It has close ties to their near and dear ones who have migrated to urban slums. Together, they constitute well over three-quarters of all voters. Rural India's share of the economy is, however restricted to 13 per cent of GDP, a decline from about 50 per cent at Independence. That is where they now stagnate, while a tiny sliver of the urban elite corners much of the fruit of faster growth.

How pathetic is their condition is unveiled in the 2015 Economic Survey, which claims that GDP has registered well over seven per cent growth in the past year of mainly the Modi government, but left agriculture lagging behind at a whisker over 1 per cent. Just 1.1 per cent. Even this minuscule one per cent advance masks the fact that while one or two commercial crops fared relatively well last year, almost all others have registered negative growth.

For all of Modi's tears and protestations that he knows poverty, the fact is that he is now much better acquainted with the fat cats of industry and infrastructure than he is with the poverty-stricken kisans and khet-mazdoor. While Gandhiji's goal for the nation was to "wipe every tear from every eye", Modi's is to shed copious crocodile tears for the poor while bringing the bright smile to the super-rich.

That is why the principal objective of the 2015 amendment to the 2013 Land Acquisition Act has been to create a "special category" of economic activity that totally exempts these sectors from the two essential provisions of the 2013 Act: one, Social Impact Assessment in consultation with the affected persons and the affected area through the gram sabhas and panchayats, on the basis of which "fair and just compensation" will be determined; and, second, exemption from first securing 70-80 per cent consent of those who will be losing their land before acquisition proceedings are initiated. Modi's amendments exempt "special category" projects from these key requirements. He does not want to give space for affected persons (both land owners and labour losing their employment and livelihood), local communities, local bodies or their elected representatives to have any voice or say in determining whether they should be forcibly deprived of their land, their chattel, their livelihood, their customs, their usages and their integrity as an organic family.

Chief among the "special category" of exempted economic actives are "industrial corridors" and "infrastructure". For what else does big business want quasi-free land? It wants cut-price land to put up manufacturing units and physical infrastructure. Neither will provide substitute employment or livelihood to those who are being forcibly deprived of their property and the employment derived from working the land. Almost all the benefit will go to those who had nothing to do with the land until it was forcibly acquired.

Big Business wants to thrive on governments filching the land from the aam kisan and handing it over to them, so that they get the land dirt cheap and then sell the surplus at hugely inflated prices. The aam kisan is to be compensated at a multiple of the circle price, when everyone knows that four times that bogus rate is not even one-fourth of what the surplus land will fetch when it is resold, as all the evidence shows it will.

This fundamental exploitation is at the heart of the "special category" that Modi has created to favour his crony capitalist friends. He has covered up his real purpose by adding "affordable housing" to the list of exemptions and started strumming his guitar with the usual chauvinistic appeal to "defence" by placing it among the exempted categories. It won't wash because none other than the Defence Ministry itself had informed the Standing Committee on Rural Development, of which I was a member, that they saw no need to exempt land acquisition for defence industries and defence purposes from the full purview of the 2013 Act. One reason that may have weighed with the Ministry then might have been the fact that nearly 1.5 lakh hectares of land acquired for defence use is lying unutilized with the defence authorities, in some cases going back half-a-century or more!

Moreover, "affordable housing" in rural villages rarely requires land acquisition because the housing is built on panchayat land or state government land; in urban areas, "affordable housing" usually comes up in the same location as the jhuggi-jhopdis. Clearly, Modi's main objective – indeed his sole objective – is land-grabbing to the detriment of the same peasants he claims to be gathering to his bosom so as to flog the land to his corporate moneybags at a fraction of the true market price and at an even smaller fraction of the anticipated rise in land values.

The kisan is no fool. He knows that it is neither a passionate desire for national defence nor housing for the poor that drives the man. They know that his innocent expression – "special category" – is really aimed at making the rich infinitely richer and gravely depriving the poor to fill party coffers.

Why is Modi in such a desperate hurry to push through his goals by ordinance and possibly by the rarely used parliamentary route of a joint session of both Houses? Is it just to secure the majority that is eluding him in the Rajya Sabha? Or is it the fundamental plank of his programme of thrusting the "Gujarat model of development" on the whole of this hapless country?

The key to the Gujarat model was rampant land acquisition to pass on land to the private sector at throwaway prices. A classic case was in Kutch where some 1500 acres were acquired by Chief Minister Modi and passed on to his favourite corporate house, who used a small portion of the land for their own use, and held on to the remainder to sell at a market price that was around 200-300 times the rate at which it was allotted to them. Another example was at the Special Industrial Zone in Hazira, where one of India's major construction companies received land at a discounted price that was zero point something of the rate at which micro-industries subsequently secured land in the same special industrial zone. (The above estimates have been obtained from knowledgeable articles in the prestigious academic publication, *The Economic & Political Weekly*).

Particularly worth noting is a huge portion of land that was acquired by Modi's Gujarat government from tribal populations. According to figures supplied by the erstwhile Planning Commission in its Twelfth Plan documents, whereas tribal people constitute only 8 per cent of the state's population, 76 per cent of those dispossessed and displaced were Gujarat's unfortunate tribals. No wonder they massively voted against him. Alas, their share of the electorate was so small that such mass deprivation did not result in electoral losses for so callous a government.

Modi, therefore, decided that the centrepiece of his economic "reforms" programme would be to replicate the "Gujarat model" all over India. Hence the tearing hurry to take the ordinance route and, failing its endorsement in the Upper House, deploy the NDA's brute majority in a joint session of both Houses. There are contra-indications from the ground.

Many of his allies and all of the Opposition are up in arms against this outrage. So are the bulk of the 60 per cent of the electorate directly adversely affected. Gujarat is not India. Compared to most of the densely-populated states of the country, there are large tracts of arid dryland and wasteland in Gujarat that can be forcibly taken over without effective political opposition. Also, Gujarat's forests are available for exploitation by any ruler as ruthless as Modi.

But India is not Gujarat. When multi-crop agricultural land is taken over, Modi is quite wrong in thinking he can ride roughshod over protesting kisans. Moreover, a united Opposition will come to the rescue of the deprived kisan and khet-mazdoor wherever and whenever there is takeover of rich agricultural land (which was prohibited under the 2013 Act). They will have to face the electoral consequences – particularly in UP and Bihar where the national destiny is crucially determined.

The newly-minted Janata Parivar is waiting in the wings to win back the states it lost to Modi in 2014. And a newly-minted Congress, immediately after its Rahul-led rally on 19 April against the land acquisition amendments, will lend its might and weight to the cause of the kisan against the depredations of the merchants of disaster.

This is the BJP's lemming moment. The countdown to the end of Modi's achhe din has begun.

NDTV.com

BJP'S MOVE TO DESTROY KASHMIRIYAT

13 April 2015

The worst of a coalition of opposites, such as we have in Jammu & Kashmir, is perhaps intended to keep the alliance going, with the partners indulging in what can only be described as "competitive communalism".

Nothing else explains how an otherwise decent Chief Minister could have made the appalling suggestion that he would construct a series of habitations in the Valley into which he would funnel returning Kashmiri Pandits, thereby reducing the proposed exclusively Pandit communities to a string of Bantustans, as the apartheid regime in South Africa had done to definitively separate White from Black. Fortunately, Mufti Sahib has now fudged his original intention by claiming he was misunderstood. But the proposal has not been withdrawn, merely kept for the moment in abeyance.

It is the BJP, partner in the coalition which is pressing for the early return of the Pandits to the Valley. Mufti Sahib's PDP is more than willing to welcome back the Pandits. Indeed, all elements of the Kashmiri polity, including the Hurriyat, assert the necessity of the Pandits returning to Valley. They do not, emphatically do not, regard the Pandits as aliens. But the Pandit community as a whole continues to be apprehensive about their security in the company of their fellow Kashmiri Muslims, and the BJP-Sangh Parivar does everything it can to aggravate these fears, however unfounded.

Hence, on the one hand, the movement for a Panun Kashmir, carved out of a portion of the Valley, where the Hindus would live isolated from, and apart from, the Valley Muslims, and not in composite neighbourhoods. It is a repudiation of the essence of Kashmiriyat, an institutionalization of the wholly bogus line that Hindus and Muslims cannot live together in the Valley, that they must remain separated.

This is the line favoured by the bulk of the Jammu BJP. Stopping short of the Panun Kashmir line, but not going so far as to draw the Hindu-Muslim divide along the Chenab river that divides Kashmir from Jammu (as the Pakistanis have sometimes suggested), the PDP has sought to bridge the two positions by placing on the table for discussion the establishment of a series of Hindu Bantustans in the Valley. In practical terms, there is little to choose between the Panun Kashmir proposal and the Mufti proposal. Both would spell the end of the spirit of Kashmiriyat and institutionalize a gulf between Pandit and Muslim that was never part of the traditional unique ethos of the state, where the two communities have lived in peaceful harmony for centuries.

The original sin was that of Jagmohan, who in his second term as Governor of J&K, that happily lasted under six months (January-May 1990), either panicked or revealed the deepest of his prejudices in facilitating the emptying of the Valley of almost all its Pandits in a matter of days in March 1990. The Pandit population in 1990 was about 1,70,000. It has now been reduced to some 7000 – but all 7000 have lived through the last terrible 25 years in the same mohallas as the Muslims, a shining beacon of secular togetherness in this most trying of times. So integral to Kashmiriyat is the imperative of the two communities living together that the separatists led by Syed Geelani have been among the loudest in affirming the importance of the Pandit community returning to the Valley and condemning the idea of Pandits-only Bantustans.

Why did Jagmohan panic? He has provided the answers himself in his book, *My Frozen Turbulence in Kashmir*, a detailed apologia for his actions during the disaster that overtook the Valley in his brief term. He arrived just as extremist elements began filling the governance void in Srinagar consequent on the elected Farooq Abdullah government resigning office and Governor Krishna Rao doing the same in the wake of the VP Singh government refusing to heed their cautionary advice against the state government releasing dreaded convicted terrorists in exchange for the release of the kidnapped daughter of the then Union Home Minister, the same Mufti who is now Chief Minister of the state.

True, night after night, the most vicious anti-Pandit propaganda was broadcast from microphones installed in mosques. True, gruesome killings accompanied the propaganda. True, eminent, secular Kashmiris, the very embodiment of Kashmiriyat, were targeted. It looked as if the only way the Pandits could save themselves would be to flee the Valley. But why? It was the duty of the administration led by the Governor to not succumb to these threats, to take appropriate action to protect the unprotected, and to take the sternest action against those who were disrupting the peace of the Valley. Instead, the Governor took fright.

On page 478 of his book, Jagmohan quotes his Additional Director-General of Police. He says that in the period between December 1989 and May 1990 (Governor Jagmohan's term), a total of 134 innocent persons were assassinated. Of these, says the Additional DG, as many as 71 were Hindus. Elementary mathematics would show, although the additional DG is not quoted as saying so, that this must mean 63 were Muslims. In other words, the number of Muslims killed was just eight less than the number of Hindus killed. This was not a communal massacre. It was a massacre of loyal Indians by thugs and terrorists. The rhetoric was communal, but the victims were almost equally Hindus and Muslims.

Much closer to the truth than the Governor was HN Jattu, president of the All-India Kashmiri Pandit Conference who was quoted in *The Hindustan Times* of 8 February 1990 – that is, in the middle of the worst atrocities – as saying that all communities suffered, the Pandits as much as the Muslims. He also said – and this is the moot point – that the Kashmiri people were suffering not because of any Hindu-Muslim incompatibility but because of "misrule and maladministration".

Whose misrule? Whose maladministration? Governor Jagmohan's, of course. He had taken undue and unwarranted advantage of the J&K Constitution to dissolve the duly elected Assembly and assume dictatorial powers of governing the state. Indeed, it was the extent and depth of his misrule that led to VP Singh recalling him within six months. There could be no more damning indictment of the suffering he caused the people of Jammu and Kashmir, specifically the Pandits whom he had deprived of home and hearth instead of throwing a protective arm around the collective shoulders of all Kashmiris, Hindu or Muslim. For a quarter of a century, we have continued to rue that misrule.

Yet, it is Jagmohan's fans and acolytes who swell the ranks of the BJP in Jammu. It is they who are advocating a Jagmohan-like solution that is worse than the problem. It is they who want the Pandits back in the Valley – but in Hindu ghettos that emphasize the Hindu-Muslim divide. That is why they must be resisted. Mufti Sahib must not let himself be deflected from his larger purpose by these half-baked proposals for the return of the Kashmiri Pandit to his homeland.

The doors and windows of all Kashmiris must be opened to all Kashmiris without regard to religion.

NDTV.com

THE RETURN OF RAHUL GANDHI

20 April 2015

I have just returned from the Kisan-Khet Mazdoor rally. What a smooth and seamless return it has been. There was no sense of disconnect between the departure of Rahul some 60 days ago and his return now. The prophets of doom find their mouths stoppered. Tragedy has not accompanied his going away. Disintegration has not heralded his coming back.

That Rahul decided, apparently suddenly, to disappear from the public sphere is not as unusual as is being made out. Mahatma Gandhi himself took "leave of absence" from politics for all of four years between 1924 and 1928 as he introspected over whether nonviolence and religious harmony could, in fact, be taught to hundreds of millions of people or whether Chauri Chaura and communal rioting symbolized the real India. For reflection, he preferred the sanctorum of his ashram at Sabarmati to the politics of the time. Indeed, he was not even contemplating a second innings. That was thrust upon him by Motilal Nehru almost begging him to attend the 1928 Calcutta session of the All-India Congress Committee to provide the elder Nehru a protective screen against his own son, Jawaharlal, who had taken up cudgels against his father's Nehru Report on a constitutional change for advocating Dominion status, not 'Purna Swaraj'. As seamless was the Mahatma's return to centre stage after absenting himself for four years, equally seamless was Rahul's re-emergence after two months. It is not necessary to always be the cynosure of all eyes to do one's political duty.

As for Rahul not disclosing his destination, it does not need a long memory to recall that when Sonia Gandhi fell ill a few years ago and had to go abroad for treatment, no one knew where she had gone and speculation was rife as to her whereabouts and the cause of her absence as well. We now have some idea of where and why she went. It was not necessary for us to know then, any more than it was necessary for us to know now, that Rahul had gone to Burma for a course of meditation.

Unlike anywhere in India or perhaps anywhere in the world, Burma is the most closeted country for anyone who seeks privacy, besides being an outstanding Buddhist centre for meditation and vipassana. Privacy is most demanded by those who have the least of it. Rahul has had to suffer the invasion of his privacy since infancy. For a child growing up in a Prime Minister's house is not easy. You are subjected to a constant scrutiny even before you have learnt your first nursery rhymes. Remember the post-Emergency ditty when little Rahul was all of seven years old:

> *Desh ki netri Indira Gandhi,*
> *Yuvaon ka neta Sanjay Gandhi,*
> *Bachchon ka neta Rahul Gandhi,*
> *Bhaad mein jaye Mahatma Gandhi.*

There are some who take to their security detail like ducks to water. They love being surrounded by gun-toting guards. There are others who hate the way their private space has been usurped by the AK 47s. For them, escaping constant surveillance is as much a relief as having Black Cats hanging around is a thrill for others. If Rahul prizes his privacy, as he has done these last two months, it warrants sympathy, not censure.

Moreover, sententiousness about politics being a 24x7 job was negated the moment Rahul walked onto the stage. The party was in readiness for him, not moping about his having been away. And, in any case, it is only in India that this nonsense about politics being 24x7 is bruited about. Prime Ministers and Presidents in most countries take time off to recharge their batteries. Those who talk of 24x7 politics are those who get most bored and feel most neglected when they are not surrounded by a thousand suitors a day – with no vision beyond their own advancement, and no interests other than the lowest forms of politicking, plus fear that if they are out of sight, they'll soon be out of mind. Rahul has no such apprehension.

It was argued that it was eccentric, at best, and thoroughly irresponsible, at worst, for Rahul to vanish just as the Land Acquisition Ordinance was capturing national attention. The confidence with which Rahul spoke at Sunday's rally, and the attentiveness with which he was heard, demonstrated that his absence notwithstanding, the Congress, under the leadership of his mother, had built up the momentum for Rahul's homecoming to be a memorable occasion. Of the speeches made at the rally, I, for one, found his intervention the most substantive – careful delineation of the arguments against the ordinance, followed by a stinging direct attack on Modi for promulgating the ordinance as payback to the "capitalists" who funded his poll campaign to the tune of tens of thousands of crores of rupees. It was a speech that nicely blended hard-nosed logic with a rousing political theme. That is the mark of leadership.

Unerringly, Rahul targeted the usurpation by the State of land belonging to subsistence farmers and the landless agricultural labourers that work the land, as being the essence of the "Gujarat model" that Modi hopes to replicate all over India. Big Business funded him in the expectation that he would return their gift manifold by seizing hundreds of thousands of acres worked by the poor to hand over to the super-rich at dirt-cheap prices. That is why this battle is not over legal technicalities, but goes to the heart of the question of whether governance in our country should be for the rich or the poor.

The Congress stands for striking the right balance while tilting towards the poor. Modi believes soothing words can pull the veil over the dirty hijack he has planned. Rahul's speech signalled a return to Nehru and Indira and Rajiv Gandhi, a definitive leftward shift in the party's public stance. It has sent Modi running for cover.

Seeing mother and son together on the platform, succeeding each other in the speaking order as per the demands of protocol, one wondered why anchors, commentators and BJP spokespersons have been tying themselves in knots predicting an imminent split in the party, even a split in the Gandhi family. It's all been idle speculation, sufficient to fill the empty hour around dinner time, but highly misleading in terms of sound political analysis. Of course, every Congressman and woman has a view on the future leadership. Some have given expression to their views. Others have kept their opinions to themselves. Most will go with the prevailing wind.

But far from spelling confusion, all it means is that a democratic political party must allow space for a bouquet of views – and the Congress is, despite being maligned to the contrary, a democratic political party. Notwithstanding attempts to paint Congress workers and leaders as automatons just waiting for one of the two ji's to tell them whether the sun rises in the east or the west, almost every Congressman I have ever met has lively views on virtually everything under the sun. They are vociferous in discussing these matters with their comrades. Media persons love listening in to the gossip. The moment the media hear two views, they start seeing dissidence.

Dissidence is not dissent. Nor is dissent equal to descent. Internal debate is lively, sometimes heated. But the genius of the party has lain in following debate with consensus, and everyone accepting the final decision, not undermining it.

That is why the spectacle of Rahul and his mother on the stage together was reassuring. Their individual posts, and the relative pecking order, are of secondary significance. The important thing is that the two are together, a duumvirate that works together as a single team with the party and the growing number of other parties that wish to join hands in the struggle against Modi.

So, Modiji, watch out! A united Congress and a united Opposition are coming after you.

NDTV.com